Stolen Motherhood

Stolen Motherhood

Aboriginal Mothers and Child Removal in the Stolen Generations Era

Anne Maree Payne

LEXINGTON BOOKS
Lanham • Boulder • New York • London

Published by Lexington Books
An imprint of The Rowman & Littlefield Publishing Group, Inc.
4501 Forbes Boulevard, Suite 200, Lanham, Maryland 20706
www.rowman.com

6 Tinworth Street, London SE11 5AL, United Kingdom

British Library Cataloguing in Publication Information Available

Library of Congress Cataloging-in-Publication Data

Names: Payne, Anne Maree, 1967– author.
Title: Stolen motherhood : aboriginal mothers and child removal in the stolen generations era / Anne Maree Payne. Other titles: Aboriginal mothers and child removal in the stolen generations era
Description: Lanham : Lexington Books, [2021] | Includes bibliographical references and index. | Summary: "This book explores the experiences of Aboriginal mothers of Stolen Generations children, providing new insights into our understanding of this era. It reflects critically on human rights processes based on truth-telling, raising important issues about who gets to speak at such processes and whose voices are heard and validated."—Provided by publisher.
Identifiers: LCCN 2021008038 (print) | LCCN 2021008039 (ebook) | ISBN 9781793618627 (cloth) | ISBN 9781793618634 (epub) | ISBN 9781793618641 (pbk)
Subjects: LCSH: Children, Aboriginal Australian—Government policy—Australia. | Women, Aboriginal Australian—Attitudes. | Mother and child. | Aboriginal Australians, Treatment of—History. | Motherhood—Australia—Psychological aspects. | Women, Aboriginal Australian—Australia—Social conditions. | Stolen generations (Australia)
Classification: LCC DU124.C45 P39 2021 (print) | LCC DU124.C45 (ebook) | DDC 362.7/789915—dc23
LC record available at https://lccn.loc.gov/2021008038
LC ebook record available at https://lccn.loc.gov/2021008039

Contents

Acknowledgments   vii

Introduction   1

1   Motherhood, Truth-Telling and the *Bringing Them Home* Inquiry   17

2   Untold Suffering? Motherhood and Silence   31

3   "To the Exclusion of the Rights of the Mother" : The Impact of Aboriginal "Protection" Legislation   53

4   "Strange Anomalies": Limitations on Aboriginal Mothers' Access to Social Security   67

5   "Forcible Removal Through Employment": The Impact of the Requirement to Work on Aboriginal Mothers   77

6   Monitored Motherhood: The Impact of State Surveillance and the Threat of Intervention in Aboriginal Families   85

7   Sitting in Judgment? Views about Aboriginal Mothering   93

8   For Their Own Good? Diverse Perspectives on Aboriginal Child Removal   117

9   Beyond Silence: Aboriginal Mothers' Experiences of Child Removal in the Stolen Generations Era   139

Conclusion   161

Appendix I: Legislation Consulted   171

Appendix II: List of Interviews Quoted   173

Bibliography   177

Index   189

About the Author   197

Acknowledgments

Like many Australians, I was shocked and moved to learn about the experiences of Aboriginal and Torres Strait Islander people who were removed from their families as children through the reports which emerged from the hearings of the *Bringing Them Home* Inquiry in 1996. In the aftermath of the publication of the *Bringing Them Home* report, I joined the estimated half a million Australians who signed a Sorry Book;[1] in my then role as director of the Equity & Diversity Unit, I cochaired the University of Technology Sydney's Reconciliation Committee and coauthored its Reconciliation Statement, one of the first of its kind in Australia. I was also involved in the nomination of Sir Ronald Wilson and Mick Dodson, the cochairs of the inquiry, for an honorary doctorate, drafting the citation for the award which they received in 1998—the only such recognition from an Australian university that their work on the Inquiry received. In 2000, when I was in the late stages of pregnancy with my first child, I was cofacilitating an anti-racism train-the-trainers session at UTS; amongst the many personal reflections and experiences which were shared, an Aboriginal participant described her devastating experience of having her baby stolen (there is no other word to describe what happened to her) when she was working as a young, single mother in Queensland in the early 1960s, which brought the reality of the impact of Aboriginal child removal home to me in a very real and powerful way.

After nearly two decades working on gender, diversity, Aboriginal employment and reconciliation initiatives in Australia, I undertook a master's degree in Human Rights at the London School of Economics over 2008–2010. This course provided me with an international context within which to better understand and reflect on the reconciliation and truthtelling processes which had been taking place in Australia over the previous two decades, and also led me to question many things which I had previously taken for granted. On returning to Australia in 2012 I enrolled in a PhD program in Australia to pursue some of my questions.

This book is the outcome of my PhD research, and of my longstanding interest in gender, human rights, motherhood, Aboriginal social justice and reconciliation. I would like to particularly thank my PhD supervisor, Heather Goodall, who has been an inspiration to me for many years; her wisdom, expertise, flexibility and ongoing support have been greatly appreciated. I would also like to gratefully acknowledge the valuable feedback I received on my research from my PhD examiners, Lynette Russell, Catherine Kevin and Fiona Paisley; and for the detailed comments on my book manuscript provided by an anonymous peer reviewer. Any errors or omissions in my work remain my own.

I would also like to acknowledge and thank a number of other people who met with me over the past decade to discuss my research into motherhood and the Stolen Generations, and provided invaluable suggestions and feedback, including Aunty Joan Tranter, Sonya Pearce, Heidi Norman, Terri Libesman, Michael McDaniel, Chris Evans, Mary Edwards, Peter Read, Belinda Russon, Juanita Sherwood, Christina Ho, Kyungja Jung and Marivic Wyndham. Thanks to many supportive current and former colleagues in the Faculty of Arts & Social Sciences at the University of Technology Sydney (in addition to the ones already named), who have generously helped me in a range of ways, particularly Nina Burridge, Burcu Cevik-Compiegne, Chris Comerford, Kay Donovan, Lucy Fiske, Chrisanthi Giotis, Amelia Johns, Mehal Krayem, Natalie Krikowa, Tim Laurie, Kais Al-Momani, Jennifer Newman, Helary Ngo, Susan Oguro, Olga Oleinikova, Jenna Price, Katrina Thorpe and Rayma Watkinson.

Several people agreed to be formally interviewed by me for this book, involving a number of hours of their time plus additional time spent reading and correcting transcripts, and I wish to extend a huge thanks to two interviewees who preferred to remain anonymous, as well as to Lily Arthur, NSW Coordinator of Origins Forced Adoption Support Network and Co-Chair of the Stolen Generations Alliance (NSW), and Peter Read. I would also like to express my sincere appreciation and thanks to all the people whose interviews in the National Library of Australia's *Bringing Them Home* Oral History Project I have drawn upon, for making their interviews available for research. As Jackie Huggins commented in relation to these interviews, "It is indeed an act of great courage and trust to speak about matters that are so close to the heart, and to allow others to explore and consider what has been revealed."[2] I hope I have done some small degree of justice to their stories. My thanks also to Fiona Milway, Reference and Administration Officer, and to all the staff in the Oral History and Indigenous Programs department of the National Library of Australia, for their dedicated efforts in obtaining permission for me to quote from the NLA interviews cited in this book. The staff of the Petherick Reading Room at the NLA were also unfailingly helpful and accommodating during a number of long days spent accessing the *Bringing Them Home* Oral History Project interviews.

A huge thanks to Michael Cook for allowing me to use his powerful and moving image, *Mother (Pram)* on the cover of the book, and to Alice McAuliffe for first drawing Michael's *Mother* series to my attention.

Thank you to the editors of *Law & History*, who kindly granted permission for me to publish some material in this book which was previously published in their journal.[3]

My husband Kevin has been an immense source of encouragement and support, and always believed in me more than I did in myself; and my children Harry and Alice kept me grounded in the real world and were a constant reminder to me of why my research was important.

Love and thanks to Colleen Almojuela, Robin Butterfield and Chris Smith, three amazing educators who I was fortunate to meet early in my career and who had a major influence on my understanding of Indigenous issues. And last but not least, this book is dedicated to Aunty Joan Tranter, dear friend, valued colleague and recently retired Indigenous Elder in Residence at UTS, who first suggested the term "stolen mums" to me.

NOTES

1. Australian Institute of Aboriginal and Torres Strait Islander Studies, "Explore the Sorry Books."
2. Quoted in Mellor and Haebich, *Many Voices*, 3.
3. See Payne, "To the Exclusion of the Rights of the Mother."

Introduction

In 2018, a public outcry arose over comments made on Australian breakfast television in relation to the adoption of Aboriginal children by white families, with one panelist commenting that the removal of children in the Stolen Generations era "was for their well-being, we need to do it again perhaps."[1] This comment reflects the ongoing view amongst some non-Indigenous Australians that Aboriginal child removal in the Stolen Generations era was both necessary and beneficial to those who were removed. Other commonly-heard arguments that have been made in relation to these removals were that they were undertaken in keeping with the "standards of the day,"[2] that there never was a generation or generations of stolen children,[3] and that in any case, Australians today should not have to accept responsibility for the actions of the past.[4] This book aims to address some of these beliefs and misconceptions and to provide a new perspective on the history of the Stolen Generations era, through a consideration of the experiences of the mothers of the Stolen Generations.

This has been a challenging topic to research. In its submission to the *Bringing Them Home* Inquiry in 1996, Aboriginal community group Link-Up NSW noted

> In preparing this submission we found that Aboriginal women were unwilling and unable to speak about the immense pain, grief and anguish that losing their children had caused them. That pain was so strong that we were unable to find a mother who had healed enough to be able to speak, and to share her experience with us and with the Commission.[5]

In launching the *Bringing Them Home* Report in 1997, Inquiry Cochair Mick Dodson noted "One thing missing from this report are the mothers' stories—but then how could a mother possibly bear to tell of her loss?"[6] This book investigates the reasons contributing to the resounding silence of Aboriginal mothers at the *Bringing Them Home* Inquiry, and reflects critically on human rights processes based on truth-telling, raising issues about who gets to speak at such processes and whose voices are heard and validated.

"Mother" is both a noun and a verb; as a noun, "mother" is typically defined as a woman in relation to a child or children to whom she has given birth; whereas "to mother" as a verb has a much broader meaning, encompassing both "to give birth to" as well as the act of bringing up a child with care and affection, a relationship that is not necessarily linked to the biological act of giving birth. "Mothering" is also defined as the act of looking after someone kindly and protectively—sometimes excessively so. One can give birth to but not "mother" a child or children, in the sense of providing care and nurturing; one can "mother" or be "mothering" without the biological act of giving birth. Not all mothers are "mothering." What does it mean to be a "good" mother; whose motherhood is supported and valued and whose is restricted; who is judged to have the capacity to mother? All of these issues are explored in this book through investigating the experiences of the mothers of the Stolen Generations.

Maternity has been described as contested terrain, a battleground on which many ideological and political battles have been waged[7]—with much at stake for the winners and losers. Debates about motherhood are central to this book, as is the understanding that motherhood is not a natural state but is rather a social construction, something that is specific to time, place and cultural context, that evolves and changes over time and that reflects the realities of power. The difficulties of rebuilding broken relationships experienced by people separated from their birth families highlight that motherhood is not a biological given but is a relationship based on lived experiences of care; as many Stolen Generations narratives attest, being reunited with your mother does not automatically lead to having a close and loving relationship with her.

This book explores some of the experiences of Aboriginal mothers of Stolen Generations children. The picture that emerges is that of Aboriginal mothers making complex and difficult choices which were context-specific, and which were often based on what they saw as being in the best interests of those for whom they had a relationship of care, within the severely constrained options which were available to them. Yet amongst the devastating stories of loss and trauma experienced by these mothers are stories of hope and resilience—the determination of mothers to retain some foothold in their children's lives, the determination of children to find their lost families and communities.

My aim is not to idealize Aboriginal mothers, and I am not attempting to argue that all child removals in the Stolen Generations era would have been completely unwarranted on child welfare grounds. However, this book highlights that perceptions of Aboriginal women as "bad" or neglectful mothers were central to the justification of child removal policies; even today such perceptions remain the foundation of the argument that Aboriginal children were removed "for their own good."

This book highlights that practices of Aboriginal child removal and the experiences and choices of Aboriginal mothers during the Stolen Generations era were far more complex than the types of situations the term "Stolen Generations" is commonly seen to encompass. The Stolen Generations era is typically defined as beginning with the passage of state-based Aboriginal "Protection" legislation in the late nineteenth and early twentieth centuries, which provided the legal basis for limiting Aboriginal parental rights and put in place discriminatory processes for the removal of Aboriginal children; and ending with the repeal of the remaining aspects of this legislation in 1969.[8]

The archetypal Stolen Generations experience is seen by many to involve Aboriginal children being "snatched," literally from their mothers' arms. However, there was a much wider range of child removal policies and practices than this archetype suggests, caused by structural barriers such as inequities in Aboriginal mothers' status as the legal guardians of their children, their lack of access to social security benefits readily available to most other Australian mothers, the requirement for Aboriginal mothers to return to work irrespective of their carers' responsibilities, and heightened state surveillance of and intervention in Indigenous families. When we consider Aboriginal child removal practices more broadly, the distinction between "forcible" and so-called "consensual" removals becomes murky, as it is difficult to meaningfully define consent in the situations that many Aboriginal mothers found themselves in.

WHY MOTHERS?

The focus of this book is on Aboriginal mothers and not on Aboriginal parents, for a number of reasons. In the Stolen Generations era, Aboriginal women were frequently heads of household and the sole parents of children, due to a range of reasons including the absence of their partners because of the nature of their itinerant labor patterns, unemployment, imprisonment or the impact of social security regulations;[9] or because in the case of white fathers of Aboriginal children, many did not live with or have an ongoing relationship with the family. Accounts from removed Aboriginal children highlight that for those living in two-parent families, the absence of the father was often seen as an opportunity or a trigger for state intervention. Mothers were also most often the focus of yearning in the tragic testimonies of removed children heard at the *Bringing Them Home* Inquiry.[10]

I acknowledge that this book's focus on Aboriginal mothers runs the risk of further marginalizing another highly marginalized group, Aboriginal fathers.[11] Feminist philosopher Sara Ruddick described fatherhood as a position of power and authority, one that is bestowed by society rather than earned through caring work or determined by children's needs; not all men get to be "fathers" in the traditional sense that society defines this role, as they do not all have access to the required power or resources associated with being a father.[12] This insight could certainly be applied to many Aboriginal fathers in the Stolen Generations era, who were denied the economic opportunities to support their family and stripped of legal recognition of their guardianship status in relation to their children. Aboriginal men have been demonized as inadequate parents and sexual predators, not something which is relegated to the distant past but which remains a feature of contemporary representations of Aboriginal masculinity.[13]

My purpose in focusing on the experiences of Aboriginal mothers is not to denigrate or deny the very real love and care provided by many Aboriginal fathers, or to discount the various roles played by both Aboriginal and non-Aboriginal fathers of Stolen Generations children.[14] An overwhelming number of the removed Aboriginal children whose experiences are discussed in this book had an Aboriginal mother; many had a white or non-Indigenous father, and a number either did not know or did not identify who their father was. These data reflect the social values of the time; relationships across racial lines were socially taboo (and subject at times to legal sanction under Aboriginal Protection legislation), however relationships did take place between white men and Indigenous women, whereas relationships between Indigenous men and white women were rare.[15]

BACKGROUND TO THE STOLEN GENERATIONS

It is important to remember that child removal policies and practices differed from state-to-state; there was not a uniform Australia-wide approach to this issue. Prior to federation each of the colonies was effectively a separate state body, and subsequent to federation the federal government was explicitly precluded from legislating for Indigenous Australians by Section 51 (xxvi) of the Constitution,[16] so it is quite difficult to construct a coherent picture of the different policies and practices being implemented in each state and territory, and it would be difficult to argue that there was a truly "national" approach to Indigenous issues prior to 1967. There were significant differences in the approach to child removal in different states and at different times; several different phases in child removal policy have been identified, including the colonial era, the era of "protection" and segregation, the era of "merging" and "absorption," and the era of assimilation.[17] Tasmania refused to acknowledge its Aboriginal population after its efforts to massacre Tasmanian Aborigines in the nineteenth century,[18] and therefore did not develop separate laws and policies targeting Aboriginal children. In Victoria, Aboriginal children were removed to "mainstream" child welfare institutions (although without the need for a court process), and a separate Aboriginal "welfare" administration did not develop.[19] From the early twentieth century in NSW, many Aboriginal children were institutionalized in "training institutions" developed specifically to accommodate Aboriginal children. In South Australia as in a number of other states with large Aboriginal populations, a state "Protector" was appointed as the legal guardian of all Aboriginal children and had sole decision-making power to remove children for training or to determine if they were "neglected."[20] In Queensland, segregation on missions rather than assimilation remained a strong focus. The Northern Territory and West Australia were home to by far the largest numbers of "full-blood" Aborigines living a "traditional" lifestyle, and these states were the major proponents of schemes designed to "breed out the colour" of their Aboriginal populations.[21] The eastern states dismantled their "protectionist" legislation much earlier than did Western Australia, the Northern Territory, South Australia and Queensland, which continued to operate a separate legislative and administrative regime for Indigenous peoples into the 1950s and 1960s.[22] However, while state policies and practices differed, it is possible to identify similarities in the ideas and beliefs underpinning the creation of the array of laws passed in the Stolen Generations era which restricted the rights of Aboriginal people.[23]

It has been argued by some that the removal of Aboriginal children in the Stolen Generations era was not racially based,[24] and that other Australian children (as well as child migrants) at that time underwent similar experiences.[25] Others see parallels between the experience of Aboriginal mothers and, for instance, young white mothers forced to relinquish their children for adoption.[26] However, one key difference between Aboriginal and non-Aboriginal mothers who experienced child removal is race. There has been extensive debate within the community on the genocide findings of the *Bringing Them Home* Inquiry, its most controversial and disputed finding, and ongoing attacks on claims that children were removed solely on the basis of their Aboriginality.[27] This book supports the contention that ideas about race were central to Aboriginal child removal, and that race was the aspect that substantively distinguished the removal of Aboriginal children from that of other non-Aboriginal children. The evidence suggests that it was the children's status of being "part-white" that often led to their increased likelihood of removal. It is important to emphasize that this is no less a racially motivated basis for removal, based on the white community's abhorrence that "near-white" children might grow up in the poverty and "abject squalor" that "full-blood" Aboriginal people were living in on a daily basis. A number of accounts relate the experiences of Aboriginal families from whom "half-caste" children were removed, but "full-blood" children were not, indicating that child removals cannot have been based solely on concerns about child neglect or abuse or perceptions of poor parenting: if this were the case, why were some children left behind?

A NOTE ON SOURCES

The difficulty of accurately identifying the number of Indigenous children removed from their families in the Stolen Generations era has long been noted, in large part because of the lack of official records documenting child removals and the unreliability of state statistics about Indigenous populations.[28] Part of the difficulty in determining numbers of children removed is that Indigenous child removals were undertaken by a number of different agencies, including church bodies, welfare officers, the police, patrol officers, and Aboriginal Protection Board personnel, and no single office had oversight of removals at a state level. In addition, informal adoptions and other child transfer arrangements in this era often took place without any paperwork.

Aboriginal people who were removed as children often expressed skepticism about the rationale for their removal contained in the "official" documentation, describing it as reflecting a lack of cross-cultural understanding and a lack of empathy for the plight of their families.[29] As Sylvia Neary commented about her experience of trying to discover the circumstances of her removal, "I realised that there was a white version, and then there was a black version of what actually happened to me. . . . I realised that the white people had their own agenda, and they had changed my name and given their version of my circumstances to suit their agenda."[30]

The other thing notably missing from official documentation about child removals is the grief of Aboriginal mothers, a point powerfully made by Christine Choo who argues that "nowhere in the official records is this devastating impact of the policy clearly visible. The pain of Aboriginal women remains hidden in the official texts."[31]

Issues around lack of records, access to records and concerns around the accuracy and reliability of those records that do exist mean that oral history accounts of child removal are an important historical source in relation to the Stolen Generations. The findings in this book are primarily based on thematic analysis of 134 oral history interviews, 130 of which were drawn from the National Library of Australia's *Bringing Them Home* Oral History Project, and four of which I undertook myself. The National Library of Australia's *Bringing Them Home* Oral History Project was established in the wake of the *Bringing Them Home* Inquiry with the stated aim to record "the diverse experiences of people directly affected by Indigenous child separation and to shed light on the policy and legislative frameworks that supported the separations."[32] Initially this project, a recommended outcome of the *Bringing Them Home* Inquiry, was intended to capture the testimonies of Indigenous people impacted upon by policies of child removal, recognizing that the *Bringing Them Home* Inquiry had not been able to hear accounts from everyone who had wanted to give evidence.[33] However the then Minister for Aboriginal Affairs John Herron insisted that the collection be broadened out to include white per-spectives on child removal, suggesting that the *Bringing Them Home* In-quiry had not provided a "rounded" account of the full history of the Stolen Generations.[34] This political intervention has, however inadver-tently, resulted in creating a resource for researchers on the attitudes and values of white Australians which underpinned child removal policies and practices in the Stolen Generations era. The National Library of Aus-tralia's interviews were collected in two phases—most over the period 1999–2002, with a second round of thirty-one interviews being undertak-en in the "Bringing Them Home after the Apology" set over the period 2009–2011.

Oral history has been described as a particularly appropriate metho-dology for telling Indigenous histories, and Indigenous peoples have their own long traditions of the oral transmission of knowledge.[35] Of course, oral history accounts (in common with other historical sources) are not objective "evidence" of the past, but rather are subjective con-structions of one person's perspective and lived experience. The different contexts, audience (or perceived audience), questioner/interviewer and the narrator's sense of the legacy of their story will all impact on the way a life story gets told; in addition to many other factors such as the vagar-ies of memory, the association of experiences or ideas that might be meaningful to the narrator but not obviously so to the interviewer or listeners, the interviewee's perceptions about how the material may be used in the future, concerns about sensitivity and confidentiality, and so on. Rather than seeing this subjectivity as a weakness, such narratives are an important source of historical information because they tell us how the storyteller makes sense of their world.[36] We need to read these texts and representations "against the grain" to determine their possible meanings, an approach I have endeavored to take throughout; while we must read with care and question the context in which such sources were produced, they remain "indispensable as detailed accounts, and as representations of subjective experience, observation or viewpoint."[37] British sociologist Les Back has described the art of listening as engaging with people with respect for the complexity of their lives and humility about the limits of our own understanding, while maintaining critical judgment;[38] it is this balance that I have striven for in my analysis of these at times widely divergent accounts about the contested history of the Stolen Generations. My focus is on what the interviews reveal about the interviewees; how they perceived what happened to them; how they described or justified the actions of themselves or others; what they believed motivated their behaviors or those of others; and how they feel about their experiences.

In addition to oral history interviews, I have considered accounts of Aboriginal child removal and Aboriginal mothers' experiences from oth-er sources, including excerpts contained within the *Bringing Them Home* Report and from various anthologies and oral history collections, as well as letters, records, and other documents reproduced in secondary sources which were relevant to my research.

Autobiographical and biographical narratives written by and about Aboriginal women have been another important source of information about Aboriginal motherhood in the Stolen Generations era.[39] Although a number of Aboriginal women's autobiographies speak powerfully about the challenges the authors faced as mothers, accounts of experiences of child removal told from the perspective of Aboriginal mothers are incredibly rare; something that is worth highlighting as this is clearly a very difficult subject area to address. I have also read several autobiographies and memoirs written by white Australians who played a role in Aboriginal child removal processes in some way during the Stolen Generations era.[40]

Another important source has been state and federal legislation impacting Indigenous parenting rights, for example, constraints on the guardianship status of Indigenous parents, and discriminatory provisions limiting Aboriginal people's access to social security benefits and payments. This research has been important in documenting the structural and systemic nature of disadvantage facing Indigenous mothers in the Stolen Generations era. Black sociologist Joyce A. Ladner called on feminist researchers exploring issues of race to redefine the "problem" they were investigating,[41] a call echoed by Indigenous academic Linda Tuhiwai Smith who argues that "many researchers, even those with the best of intentions, frame their research in ways that assume that the locus of a particular research problem lies with the indigenous individual or community rather than with other social or structural issues."[42] Rather than seeing child removal as arising from the "problem" of Aboriginal parenting, this book focuses on identifying and exploring the structural barriers experienced by Aboriginal mothers in the Stolen Generations era, highlighting the impact of institutionalized racism expressed through legislation and the policies implemented by welfare agencies, government departments, mission officials and others involved in the administration of Aboriginal affairs at this time.

In writing about silence and the consequences of speech, it was important to take great care in terms of my source material. As I am aware of the consequences when people feel they lose control of their stories after telling them, I have only included accounts of child removal (whether from Aboriginal or white perspectives) that have previously been published and are in the public domain, or where interviewees had consented for their material to be available for public use; in cases where there were restrictions on the use of interview content, I obtained specific permission from the interviewee or their next of kin to quote from their interview in this book.

WHITE RESEARCHERS AND ABORIGINAL HISTORY

In *Decolonizing Methodologies*, Linda Tuhiwai Smith expressed the concern of many Indigenous peoples about the exploitative nature of academic research.[43] Assumptions about what is knowable to a non-Indigenous researcher, and who has the right to know, are also critical; Martin Nakata observes that non-Indigenous research about Indigenous peoples runs the risk of only charting the surface level of knowledge, and not being able to "illuminate the shadowy corners."[44] As a white historian researching the history of the Stolen Generations, it has been important for me to have a self-awareness that there are aspects of cultural understanding and knowledge that I as a non-Indigenous researcher will necessarily lack. Nakata comments that in researching the Indigenous "other," we are ultimately learning more about the limits of our own knowledge practices; this, as he states, may be "the most valuable exercise of all."[45]

In keeping with the Australian Institute of Aboriginal and Torres Strait Islander Studies' *Guidelines for Ethical Research in Australian Indigenous Studies,* I sought to engage with the key community organizations involved in providing services and support to members of the Stolen Generations at the outset of my research. I contacted Link-Up NSW and the NSW Convenors of the Stolen Generations Alliance, the two key representative groups of members of the Stolen Generations in NSW, advising them of my proposed research and offering the opportunity for feedback, input or participation. I also contacted a number of other community groups working on Stolen Generations issues, including Reconciliation Australia, the National Sorry Day Committee and the Healing Foundation, advising them of my research, inviting them to comment or to be further involved as they saw appropriate. I received responses from all of these organizations except the National Sorry Day Committee; responses ranged from requests for further information or clarification to expressions of in-principle support for my research.

My aim in undertaking this research has been to listen rather than trying to speak on the behalf of Indigenous people. The Aboriginal concept of *dadirri,* which has been described as "a deep contemplative process of 'listening to one another' in reciprocal relationships,"[46] is relevant here. Miriam-Rose Ungunmerr-Baumann, who first wrote about the concept of *dadirri,* describes listening as a vital life-skill that Aboriginal people learn from an early age, but one that is not often reciprocated by white Australians.[47]

I have endeavored throughout this book to listen deeply to the accounts of child removal by both Aboriginal and non-Aboriginal people, to recognize the importance of the context in which they are speaking, their perception about who is listening, and their wishes about what the legacy of their testimony will be. I have also kept in mind Joan Scott's advice: "Experience is at once always already an interpretation and something that needs to be interpreted."[48]

TERMINOLOGY

Throughout this book I have primarily used the term "Aboriginal" rather than "Indigenous" for several reasons: firstly because many Indigenous Australians find the term Indigenous "too generic";[49] secondly because Aboriginal and Torres Strait Islander peoples represent two distinct cultural groups (though with great diversity within each),[50] with different histories and experiences which are occluded by the term "Indigenous Australians"; and thirdly because all the Indigenous interviewees whose oral history accounts are quoted in this book identified as Aboriginal. This book is a study of Aboriginal mothers and mothering rather than "Indigenous Australian" mothering as all of my research material about Stolen Generations mothers relates specifically to Aboriginal women. I do however at times use the term "Indigenous" where referring to policies and practices that encompassed both Aboriginal and Torres Strait Islander peoples.[51]

I also at times use historical terminology based on pseudo-scientific "racial" categories such as "half-caste," "full-blood," "quadroons," and so on. These terms, applied to people of "mixed" descent by the white community, are a clear reflection of the prevailing Social Darwinist and eugenicist thinking of the time in which they were devised. I have chosen to include them as they are the terms used by the interviewees, and in this specific instance I felt their use was warranted, indeed essential, as white ideas about race are critical to understanding the history of the Stolen Generations. It has been identified that "no less than 67 identifiable classifications, descriptions or definitions"[52] of Aboriginality were used in Australian legislation from the colonial era to the present day, a figure that undoubtedly reflects extreme white Australian anxieties about racial miscegenation.

Gender has also been identified as a significant element in the (white) construction of Aboriginal identity, and one in which motherhood played a key role, with Aboriginal people of "mixed" descent being defined by the racial category of their mother, rather than their non-Aboriginal relatives.[53]

It is important to note that the policies and practices of child removal sustained over many decades have impacted significantly on all three aspects of contemporary Aboriginal identity—knowledge of genealogical descent, the capacity to self-identify and the capacity to demonstrate community recognition/acceptance.[54] It is estimated that there are many Australians today who remain unaware of their Aboriginal ancestry as a consequence of child removal practices;[55] and in the course of researching and writing this book I met a number of people who disclosed to me that they were aware they had Aboriginal ancestry but they did not identify as Aboriginal because their connections to community had been broken.

The term "Stolen Generations" is also contested by some. The first use of the term is attributed to historian Peter Read, one of the earliest academic researchers to document the removal of Indigenous children. It has been challenged by conservative commentators on the grounds of the alleged inaccuracy of both the terms "stolen" and "generations."[56] I use it throughout this book as it is the term that those directly impacted by child removal policies and practices are most likely to use to describe themselves, though it is important to note that the usage of this term and debates about who can claim it are a significant issue for both Aboriginal and white people.[57]

STRUCTURE OF THIS BOOK

This book in some senses starts at the end—with an analysis in chapter 1 of the limited testimony from mothers heard at the *Bringing Them Home* Inquiry, and an exploration in chapter 2 of the reasons which may have contributed to Aboriginal mothers' unwillingness to speak about their experiences of child removal. These chapters identify the definitional limits created by the *Bringing Them Home* Inquiry process; the difficulty of finding a position from which mothers were willing and able to speak; constraints on mothers about speaking of experiences of sexual violation; the impact of shame, self-blame and the blame of others; the fear of damaging the fragile bonds which have been reestablished with their now-adult children; or because some stories may be too painful to be spoken.

Fundamental to my argument about the enduring silence by Aboriginal mothers about their experiences is my belief that there is a lack of understanding by many people in the Australian community about the structural barriers to Aboriginal motherhood in the Stolen Generations era. Chapter 3 details the impact of Aboriginal Protection legislation and inequalities in Aboriginal mothers' status as the legal guardians of their children. Although issues such as parental "consent" have often been the focus of public debate about child removals in the Stolen Generations era, this chapter highlights that Aboriginal mothers at this time often had limited parental rights in relationship to their children. Indigenous parental rights were overridden through the appointment of Chief Protectors (or equivalent positions), who were in a number of states the legal guardians of all Indigenous children, leaving Indigenous parents without any legal recourse in the event of the removal of their children. Chapter 4 addresses Aboriginal mothers' lack of access to social security benefits readily available to many other Australian mothers, highlighting the contribution of white authorities to creating the conditions of "neglect" that led to Aboriginal child removals. Where benefits were available to Aboriginal mothers in the Stolen Generations era they were often paid in the form of rations rather than money; and some Aboriginal families faced bizarre situations where different family members were eligible for different forms of support based on the "percentage of Aboriginal blood" they were deemed to possess. Chapter 5 explores the requirement for some Aboriginal mothers living on missions and reserves to return to work irrespective of their carers' responsibilities, while chapter 6 considers the impact of the heightened state surveillance of Indigenous families, and the pervasive fear of child removal experienced by Aboriginal mothers in the Stolen Generations era.

Chapter 7 explores issues of consent, the concept of "forcible removal," and white attitudes towards Aboriginal mothers, highlighting how characterizations of Aboriginal mothers as neglectful, uncaring and disinterested parents were integral to the justification of child removal policies and processes in the Stolen Generations era and continue to be used by some to justify these past practices today. Chapter 8 examines the differing explanations for Aboriginal child removal during the Stolen Generations era that have been put forward by people who were removed as children and by white people involved in these child removals. These diverse perspectives on child removal highlight that for many, the Stolen Generations era remains a period of contested history, where there seems little if any common ground between the main parties involved as to what actually happened and who, if anyone, was to blame. White people involved in the removals process typically emphasized social disadvantage and parental neglect as key factors in Aboriginal child removal, tending to highlight what they saw as the "positive benefits" accruing to Aboriginal children subsequent to their removal. However, only a minority of Aboriginal people who were removed as children identified parental neglect as a significant factor in their removal. Overall, members of the Stolen Generations related few benefits resulting from their removal and many harms, including loss of language, cultural knowledge and identity; damage to self-esteem; physical and sexual abuse; substandard material provisions for their care; and poor educational and work opportunities.

What we learn in chapter 9 about the complex experiences of some Aboriginal mothers of Stolen Generations children highlights their struggles to make choices in the best interests of their children despite the constrained options available to them. These powerful accounts from the mothers of removed children go to the very heart of key issues in the contested history of the Stolen Generations: to what extent did mothers "consent" to the removal of their children, what were the circumstances in which children were removed, what "choices" were indeed open to Aboriginal mothers, who were in many cases young single parents living in poverty, required to work to support themselves and denied the social security support and legal protections available to non-Indigenous parents? This chapter also identifies the circumstances that have enabled some Aboriginal mothers to speak about their experiences of child removal.

As Kevin Rudd noted in his "Apology to Australia's Indigenous Peoples," "the hurt, the humiliation, the degradation and the sheer brutality of the act of physically separating a mother from her children is a deep assault on our senses and on our most elemental humanity."[58] While some may argue that the removal of Indigenous children was based on what was perceived to be in the best interests of the child, it is never possible to argue that such removals were in the best interests of their parents, whose subsequent lives often bear stark witness to the trail of destruction and trauma wreaked by the loss of their children.

Issues of motherhood are at the very heart of Stolen Generations policies and practices. Concerns about the prospective motherhood of Aboriginal girls and racially based fears about miscegenation were integral to child removals in many states. Characterizations of Aboriginal women as negligent and corrupting mothers were used to justify the removals. Returning to "Mother" was the embodiment of coming home for many Indigenous people who were removed as children; the *Bringing Them Home* Report poignantly states that "A number of witnesses told the Inquiry of their feeling of being 'at home at last' when they finally met their birth parent, usually their mother."[59] As this book will highlight, the experiences of the mothers of the Stolen Generations are crucial to our understanding of this era of Australia's history, and its ongoing impacts on Indigenous families today.

NOTES

1. Prue MacSween quoted in Carmody, "'So many mistruths.'"
2. In a submission made to the UN Human Rights Committee, the Human Rights and Equal Opportunity Commission noted that "racial discrimination and genocide were 'standards of the day' against which forcible removal policies should be evaluated." Human Rights and Equal Opportunity Commission. "The National Inquiry into the Separation of Aboriginal and Torres Strait Islander Children from Their Families, Bringing Them Home," 5.
3. A claim made by former Minister for Aboriginal Affairs John Herron in a submission made on behalf of the Federal government to a Senate Inquiry into the Stolen Generations, which stated that there never was a generation of stolen children and that the proportion of separated Aboriginal children was no more than 10 percent. See Dow, "Sorry: The Unfinished Business of the Bringing Them Home Report."
4. See for example former Prime Minister John Howard, quoted in Simkin, "Debate rages over Stolen Generations phrase." Robert Manne has argued that there was a concerted campaign by right-wing commentators, aided and abetted by senior representatives of the Howard government, to discredit the findings of the *Bringing Them Home* Inquiry—see Manne, *The Stolen Generations and the Right*.
5. Human Rights and Equal Opportunity Commission, *Bringing Them Home*, 212.

6. Dodson, "National Inquiry into the Separation of Aboriginal and Torres Strait Islander Children from Their Families."

7. Greenfield, "Introduction," 8.

8. Australian Human Rights Commission, "Submission to the United Nations Human Rights Committee."

9. Pettman 1992, 65–66.

10. Human Rights and Equal Opportunity Commission 1997, 235. In the publication *Many Voices,* Mellor and Haebich also highlight "the central importance of a mother's love" in the interviews collected by the National Library of Australia's *Bringing Them Home* Oral History Project. They note "when a longing to find family was expressed, most often it was a mother who was being sought; when people spoke about missing family, it was their mother they referred to, or remembered crying for as a child. The ironic counterpoint to this longing was that it was often an unknown and disengaged white paternal heritage that had determined their fate, both within their family and at a broader policy level" (2002, 8).

11. A point made by Victoria Haskins, who highlights that the stereotype of the "fatherless" mixed race child underpinned the State taking on "patriarchal authority" over Aboriginal children; she cautions that in continuing to exclude Aboriginal fathers we run the risk of replicating the historical denial of Aboriginal fatherhood. See Haskins 2008.

12. Ruddick 1989, 42–43.

13. For example, the infamous 2016 cartoon by Bill Leak, see https://www.abc.net.au/news/2016-08-04/cartoon-an-attack-on-aboriginal-people,-indige-nous-leader-says/7689248; Shino Konishi also argues convincingly that both the government and the media have represented Aboriginal men as sexual predators and threats to Aboriginal children, see Konishi 2011, 27.

14. Research undertaken on fatherhood and the Stolen Generations includes the aforementioned articles by Victoria Haskins (2008) and Shino Konishi (2011); and Fiona Probyn (2003) addresses the role of "the invisible white fathers" (62) and the state as "good White Father" (73).

15. Katherine Ellinghaus notes that "Many historians have recognized how seldom relationships involving white women and indigenous men occurred" (Ellinghaus 2006, x).

16. Markus, "Legislating White Australia, 1900–1970," 239.

17. Human Rights and Equal Opportunity Commission, *Bringing Them Home,* 27–33.

18. Brock, "Aboriginal Families and the Law in the Era of Segregation and Assimilation," 136; see also Human Rights and Equal Opportunity Commission *Bringing Them Home,* 29.

19. Swain, "History of Child Protection Legislation," 17.

20. Swain, "History of Child Protection Legislation," 19.

21. Manne, "Aboriginal Child Removal and the Question of Genocide, 1900–1940," 227–228.

22. Human Rights and Equal Opportunity Commission, *Bringing Them Home,* 250.

23. Brock, "Aboriginal Families and the Law in the Era of Segregation and Assimilation," 136.

24. Windschuttle, *The Fabrication of Aboriginal History,* 17.

25. Cuthbert and Quartly note that non-Indigenous groups have at times co-opted the terminology and strategies of members of the Stolen Generations, referring to themselves as "the other" or "white" Stolen Generations. Cuthbert and Quartly, "'Forced Adoption' in the Australian Story of National Regret and Apology," 179.

26. Cuthbert and Quartly also report that some mothers who experienced forced adoption have "rallied under the name of the Mothers of the White Stolen Generations." Cuthbert and Quartly, "'Forced Adoption' in the Australian Story of National Regret and Apology," 179.

27. See, for example, Bolt "High Price of not Testing the Truth on 'Stolen Generations.'"

28. Read, "How Many Separated Children?," 155.

29. Ryan Kelly disputed the version of his removal contained in his "official" file; despite the ongoing efforts of his parents to reclaim their children, documented in letters on his file, he commented that the departmental officials "were relentless in their ignorance." Ryan Kelly interviewed by John Maynard, 1 April 2001, ORAL TRC 5000/240, National Library of Australia, 16.

30. Sylvia Neary interviewed by Jane Watson, 16 March 2001, TRC 5000/251, National Library of Australia, 46.

31. Choo, *Mission Girls*, 152.

32. National Library of Australia's *Bringing Them Home* Oral History Project.

33. Human Rights and Equal Opportunity Commission, *Bringing Them Home,* 651.

34. Human Rights and Equal Opportunity Commission, "Submission to the Senate Legal and Constitutional References Committee's Inquiry into the Stolen Generation," 9.

35. Poff, "The Importance of Story-Telling," 27.

36. Feldman et al., "Making Sense of Stories," 148.

37. Woollacott, *Gender and Empire*, 2.

38. Back, *The Art of Listening*, 163.

39. Biographical and autobiographical sources considered include Barnes, *Munyi's Daughter. A Spirited Brumby*; Clare, *Karobran. The Story of an Aboriginal Girl*; Clements, *From Old Maloga (The Memoirs of an Aboriginal Woman)*; Crawford, *Over My Tracks*; Cummings, *Take This Child . . . From Kahlin Compound to the Retta Dixon Children's Home*; Edmund, *No Regrets*; Hegarty, *Is That You, Ruthie?* and *Bittersweet Journey*; Huggins and Huggins, *Auntie Rita*; Kartinyeri, *Kick the Tin*; Kennedy, *Born a Half-Caste*; Langford, *Don't Take Your Love to Town*; McDonald, *When You Grow Up* and *Finding Myself*; McGee-Sippel, *Hey Mum, What's a Half-Caste?*; Mok, *Cherbourg Dorm Girls*; Morgan, *My Place*; Mum Shirl, *Mum Shirl. An Autobiography*; Nannup, Marsh and Kinnane, *When the Pelican Laughed*; Pilkington, *Follow the Rabbit-Proof Fence* and *Under the Wintamarra Tree*; Read, *Tripping Over Feathers*; Roughsey, *An Aboriginal Mother Tells of the Old and the New*; Simon, *Through My Eyes*; Terszak, *Orphaned by the Colour of My Skin*; Tucker, *If Everyone Cared*; Vicenti and Dickman *Too Many Tears*; Walker, *Me and You*; Ward, *Wandering Girl* and *Unna You Fullas*; West, *Pride against Prejudice*; and Woodrow, *One of the Lost Generation*.

40. Clarke, *Things Are So Much Better than They Used to Be*; Macleod, *Patrol in the Dreamtime*.

41. Ladner, "Introduction to Tomorrow's Tomorrow. The Black Woman," 77.

42. Tuhiwai Smith, *Decolonizing Methodologies*, 95.

43. Tuhiwai Smith, *Decolonizing Methodologies*, xi.

44. Nakata, *Disciplining the Savages: Savaging the Disciplines*, 2.

45. Nakata, *Disciplining the Savages: Savaging the Disciplines*, 225.

46. Atkinson, *Trauma Trails*, 15.

47. Ungunmerr-Baumann, "Dadirri. Inner Deep Listening and Quiet Still Awareness."

48. Scott, "The Evidence of Experience," 797.

49. Australian Institute for Aboriginal and Torres Strait Islander Studies, "Indigenous Australians."

50. Australian Institute for Aboriginal and Torres Strait Islander Studies, "Indigenous Australians."

51. Australian Institute for Aboriginal and Torres Strait Islander Studies, "Indigenous Australians."

52. McCorquodale, "The Legal Classification of Race in Australia," 9.

53. Brock, "Aboriginal Families and the Law in the Era of Segregation and Assimilation," 134.

54. Australian Law Reform Commission 2003, my emphasis.

55. Jopson, "A Real Nowhere Man."

56. Gigliotti, "Unspeakable Pasts as Limit Events," 177.

57. See Payne, "Untold Suffering," Appendix 4: Who Can Claim the Status of Being "Stolen"?, 338–345.

58. Rudd, "Apology to Australia's Indigenous Peoples."

59. Human Rights and Equal Opportunity Commission, *Bringing Them Home,* 235.

ONE

Motherhood, Truth-Telling and the *Bringing Them Home* Inquiry

This chapter investigates the reasons for the lack of testimony from mothers at the *Bringing Them Home* Inquiry. While the *Bringing Them Home* Report attributed the lack of participation in the Inquiry by Indigenous parents to the lasting impact of their grief, I explore the possibility that the framing of the issue of child removal by the Inquiry itself may in part have contributed to silencing the testimony of mothers who had experienced child removal. Drawing on the feminist critique of human rights mechanisms as well as themes identified from the oral history interviews and other sources, a number of issues are identified that may have impacted on Aboriginal mothers' willingness to speak about their experiences of child removal.

While people may choose to remain silent about their experiences of human rights violations for diverse reasons, research shows that such silence can be gendered;[1] and the reasons why mothers are silent may be different at least in part from those of others who choose to keep their suffering secret. The focus here is on motherhood, but it is important to acknowledge the impact of social disadvantage and racism in silencing Aboriginal people; these issues are not limited to Aboriginal mothers only. Reflecting critically on the *Bringing Them Home* Inquiry process and its intended and unintended outcomes is of value in considering the design of inclusive truth-telling processes which enable a diversity of opinions and perspectives to be spoken, vital in the context of the recent focus on truth-telling in Australia emerging from the Referendum Council of Australia's regional dialogues and the Uluru Statement from the Heart.[2]

THE *BRINGING THEM HOME* INQUIRY

Australia's *National Inquiry into the Separation of Aboriginal and Torres Strait Islander Children from Their Families*, undertaken by the Australian Human Rights and Equal Opportunity Commission in 1996, documented an under-recognized aspect of Australian history, and attempted to reconfigure community attitudes towards Aboriginal child removal practices that had previously been seen as unproblematic, but which the Inquiry now concluded constituted genocide.[3] This Inquiry took place within the context of burgeoning international interest in the use of "truth-seeking" models to examine both contemporary and historical injustices. The *Bringing Them Home* Inquiry is part of a longer history of activism by both Indigenous and non-Indigenous Australians on issues of Indigenous rights throughout the twentieth century, addressing issues such as land rights, dispossession, segregation, and child removal, as well as the Maralinga Royal Commission into British Nuclear Tests in Australia and the Royal Commission into Aboriginal Deaths in Custody.[4]

The main focus of the Inquiry, or at least of the Report that is its primary public product, was on the experiences and testimony of people who were forcibly removed as children. The voices of these adult survivors of child removal are a key feature of the Report, however there is very little testimony included within the *Bringing Them Home* Report from Indigenous parents whose children were removed. This strong focus on the removed children shapes the Inquiry, in terms of evidence collected, the people interviewed, and the Report's findings and recommendations.

The *Bringing Them Home* Report acknowledged the lack of parental testimony at the Inquiry, describing it as a consequence of both the devastating impact of child removal on the lives of Indigenous parents, and the unwillingness of those still living to talk about their experiences: "Few of the parents have survived to tell their own stories. Many of those who have feel such guilt and despair that they were unable to come forward."[5] Mick Dodson, cochair of the Inquiry with Sir Ronald Wilson, commented at the launch of the Report at the National Reconciliation Convention that "One thing missing from this report are the mothers' stories—but then how could a mother possibly bear to tell of her loss?"[6] The Report contained an extract from a submission by the Aboriginal community-based organization Link-Up NSW, which specifically addressed the issue of the nonparticipation of mothers in the Inquiry:

> we realize that here is where our mothers were hurt most deeply. Here is where they were shamed and humiliated—they were deprived of the opportunity to participate in growing up their next generation. They were made to feel failures; unworthy of loving and caring for their own children; they were denied participation in the future of their community.[7]

The following statement included in the Report, an extract from the confidential testimony of one woman who was herself removed as a child and placed in multiple foster care arrangements, is one of the few voices of Aboriginal mothers who experienced child removal quoted in the entire 689-page Report:

> I'm a rotten mother. My own husband even put my kids in the Home, and I fought to get them back. And then I was in a relationship after that, and he even put my kids in the Home. I think I've tried to do the best I could but that wasn't good enough. Why? Because I didn't have a role model for a start.[8]

This statement addresses the intergenerational impact of child removal which was also highlighted within the Report; more than one third of Stolen Generations respondents in one study undertaken by the Aboriginal Legal Service of WA indicated that their own children had been removed.[9] Statistics such as these suggest that at least some of the witnesses who gave evidence to the Inquiry about their experiences of being removed as a child could also have testified about their experiences as a parent of having their children removed, if these questions had been asked by the Inquiry. The *Bringing Them Home* Report itself acknowledged that "Due to the intergenerational dimension of child removal, many of the people who gave testimony of their own experiences of removal presumably may also have experienced removal of their own children."[10]

DEFINITIONAL LIMITATIONS

It is worth noting that nothing in the Inquiry's mandate limited it to only investigating the child victims of removal practices; indeed, the Report itself noted "Term of reference (a) does not confine the Inquiry to dealing only with children removed from their parents."[11] Elsewhere, the Report stated that "The effects on the families left behind and on the entire Indigenous community must also be acknowledged,"[12] including recognition of the traumatic long-term impact of the removals on parents, who, it was noted, "could generally find no meaning in the forcible removal."[13]

The Inquiry utilized an incredibly broad definition of what constituted an Aboriginal family: "For Indigenous children their 'families' were constituted by their entire communities . . . the practices relevant to us do not require us to distinguish 'families' from 'communities.' Children removed from their families were also removed from their communities."[14]

By avoiding distinguishing between the loss resulting from child removal experienced by individual families and the loss experienced by Indigenous communities, the Inquiry was following a common pattern that has been identified in transitional justice of attributing harms done to women as harms done to the broader community. Rashida Manjoo, former UN Special Rapporteur on Violence Against Women, has argued that "Women's roles as mothers and bearers of children, or as bearers of collective identity, often render women as targets of specific policies and practices," and that this leads to "a general lack of accountability for crimes against women," as it is *the community* that is seen as the principal victim.[15] The Inquiry's focus on child removal as a *community loss* was essential to the genocide case it was constructing: "When a child was forcibly removed that child's entire community lost, often permanently, its chance to perpetuate itself in that child. The Inquiry has concluded that this was a primary objective of forcible removals and is the reason they amount to genocide."[16]

It is also important to note that the Inquiry did not investigate child removals that might have taken place *within* Aboriginal families or communities:

> The broad definition of the Indigenous family adopted by the Inquiry means that some experiences of separation from parents are beyond our terms of reference. Typically, too, these did not involve the application of laws, practices and policies of forcible removal. One example is the child reared by her maternal grandparents who now seeks to trace her father without assistance from her mother or her family. . . . Another is the woman whose own mother has raised her children and refuses to return them to their mother.[17]

As we will see in further detail when we consider the experiences of Aboriginal mothers in chapter 9, informal fostering arrangements where Aboriginal mothers placed a child or children with a trusted friend or relative for either a short or extended period of time were not unusual during the Stolen Generations era, and such caring arrangements have been described by some researchers as a characteristic of Aboriginal and other nonwhite families.[18] Evidence from the interviews and autobiographical sources indicates that such arrangements usually arose because the mother had only limited alternatives available to her; however the Inquiry made it clear in this statement that such arrangements were not included within its definition of what constituted being "stolen" or forcibly removed.

Another important aspect of the Inquiry's terms of reference was the requirement to investigate Aboriginal and Torres Strait Islander child removal "by compulsion, duress or undue influence." In the initial section of the Report outlining the scope of the Inquiry, an attempt was made to define these terms, with compulsion being defined as meaning "force or coercion," whether legally or illegally exercised;[19] duress was defined as not requiring the application of force but involving "threats or at least moral pressure";[20] and undue influence was defined as "putting improper pressure on the family to induce the surrender of the children."[21] It was also noted that "for ease of reference" the umbrella term "forcible removal" was used throughout the Report.[22] An early example in the Report highlighted what was described as common child removal practice; "to remove the child forcibly, often in the absence of the parent but sometimes even by taking the child from the mother's arms."[23]

A number of people interviewed in the NLA's *Bringing Them Home* Oral History Project believed that to legitimately describe oneself as a member of the Stolen Generations, a child had to be literally "snatched" from their mother's arms.[24] Although the Inquiry has been criticized for its "extraordinarily wide conception of 'forcible removal,'"[25] I would argue that the emphasis on "forcible removal" actually limited the Inquiry's capacity to investigate some of the broader systemic issues that contributed to Aboriginal child removal, such as those that are outlined in chapters 3 through 6 of this book. The Inquiry's focus on "forcible" removals also implicitly suggested that some Indigenous child removals were "voluntary" or "unforced." However, how many removals could be described as truly "voluntary" within the context of the time, in which Aboriginal mothers had extremely limited options available to support their children, Aboriginal parents had legal limitations on their parental rights and were discriminated against in access to social security benefits, and Aboriginality was automatically equated with poor parenting and neglected children?

Whilst I have no wish to denigrate the important work undertaken by the *Bringing Them Home* Inquiry under what were no doubt great financial and political constraints, I have outlined the Inquiry's terms of reference and the way it conceived of and constructed the issue of Aboriginal child removal in some detail here to emphasize that choices were being made about what policies, practices and experiences would be investigated, and those which would not, highlighting the ways in which a human rights violation is constructed to address particular or politically palatable wrongs, rather than all the wrongful behavior or violation of rights that might have taken place.[26] Possibly the Inquiry highlights limitations inherent within the concept of human rights, the need to reconceptualize victims beyond the human rights paradigm of the right holder and to assess the collective impact of a human rights violation.[27]

"OPENING WOUNDS": PARTICIPATING IN THE *BRINGING THEM HOME* INQUIRY

Women often participate in human rights inquiries to testify about the harms done to others, rather than themselves; Katherine Franke describes women testifiers as "repositories of memory for the suffering of others."[28] For example, approximately equal proportions of men and women testified at the South African Truth and Reconciliation Commission, but women largely spoke about the sufferings of male relatives, whereas men spoke about their own experiences.[29] This was in no small part due to the way in which the South African Truth and Reconciliation Commission defined its focus exclusively on *"political* violence," in a way that excluded the "everyday" violence and degradations of apartheid that were primarily experienced by women.[30]

A number of interviewees in the National Library of Australia's Oral History Project spoke about their experience of taking part in the *Bringing Them Home* Inquiry. Despite a widespread perception that "speaking out" about injustice is an essential precursor to healing, it is evident from the transcripts that not all of the interviewees who testified found the experience of participating in a human rights inquiry a positive one.

One interviewee, Carol Kendall, worked for a community organization and was involved in the Inquiry as a state representative. She reflected on the impact of limited finances on the facilitation of community input into the Inquiry process; nevertheless, she felt that the process was important and that significant input was achieved. However, she commented that the negative reception of the Report by the federal government contributed to re-traumatizing some people in the community; rather than the truth of their stories being acknowledged, many people in the federal government and the wider community did not want to hear the "truths" the Inquiry was telling as they challenged other dominant narratives about the Australian nation:

> The things that were achieved were, I believe, that people came, opened up their wounds with great courage and strength, and talked about their pain with the hope that the truth would finally be acknowledged. Now, from that we've had people retraumatised, because prior to the findings of the inquiry the Prime Minister, Mr Howard, tried to discredit that document, which then, in effect, gave people the view that people had come there and lied. That somehow it wasn't really the truth. It wasn't really what happened. It wasn't really what people wanted to hear, is what the issue is. It didn't show this country in the light that we all like to think, that we live in the lucky country. I believe the lucky country is only lucky for some, you know, and that's very true. There are still issues that haven't been addressed. [31]

It is likely that official rejection of the findings of the Inquiry by the federal government contributed to silencing other victims.[32] The failure to show empathy towards others' suffering has been described as an unavoidable feature of the human response to pain. In her sociological study of the nature of physical suffering, Elaine Scarry noted that "to have great pain is to have certainty; to hear that another person has pain is to have doubt," and that this doubt has the impact of amplifying the suffering of those in pain.[33] Others have emphasized the under-recognized social and relational dimensions of pain, and the invisibility of racialized pain;[34] historically, black women's capacity to experience pain has often been downplayed, as we will see in chapter 8 in the perception of some white Australians during the Stolen Generations era that Aboriginal mothers were not capable of experiencing the same depth of grief and loss on the removal of their children that a white mother would experience.

Yvonne Mills spoke about her experience participating in a family session at the Inquiry with her siblings, all of whom had been removed from their mother as children. In her case, although present at the Inquiry, she was silenced due to being overwhelmed by her emotions, as the realization of what her mother must have gone through finally hit her:

> That's when it really hit me, it really hit me at that meeting that this wasn't all my mother's fault. You know, I was hearing all these things and I suddenly start thinking after all these years, I had sort of been thinking of myself and what all of this had done to me. And I never once had thought what happened to my mother, what was she going through? You know, how did she feel with all these things that were happening to her. And I suddenly realised that in this, what was supposed to be this telling of what happened to our family, and I started crying and I cried through the whole session.
>
> When it was my turn to talk, when they asked me what I would like to say I just couldn't say anything. . . . And when the opportunity came for me to talk I couldn't talk because I was so emotionally upset because for the first time I'd realised gee, you know, what did my mother go through?[35]

Mary Terszak's experience of childhood removal and subsequent dislocation resulted in her living interstate and far removed from her own community. When she participated in a *Bringing Them Home* community consultation, she reported feeling that her story and her experiences were not valued by the community in which she now lived, leaving her with ambivalent feelings about her participation:

> When I went to the Bringing Them Home meeting in Redfern I sat there, and because they're Kooris, I'm a Nyungah. I don't understand. We're still Aboriginal people. They don't care how I feel. . . . I sat there. I listened to it all. I did have input into the Bringing Them Home. I produced a picture which was put into the small book on a few of us kids from Sister Kate's, but the way I felt I don't think she was particularly interested in what I was saying, even though I was sad and giving over a bit of how I was feeling. I was a bit jumbled up, I think, in what I was saying. I don't know.[36]

Rather than feeling validated and part of a community of people who had suffered similar experiences, Mary felt alienated and that her story was not valued or of interest. Researchers have investigated similar instances of "outlier" or "non-fitting" narratives within human rights inquiries. One case is the testimony of Mrs. Konile, the mother of one of the "Gugulethu 7" killed by the apartheid regime, at the South African Truth and Reconciliation Commission (SATRC). Arguing that the SATRC "was looking for a certain kind of story: that of a brutal regime, stoic struggle, resilient mothers and families, and an eventual triumph over evil,"[37] Krog et al. highlight that Mrs. Konile's testimony was instead seen as incoherent and confusing, in part because of issues with translation but also because the imagery and metaphor Mrs. Konile used to describe her experiences were meaningless to the tribunal, which lacked the cultural background to understand her. The researchers comment:

> within a postcolonial context, a woman may appear either incoherent because of severe suffering or unintelligible because of oppression— while in fact she is neither. Within her indigenous framework, she is logical and resilient in her knowledge of her loss and its devastating consequences in her life. She is not too devastated to make sense; she is devastated because she intimately understands the devastation that has happened to her. However, the forum she finds herself in and the way narratives are being read make it very hard for her to bring the depth of this devastation across.[38]

Judith Stubbs described the negative after-effects of her experience of testifying before the *Bringing Them Home* Inquiry. Her participation in the Inquiry brought up a lot of issues she didn't want to deal with, and details about her testimony were published in the Report, which led her to feel that her confidentiality had been breached:

> Interviewer: With giving evidence in the Stolen Generation, for the Stolen Generation Report, that was a pretty powerful political thing you did.
>
> Judith: Yeah it was but in some ways I'm sorry I did that.
>
> Interviewer: Why?
>
> Judith: It just opened up a lot of things that I didn't want opened up. It made my life miserable, it made it terrible.
>
> Interviewer: Do you feel they abused your confidence?
>
> Judith: Yeah, 'course they did.[39]

For some interviewees, talk changes nothing; what they sought as an outcome from their truth-telling was compensation that would help them to address some of the damages that had been inflicted.[40] This remains part of the "unfinished business" of the Inquiry.[41]

A number of white interviewees were also highly critical of the *Bringing Them Home* Inquiry, either because of what they saw as procedural flaws in the Inquiry process, or because they believed their testimony was unwanted.[42] From the perspective of former patrol officer Les Penhall, the Inquiry was one-sided and could not claim to tell "the truth" about Aboriginal child removals because it had not sought out all perspectives:

> So I find that the credibility of the whole report is certainly subject to query. Also that no attempt was made to find out the other side of the story. Because everything was given *in camera*, no-one can query what was told to the inquiry, and to me most of it is half-truths. They haven't told the whole truth. I think that the report should be ignored. . . . Because it just gives the wrong impression altogether of what actually happened.[43]

There are strong parallels here with the reception of the South African Truth and Reconciliation Commission's multi-volume report, which was widely received by opposition parties in South Africa "as an ideological advertising campaign for the ANC's version of the past."[44] In a similar vein to criticisms of the *Bringing Them Home* Inquiry, the South African Truth and Reconciliation Commission was also criticized for failing to uphold "legal standards of investigation,"[45] highlighting fundamental misunderstandings about human rights inquiry processes, particularly those which utilize restorative justice mechanisms which place an emphasis on victim narratives.

Traditional Western approaches to law have been critiqued by Indigenous academics as being hierarchical, adversarial, win-lose, individualistic and divisive.[46] This is contrasted with the promise of restorative justice, which is seen by some to be an approach more compatible with Indigenous approaches to justice.[47] The concept of "truth-telling" emerges from restorative justice processes designed to bring victims and perpetrators together. Restorative justice tries to incorporate the experience of victims (retributive justice processes are seen to be focused on perpetrators), and truth-telling in the context of transitional justice is typically based on acknowledging the truth of victim accounts in the face of previous state denial. Truth is often associated with "healing" based on assumptions about the cathartic process of giving testimony (although it is important to note here that some question whether testifying is in fact healing for all victims).[48]

There has been growing recognition of "the right to truth" within the international human rights framework, with the UN Human Rights Committee passing a Resolution on the Right to the Truth in 2009, an International Day for the Right to the Truth Concerning Gross Human Rights Violations being established by the UN General Assembly in 2010, a Special Rapporteur on the promotion of truth, justice, reparation and guarantees of non-recurrence being established in 2012, and a UN Resolution on the Right to Truth being passed by the General Assembly in 2013.

Truth-telling is part of a wider movement of recognition about the ongoing legacy of the past. In transitional justice truth-telling processes, the past is being revisited as a way to move forward; or as Stan Cohen expresses it, "You discover the truth about the past in order to achieve justice in the present."[49] However, it is important to note that truth-telling does not necessarily result in either justice for victims or punishment for wrong-doers. There is a danger that the truth will be a form of "phantom justice," offering "an apparition of redress without material substance."[50] Acknowledgment has been described as the bridge between knowing about past injustice and doing something about it; Cohen argues that "Acknowledgement is what happens to knowledge when it becomes officially sanctioned and enters the public discourse."[51] In Australia, there have been ongoing calls by Aboriginal and Torres Strait Islander peoples for truth-telling, to acknowledge the multiple ways in which the past is replicated in the present-day experiences of Indigenous Australians.[52]

Reactions by some of the white interviewees in the NLA's *Bringing Them Home* Oral History Project highlight that there was a failure to understand that the *Bringing Them Home* Inquiry was not operating in a traditional retributive justice mode, with the evidentiary standards and cross-examination of witnesses that such a model requires. The hostility expressed by some white interviewees is more understandable with the realization that from their perspective, they felt they had been judged and found guilty without the benefit of a "fair trial." Perhaps there was a need to hear all stories and perspectives, to at least minimize the possibly inevitable perception that the Inquiry was one-sided. As these criticisms demonstrate, human rights inquiries do not operate in a political vacuum—the power dynamics of the political context impact upon their operations and investigations, and on the way their findings are received and understood.

"Truth-telling" about Australia's colonial history has recently (re)emerged as a significant issue in Australia, with some arguing that this "moment of truth"—the opportunity to engage with the history of relations between Indigenous and non-Indigenous Australians—will have major implications for the ongoing legitimacy of the Australian nation.[53] The Uluru Statement from the Heart (2017), the outcome of an unprecedented process of dialogue with Indigenous communities nationally,[54] outlined the call from Indigenous community representatives for the establishment of truth-telling mechanisms to explore Aboriginal and Torres Strait Islander perspectives on Australia's colonial past. The demand for truth-telling from the process participants emerged spontaneously (it was not an option in the Referendum Council's discussion paper) and was unanimous at every Dialogue;[55] one of the Guiding Principles emerging from the First Nations Regional Dialogues was that a reform option should only proceed if it "Tells the truth of history."[56] Appleby and Davis have reminded us that truth-telling "has not been absent in the relationship between Indigenous and non-Indigenous Australia."[57] However, despite a seeming plethora of truth-telling, the process remains "ad hoc and piecemeal over the decades, and there is little coherency across the federation."[58] Reconciliation Australia's Reconciliation Barometer has recently identified that around one-third of Australians are either unaware of, or reject, significant aspects of Australia's colonial history, including frontier massacres and the forcible removal of Indigenous land and children.[59] Research suggests that the barriers to learning historical "truths" are attitudinal as well as structural,[60] and researchers have lamented the piecemeal nature of current educational approaches as well as the levels of "disaffection, disinterest and denial of Aboriginal and Torres Strait Islander history in Australia."[61]

The Joint Select Committee on Constitutional Recognition relating to Aboriginal and Torres Strait Islander Peoples Final Report (2018) described truth-telling as a process encompassing multiple dimensions, including as a foundational requirement for healing and reconciliation, a form of restorative justice, a process for Indigenous people to share their culture and history with the broader community and to build wider understanding of the intergenerational trauma experienced by Indigenous Australians, and to build awareness of the relationship between past injustices and contemporary issues.[62] Truth-telling is not imagined here simply as an historical process designed to set the record straight—there is an ongoing need for "transition" within the call for truth-telling about Australian history to re-set the relationship between Indigenous and non-Indigenous Australians.[63] June Oscar recently described the capacity of truth-telling processes to shift expectations and perspectives, to transform relations and to "develop a national narrative of equality."[64]

Although there was overwhelming support for truth-telling at the First Nations Regional Dialogues, special measures may be required to minimize the trauma caused to Indigenous peoples by asking them to remember painful past histories.[65] Some researchers are optimistic about the potential for truth-telling processes, arguing that they "offer dramatic images of honouring Indigenous experiences, overturning colonial structures, and challenging their legitimacy."[66] However, as we will see in chapter 2, not everyone is comfortable in telling their truth, and it has been noted that "Silence may operate as an effective shield in a sociopolitical environment unwilling to listen to the voices of the victims."[67] Noting that "Indigenous attempts to reclaim land, language, knowledge and sovereignty have usually involved contested accounts of the past by colonizers and colonized," Tuhiwai Smith warns that "a thousand accounts of the 'truth' will not alter the 'fact' that indigenous peoples are still marginal and do not possess the power to transform history into justice."[68] She highlights that "Sharing knowledge is a long-term commitment,"[69] arguing that "This form of remembering is painful because it involves remembering not just what colonization was about but what being dehumanized means for our own cultural practices,"[70] words which resonate strongly in the context of the history of the Stolen Generations in Australia.

While it is important to reflect on truth-telling and the experiences of those who testified at the *Bringing Them Home* Inquiry, it is also important to consider the experiences of those who didn't even consider speaking at the Inquiry, and why they might have chosen to remain silent—their experiences will be explored in the following chapter.

NOTES

1. Nesiah, "Gender and Truth Commission Mandates," 1.
2. Commonwealth of Australia, "Final Report of the Referendum Council," 15.
3. Human Rights and Equal Opportunity Commission, *Bringing Them Home,* 218.
4. Goodall 2006.
5. Human Rights and Equal Opportunity Commission, *Bringing Them Home,* 212.
6. Dodson, "National Inquiry into the Separation of Aboriginal and Torres Strait Islander Children from Their Families."
7. Human Rights and Equal Opportunity Commission, *Bringing Them Home,* 212.
8. Human Rights and Equal Opportunity Commission, *Bringing Them Home,* 226.
9. Human Rights and Equal Opportunity Commission, *Bringing Them Home,* 226. In comparison, a more recent national study undertaken by researchers at the UNSW found that 13.1 percent of respondents (both Indigenous and non-Indigenous) who had spent their childhood in out-of-home care had their own children taken into care. Fernandez et al., *No Child Should Grow Up Like This,* 13.
10. Human Rights and Equal Opportunity Commission, *Bringing Them Home,* 222.
11. Human Rights and Equal Opportunity Commission, *Bringing Them Home,* 11.
12. Human Rights and Equal Opportunity Commission, *Bringing Them Home,* 15.
13. Human Rights and Equal Opportunity Commission, *Bringing Them Home,* 214.
14. Human Rights and Equal Opportunity Commission, *Bringing Them Home,* 11.
15. Manjoo, "Gender Injustice and the South African Truth and Reconciliation Commission," 137–138, my emphasis.
16. Human Rights and Equal Opportunity Commission, *Bringing Them Home,* 218.
17. Human Rights and Equal Opportunity Commission, *Bringing Them Home,* 12.
18. See Eades, *Courtroom Talk and Neocolonial Control*; Stack, *All Our Kin.*
19. Human Rights and Equal Opportunity Commission, *Bringing Them Home,* 5.
20. Human Rights and Equal Opportunity Commission, *Bringing Them Home,* 6.
21. Human Rights and Equal Opportunity Commission, *Bringing Them Home,* 9.
22. Human Rights and Equal Opportunity Commission, *Bringing Them Home,* 5.
23. Human Rights and Equal Opportunity Commission, *Bringing Them Home,* 5.
24. See Payne 2016, "Untold Suffering," 338–345.
25. McGregor, "Governance, not Genocide," 292.
26. Barkan, *The Guilt of Nations,* xx.
27. Rubio-Marín, "What Happened to the Women?," 31.
28. Franke, "Gendered Subjects of Transitional Justice," 822.
29. Ross, *Bearing Witness,* 17.
30. Ross, *Bearing Witness,* 15.

31. Carol Kendall interviewed by John Maynard, 5 April 2001, ORAL TRC 5000/246, National Library of Australia, 44.

32. Gigliotti "Unspeakable Pasts as Limit Events," 177.

33. Scarry, *The Body in Pain*, 7.

34. Fannin, "Labour Pain," 25.

35. Yvonne Mills interviewed by Colleen Hattersley, 15 August 1999, ORAL TRC 5000/37, National Library of Australia, 26.

36. Mary Terszak interviewed by John Bannister, 4 November 1999, ORAL TRC 5000/61, National Library of Australia, 4.

37. Krog et al., "The South African Truth and Reconciliation Commission," 541.

38. Krog et al., "The South African Truth and Reconciliation Commission," 544.

39. Judith Stubbs interviewed by Ann-Mari Jordens, 22 October 2000, ORAL TRC 5000/175, National Library of Australia, 67.

40. See, for example, Deirdre Heitmeyer interviewed by John Maynard, 4 March 1999, ORAL TRC 5000/11, National Library of Australia, 6–7; Judith Stubbs interviewed by Ann-Mari Jordens, 22 October 2000, ORAL TRC 5000/175, National Library of Australia, 58; Mary Terszak interviewed by John Bannister, 4 November 1999, ORAL TRC 5000/61, National Library of Australia, 40–42.

41. Reys, "Unfinished Business—Reparations and Reconciliation."

42. Penhall relates his experience of attending the Inquiry and offering to give evidence when it met in Darwin. He states that he was told that time didn't allow for this and he was told that "I should put in a written submission. I felt that while I felt strongly about the whole thing, I didn't feel sitting down and writing a submission to the inquiry, because I thought that, you know, I was there and volunteered to give evidence." Les Penhall interviewed by Francis Good, 25 January & 1 Feb 2000, ORAL TRC 5000/105, National Library of Australia, 44.

43. Les Penhall interviewed by Francis Good, 25 January & 1 Feb 2000, ORAL TRC 5000/105, National Library of Australia, 43–44.

44. Wilson, *The Politics of Truth and Reconciliation in South Africa*, 39.

45. Wilson, *The Politics of Truth and Reconciliation in South Africa*, 33.

46. McCaslin and Breton, "Justice as Healing. Going Outside the Colonizers' Cage," 524.

47. McCaslin and Breton, "Justice as Healing. Going Outside the Colonizers' Cage," 528.

48. See for example Aolain and Turner "Gender, Truth & Transition," and Brounéus, "Truth-Telling as Talking Cure?"

49. Cohen, "States of Denial," 242–243.

50. Lugosi, "Truth-Telling and Legal Discourse," 312.

51. Cohen, "States of Denial," 225.

52. Oscar, "June Oscar's 2020 Vision."

53. Davis, "Moment of Truth: Correspondence"; McKenna, "Moment of Truth."

54. Commonwealth of Australia, "Final Report of the Referendum Council."

55. Commonwealth of Australia, "Final Report of the Referendum Council," 15.

56. Commonwealth of Australia, "Final Report of the Referendum Council," 22.

57. Appleby and Davis, "The Uluru Statement and the Promises of Truth," 501.

58. Appleby and Davis, "The Uluru Statement and the Promises of Truth," 502.

59. Reconciliation Australia, "Truth-Telling about the Past, the Present and the Future."

60. Clark, *History's Children*.

61. Appleby and Davis, "The Uluru Statement and the Promises of Truth," 502.

62. Joint Select Committee on Constitutional Recognition, "Final Report."

63. Appleby and Davis, "The Uluru Statement and the Promises of Truth," 507.

64. Oscar, "June Oscar's 2020 Vision."

65. Tuhiwai Smith, "Decolonizing Methodologies," 147.

66. McCaslin and Breton, "Justice as Healing," 521.

67. Vatan and Silberman, "After the Violence: Memory," 3.

68. Tuhiwai Smith, "Decolonizing Methodologies," 35.
69. Tuhiwai Smith, "Decolonizing Methodologies," 16.
70. Tuhiwai Smith, "Decolonizing Methodologies," 147.

TWO

Untold Suffering? Motherhood and Silence

Silence is complex and multifaceted, and cannot be simply interpreted as the absence of speech; it can be the result of a deliberate choice, due to reticence, or because of constraints imposed by others on who can speak and what can be discussed.[1] Noting the ambiguous relationship between silence, secrecy and power, Foucault commented that "Silence and secrets are a shelter for power, anchoring its prohibitions; but they also loosen its holds and provide for relatively obscure areas of tolerance."[2]

Choosing to remain silent infers a position of power and the withholding of knowledge and information—a strategy Indigenous people have used effectively in colonial and post-colonial contexts to retain control over their knowledge[3]—whereas *being silenced* carries the association of victimhood and oppression.

The human rights literature often unproblematically promotes the need to "speak out," to testify, as a positive and healing.[4] Indeed such personal testimony forms the basis of most human rights mechanisms that enable redress for violations and past harms. Remaining silent, if an active choice, has significant consequences within the processes currently in place to address violations of human rights.

However, some human rights researchers have argued that there is very little empirical evidence to support the common assumption that "speaking out" or truth-telling leads to resolution or healing, particularly in the absence of a sympathetic listener and a safe environment in which to testify. Karen Brounéus, whose research analyzes the experiences of women who testified in *gacaca* courts in Rwanda, postulates that truth-telling may entail more risk for women than for men.[5] In post-genocide Rwanda, the social stigma attached to women's experience of sexual violence, the complexity of victim/perpetrator relationships occurring even

31

within families, and the ongoing insecurity of the women's environment constituted heightened risks for women in publicly testifying about their experiences of human rights violations, resulting for some women in their re-traumatization, ill-health and social isolation.[6]

In her research about Australians' perception of the past, Heather Goodall has identified an understandable reluctance by Indigenous Australians to relinquish custodianship of their stories, as well as a perception that it was "too early" in the Reconciliation process for some stories to be shared.[7] Other researchers have emphasized that there is at times a deliberate withholding of some information within stories told to the broader community by Aboriginal people, to emphasize that some knowledge is not for sharing;[8] some stories "are as much about 'secrecy and strategic non-disclosure' as they are about the giving of information."[9]

Diane Eades describes silence as a much greater feature of Aboriginal English than it is of non-Aboriginal English; it does not have the negative association that is often attributed to silence in Western discourse, but is rather "a positive and productive feature of many interactions."[10] Differentiating between "active silence" and "passive silence," Deborah Bird Rose has also noted that silence in Aboriginal discourse has been wrongly interpreted as an absence, but rather is used as a strategy of knowledge management; "Silence is crucial: control is exercised through judicious management—opening and closing, revealing and concealing."[11]

In this chapter I apply these theories about the relative benefits and consequences of silence and speaking out about human rights violations to the evidence about the experiences of Aboriginal mothers in the Stolen Generations era, to determine if there are particular aspects unique to women's status as mothers that impact on their decision to speak or remain silent about their own experiences of human rights violations.

"HAVING NO VOICE": CONSTRAINTS ON SPEAKING ABOUT SEXUAL ASSAULT

Feminist theorists have criticized human rights processes for a "narrow" interpretation of gender analysis that only focuses on sexual violence.[12] Some have identified the costs involved to women when speaking about their experiences of sexual violation; this is seen primarily as the social cost of losing the "benefits that accrue to perceived purity."[13] Women may also be fearful about the possible consequences of their speech, as Urvashi Butalia's research into the ongoing silence of women who were abducted during the partition of India and Pakistan has identified:

> For women who had been through rape and abduction the reluctance to speak was of another order altogether. Sometimes these histories were not known even to members of their own families. . . . Speaking

about them, making them public, this not only meant opening up old wounds, but also being prepared to live with the consequences—perhaps another rejection, another trauma.[14]

However, there is another potential constraint specific to mothers speaking about their experiences of rape and sexual abuse that has emerged from my research: concern about the impact of such revelations on their children. Ruby[15] identified her concern about the impact that speaking about the circumstances of her falling pregnant through nonconsensual intercourse may have on her son and on other family members. She related her experience of falling pregnant in extremely difficult circumstances without any immediate family support:

> I got myself, found myself in a situation that I couldn't get out of and then I had [my son], you know. But I could never say anything to anybody, I had no family there to support me. . . . And, everyone believed it was consensual. I didn't say anything different. . . . I just let people think what they said. I had no family to back me up. . . . I just didn't say anything. They knew. They knew who [the father] was. . . . And I didn't know how, I couldn't tell anybody, I had no family. Because when you're on an Aboriginal community, you've got to have a mob behind you to back you up. . . . So I had no one. So I just kept that in, you know, I let people think what they thought, whatever they thought about me, and I didn't contest it.[16]

Ruby did not disclose the nonconsensual nature of the intercourse that resulted in her pregnancy at the time because she felt isolated and without the support of any immediate family. After the birth of her son, her concerns about speaking about the incident became focused on the impact it would have on him and other family members if she revealed the circumstances of his conception:

> I didn't want to hurt my son. He's got a very close relationship with his siblings . . . he's got a very very good relationship with them, and I didn't want to hurt any of them. . . . So I just left them to think what they wanted to think. . . . I never spoke to anyone about it. . . . I never said, because, while [my son]'s still alive, I never want to hurt him, you know. . . . So, he's very close to that [family], and I'd never, you know, in a million years try to jeopardise that. . . . He doesn't know anything about it. I never ever said anything about it. I let him believe what he's been told, or whatever he's been told. I don't know what he's been told . . . it would have been pointless me saying anything because so many people would get hurt. So I just carried that all these years. . . .
>
> Interviewer: And what do you think, um, you know, have you ever spoken to [your son] about it, or is that a no-go area? How does he feel about it now, do you think, does he understand what you did, or is it a little bit of a soft spot, or . . . ?

Ruby: I never had that conversation.

Interviewer: No.

Ruby: I didn't want to get into the area about the relationship with his father . . . Because I don't know how I would have responded to that.

Interviewer: If he started asking you questions about that?

Ruby: Yeah, whether I'd skip over that. I think there's an assumption about what happened . . . I couldn't say that to [my son], his father's a sleaze, and especially when he's got his brothers and sisters and they all look up to him as well, you know. So I couldn't say anything like that . . . I had no voice, you know.[17]

PLUMBING THE GREAT DARK DEPTHS: DAISY CORUNNA'S STORY

Another Aboriginal mother who felt heavily constrained from speaking about the circumstances of her child's parentage and conception was Daisy Corunna, Sally Morgan's grandmother. A dominant theme throughout Sally Morgan's celebrated autobiography *My Place* is the ongoing refusal of her Nan to speak to her family about her past life and experiences; one aspect of this is the suppression of her grandchildren's knowledge of their Aboriginality. In the moving concluding section of the book, Daisy, dying of lung cancer, finally agrees to speak—although not fully:

> I don't want to talk no more. I got my secrets, I'll take them to the grave. Some things I can't talk 'bout. Not even to you, my grand daughter. They for me to know. They not for you or your mother to know.
> I'm glad I won't be here in body when you finish that book. I'm glad I'm goin'. You a stirrer, you gunna have a lot of talkin' to do. I can't stick up for myself, you see. It's better you do it. Look out for your mother, she's like me.[18]

Daisy's prediction that Morgan's account of her family's past experiences would be controversial was accurate; Morgan's book has been criticized in terms of the accuracy of her claims about her family history and her failure to make the recordings of her interviews with her grandmother, mother and uncle available to other researchers to "prove" their accuracy.[19] Aboriginal critiques have also abounded, and cultural theorist John Docker describes *My Place* as "a flashpoint and a challenge, not only to local Australian arguments concerning the body, ethnicity, and identity, but to the wider unresolved centuries-long post-1492 colonial and post-colonial histories of conversion and assimilation, exile and diaspora."[20] However, one potential reading of *My Place* is as a study of an Aboriginal woman's silence. What is of interest here are the factors that contributed to Daisy's ongoing silence, sustained over many decades. For me, re-reading *My Place* after many years and considering it within the context of my research, the emotional heart of the book was not Morgan's discovery of her Aboriginal identity, but the decision by her dying Nan to at last speak about her experiences after a lifetime of suppressing her stories.

There are a number of possible reasons explored within the text for Daisy's refusal to talk even to close family members about her life. The suggestion of incest is hinted at without being directly addressed, as is the vulnerability of Aboriginal women working as domestic servants to rape. As I have outlined above, when the circumstances relating to the conception and birth of a child are potentially distressing to either the mother or the child, this operates as a constraint on the mother's ability to speak about the past. When speaking about her search for her father, one interviewee mentions her search opening up "some very unspeakable indignities that happened within the family that I won't put in here."[21] Peter Read reminds us that not all family reunions were happy ones; his experience working to reunify Aboriginal families separated by child removal included mothers rejecting their now-adult children who were seeking out their family, "particularly when there was rape, or incest, incest-rape worst of all, because of, you know, that's just so explosive in the family."[22]

There is a tension in *My Place* between women's traditional role as the preservers and transmitters of cultural and family knowledge, and women suppressing this knowledge, "between women as bearers of family history, and women forced to conceal kinship connections or create false genealogies."[23] After hearing Daisy's story, Morgan reflects on how much is still being withheld; learning part of her Nan's history had "only made me even more aware of how much we still didn't know . . . I knew there were great dark depths there, and I knew we would never plumb them."[24] The "Great Dark Depths" of some of her Nan's experiences remain forever unspoken.

Throughout *My Place*, Daisy is described often somewhat comically as being afraid of people in positions of authority—government officials, doctors, even the man who comes to collect the rent—and fearful of the consequences of her granddaughter writing down the family history:

> You don't know what the government's like, you're too young. You'll find out one day what they can do. You never trust anyone who works for the government, you dunno what they say about you behind your back.[25]

> You won't ever tell them anything about me, will you, Sally? I don't like strangers knowing our business, especially government people. You never know what they might do.[26]

Daisy is aware that others may see her fears as irrational, however her fear is based in the reality of her life experiences; she comments to Morgan, "You different to me. I been scared all my life, too scared to speak out. Maybe if you'd have had my life, you'd be scared too."[27]

In her research undertaken with women involved in the South African Truth and Reconciliation Commission, Fiona Ross identified some who were resistant to testifying; Ross postulates "It may be that through their silence, women testifiers continue to resist an incursion of the state, perhaps now benevolent, but an incursion nevertheless."[28] In the Australian context, in which many Aboriginal people's lives were marked by constant and intrusive state interventions within their families, lack of confidence in state mechanisms as organs of justice or fear of the consequences of participation are highly likely to have been factors preventing some mothers from participating in Stolen Generations inquiry processes.

In contrast to Daisy's fear of speaking out, Morgan sees truth-speaking as an essential precursor to justice, and she is relentless in her pursuit of Daisy's story.[29] However, by the end of her story, Daisy is apparently reconciled to the need to speak out, at least about some things:

> I'm not frightened for you anymore, Sal, you'll be protected. I think maybe this is a good thing you're doin'. I didn't want you to do it, mind. But I think, now, maybe it's a good thing. Could be it's time to tell. Time to tell what it's been like in this country.[30]

Contained within "Daisy Corunna's Story," located as the climactic ending of *My Place*, is Daisy's account of the removal of her daughter, Gladys, at around three years of age, when the family for whom she worked as a domestic servant refused to allow her to keep Gladys with her any longer:

> I'd been 'spectin' it. Alice told me Gladdie needed an education, so they put her in Parkerville Children's Home. What could I do? I was too frightened to say anythin'. I wanted to keep her with me, she was all I had, but they didn't want her there. Alice said she cost too much to feed, said I was ungrateful. She was wantin' me to give up my own flesh and blood and still be grateful. Aren't black people allowed to have any feelin's?
>
> I cried and cried when Alice took her away. . . . How can a mother lose a child like that? How could she do that to me? I thought of my poor old mother then, they took her Arthur from her, and then they took me. She was broken-hearted, God bless her.
>
> When Gladdie was in Parkerville I tried to get there as often as I could, but it was a long way and I had no money. . . . I knew she didn't want to stay there, but what could I do? It wasn't like I had a place of my own. It wasn't like I had any say over my own life.[31]

It is interesting to contrast Daisy's account of Gladys's removal with the earlier words attributed to Daisy's former employer, Alice Drake-Brockman, who is reported by Morgan as saying that Gladys went to "a charity home for the ones that had no parents, we sent Gladys there. She grew up with just as nice manners as anybody could wish . . . She never looked back."[32]

There are many parallels here with the accounts of white interviewees involved in child removal explored in detail in chapter 8. In Drake-Brockman's version of events as recounted by Morgan, there is no mention of forcible removal—or even of Daisy having any feelings or opinions on the matter at all, which parallels Daisy's own bitter comment on Drake-Brockman's attitude towards the whole affair. Parkerville is described as "a charity home for the ones that had no parents"; Drake-Brockman seems oblivious to the reality that Gladys of course does have at least one parent (and there is also the unspoken possibility that Drake-Brockman's own husband, who Gladys apparently bears a striking resemblance to,[33] is in fact both Gladys' father and grandfather).

Gladys's removal is seen as something that happens to Gladys, not to both Gladys and Daisy; and is seen as being for Gladys's own good. Drake-Brockman emphasizes the benefits Gladys received from having this "opportunity"—Parkerville here sounds more like a finishing school than an institution that was established to care for "waifs and orphans."[34] In contrast with Drake-Brockman's account of a victimless removal, Daisy's account emphasizes her powerlessness to prevent Gladys's removal or to provide a home for her daughter; the practical difficulties of maintaining contact with Gladys after her removal; and the parallels of this removal with her own experience of being separated from her mother as a young girl—through her own pain at losing Gladys, she connects with what she believes her own mother must have experienced.[35]

SILENCE WITHIN FAMILIES

As the above accounts emphasize, there can be "no go" areas even within close family relationships that operate to limit what is said by mothers about their experiences and the circumstances in which their children were removed, and also in some cases that prevent their now-adult offspring from asking too many questions about the exact circumstances of their removal. Families who have experienced human rights violations sometimes use silence as a coping mechanism to deal with information that is too painful or too difficult to speak about; as Fiona Ross comments,

> A space of silence exists within the family. It may be respectful, a kind of will to silence, generated to protect one another from the knowledge of the extent of hurt. It may also be the silence of being unable or unwilling to meet the extent of pain suffered. Here, one can only ac-

knowledge the strategies used to cope with violence, acknowledge the need for silence and amnesia of particular kinds.[36]

Lesley McLennon related how she had not asked her son questions about his life since they had been reunited, and he had not asked her about why she gave him up, in a seemingly unspoken but mutual understanding that it was better not to probe too deeply:

> Interviewer: Did you have some questions to ask [your son], what is he doing and what has happened to him?
>
> Lesley: [My son] never asked any questions, ay, never. He just sort of was happy to meet us . . .
>
> Interviewer: Was he happy to know that you were looking for him?
>
> Lesley: I never asked [my son] that, ay, he never asked any question, ay, he was just glad to meet his mum and his brother and his granny, and you know . . . I never asked him and he never asked me.[37]

Similarly, other interviewees who were removed as children emphasized that they had never broached the circumstances of their removal with their mothers:

> But we never talked with our mother about what had happened. And I think it was because we had respect for her not to mention it, although at the same time we still had that understanding that she didn't want us. But there was no hate there, there was no hate as far as I am concerned, there wasn't any hate from me about what had happened, I just still accepted it as it was.
>
> And consequently we never talked about and I wish now that we had've. Because since the Inquiry came about and we looked at getting our records, it's all different. It wasn't the case, our mother did want us.[38]

Suffering in Silence

A number of interviewees who were removed as children highlighted their mothers' refusal to talk about their past experiences. Some attributed their mothers' silence to the deep hurt they had suffered:

> Eventually my mum came up and stayed a bit, but she wouldn't talk. I tried to ask questions but she was just a closed book. She didn't want to talk about anything that had happened in the past because it was too hurtful to talk about it.[39]

> And it's a very painful time for her because I couldn't get too much out of her.[40]

I think she finds it really hard though, to talk about it. Like um, because sometimes she gets really upset too, you know like, when she hears things or see things she gets a bit upset about it. Especially to do with family.[41]

For Julie Wilson, who was adopted as a baby, the discovery that her mother never mentioned her existence to her older sister who her mother managed to keep, the man she eventually married or the children she then had with him, was evidence of the depth of her mother's pain:

Once that decision was made and once I had been adopted out she never spoke a word of it ever, in all of the years to come. From 1958 through to her death in 1987 never spoke a word of it. To me that bears the mark of incredible pain, to bury it so deeply like that, and to marry a man and never to have mentioned it to him either. . . . So I think I respect whatever her decisions were and I think as a woman they would have been hard decisions to have made.[42]

Julie was working for Link-Up at the time of her interview and described the weight of silence pressing heavily on her mother and on her other clients, to the extent that it impacted on their physical as well as mental health:

Interviewer: At the same time aren't you just a little bit angry with your mother for maybe not trying to find you?

Julie: No, no, I'm not, I truly aren't. I could face her right now. All I want to say to her is that it's okay and I made it. That whatever her reasons were, I found it okay, I found my way and I'm here. So, you know, I'd send that to her. No, I'm not angry with her. I feel terribly sad for her. That's all.

Interviewer: Because she had that secret all her life. She kept that, she never told anybody.

Julie: Not a word.

Interviewer: It must've been a big burden for her, don't you think?

Julie: I think a huge burden. I think maybe physically part of her heart attack was bearing her grief for all those years—for locking it. I truly believe in spiritual terms that grief like that, deep grief, if it's not allowed to go out physically actually eats away. It's like a cancer. I believe that that's what happened to her all those years. I think in my job here as a counsellor for people going through it, the most important part of it is talking it out, getting it out, because for so long it's been packed away and bottled away. No-one's been given permission to speak. So I'm not angry with her. I just feel sad that she couldn't have done that, and I wished that her life was different in that she could've had more freedom to do that.[43]

John Alexander described the difficulties he had in pinning his mother down to tell him about the circumstances in which he was removed:

> I can remember my mum saying, "I've never ever forgotten you, always had you in my mind. I'm sorry. I didn't mean it to happen. There's nothing I could have done about it," and this incredible guilt all the time . . . So my questioning of her was probably fairly clumsy, but it's very difficult to get the truth out of her . . . the only thing she keeps saying to me was, "I wasn't allowed to keep you. Sorry, I should have tried to come back for you, but I wasn't allowed to keep you."[44]

John had to live with the likelihood that he would never know the true circumstances of his removal; he stated that he had come to terms with that, and was no longer so sure that "the truth" is so important anyway:

> Whether I'll ever know the truth about the separation is . . . in all honesty it's hard to imagine Mum telling me the truth. She may one day. She's eighty-two now. She lives 1500 kilometres away, so we're not in close contact. It's not the sort of thing you're going to ask someone over the phone. Whether I'll ever find the truth out I don't know, and I'm not so sure that it's important. I think there's enough documentation to say that she had very little control over the matter . . . she's always saying, "I'm sorry, I'm sorry, but I couldn't keep you. They wouldn't let me keep you" and things like that, [that] shows she was under a fair bit of duress.[45]

For some mothers, silence remains the safest option, as in the case of one interviewee who refused the invitation made by the interviewer to discuss the removal of three of her daughters:

> Interviewee: I've got four daughters um, but I've only got one, [name], in my marriage. They were taken from me. Oh, one I had adopted . . . The others have been coming back into my life in the last couple of years, but I won't let myself get close to them.
>
> Interviewer: Did you voluntarily give them up?
>
> Interviewee: No, one I did. One I did, I've told her that . . .
>
> Interviewer: Do you want to talk about losing the other children?
>
> Interviewee: No.[46]

This interviewee agreed to be part of a national oral history project collecting Stolen Generations stories and speaks about her childhood removal from her mother; however, her experiences as a mother of having her own children removed were something that she did not want to share.

Another autobiographical account dealing with Aboriginal women's silence is *Auntie Rita*, which incorporates both Rita Huggins's memoirs and her daughter Dr. Jackie Huggins's reflections and commentary. Although Rita simply states that her daughter was born during her domestic service, Jackie suggests that there may be traumatic experiences in her mother's past that even to this day she is not willing or able to talk about:

> My mother does not want to talk even to me about the kinds of bitter treatment she experienced. I respect that, but I will not forget nor forgive the people who inflicted that pain . . . I cannot speak of those years for my mother. What stops Rita speaking about them herself is not unusual—it's the same thing that stops other people speaking about profound suffering they have experienced. The oppression and pain can be so fierce as to make people mute. They close this experience inside themselves and don't want anyone to touch it. I will not force an entry but I have done my damnedest to get inside her pain, short of breaking down the door.
>
> Guilt and shame are manifest in women who have suffered like this, and there is a self-blaming that makes them see their situations as their fault, or the fault of their race. They feel that they have gotten themselves into this mess, and are responsible for finding ways out. The sense of guilt will remain as a terrible weight to be carried all their lives unless they can allow themselves to challenge it and speak it. Women of my generation are freer to express our anger and pain because now there is a more general acceptance of the right to speak about child abuse; it's politically correct to address the maltreatment of Aboriginals; honourable to elaborate my oppression as a Black woman, etc. Still, Aboriginal women have to find our own ways of speaking about these things. The healing time can then begin. [47]

Similarly to Sally Morgan, Jackie Huggins sees speaking about the experience of suffering as a path to healing; she identifies the need to find an independent, women-centered and culturally authentic process to facilitate this kind of healing talk by Aboriginal women.

SHEETING HOME THE BLAME

One issue facing many Aboriginal mothers who experienced child removal during the Stolen Generations era was the tendency for the mothers of removed children to be blamed for their failings as carers, rather than a more structural analysis being undertaken examining broader systemic issues such as poverty and racism, and how these factors may have impacted on mothers' ability to care for their children. In adoption scenarios the birth mother is frequently judged to have failed her children; Denise Cuthbert describes the perception that these mothers are "neither strong nor protective enough; in other words, not a sufficiently 'good mother,' irrespective of her actual circumstances, to have kept her baby with her."[48] Despite the broad range of circumstances that might lead to mothers and children being separated, Carol Sanger notes that "maternal absence is often characterized less as a separation than as *abandonment*."[49] This sense of abandonment is highlighted in a comment made by Darren Perry:

> I suppose just that feeling of, yeah, being abandoned, of somebody who's supposed to love you the most in the world. How could you be worth anything if they could give you up. You know, you hear everywhere that a mother's love is the most precious thing in the world and a child to a mother is the most precious object and all that. You know, it makes you question yourself. If I'm such a precious object, how could somebody give that up, sort of thing? Yeah, you know, it's taken a lot to deal with, those feelings.[50]

Although some families preserved a fragile silence around their experiences of child removal, choosing not to ask or not to tell, other people who were removed as children described their feelings of anger and resentment towards their mothers, and it was evident that they blamed their mothers, at least in part, for their removal. This extract from "Evie's Story," incorporated into Carmel Bird's collection of autobiographical accounts by members of the Stolen Generations, highlights Evie's experience of her now-adult daughter refusing to listen to her mother's explanations about what happened:

> And with my daughter, well she came back in '88 but things aren't working out there. She blames me for everything that went wrong. She's got this hate about her—*doesn't want to know*. The two boys know where I am but turned around and said to us, "You're not our mother—we know who our real mother is."
>
> So every day of your bloody life you just get hurt all the time.[51]

Lesley McLennon discussed her brother's inability to reconcile with their mother; she believed that he still blamed their mother for his removal:

> My brother is very hurt about that. He don't want to talk about it, he's very hurt, and he'll always be hurt, and he don't want to talk about it. I think he just said because he got put in the home, you know, Mum couldn't take care of us, so I think that's where he's taking it out on Mum, ay.[52]

Lesley had herself relinquished one of her two children for adoption, and had subsequently been reunited with him, giving her insight into and compassion for her own mother's experiences.

Julie Wilson, who was adopted as a child, spoke about her half-brother's anger with their mother because she never disclosed Julie's existence to her other children:

> He was angry with our mother—very angry. He felt she'd betrayed all of them, my siblings, by not ever talking about me. He wondered why

she never trusted them. That's how he felt, betrayed, and that she didn't trust him enough to say, "You have a sister out there some-where." He was so angry because of the thirty-two years we'd lost.[53]

Some people who were removed as children seemed to focus their anger at their removal on their mother more than on any other family member, possibly because of the social expectation that your mother is meant to be self-sacrificing and the one who loves and cares for you above all others. Murray, who was institutionalized on Palm Island with his siblings, spoke about his childhood feelings of rage and hate towards his mother:

> I remember when I learnt to write letters, I wrote to my mother furious-ly pleading with her to come and take us off that island. I wrote to her for years, I got no reply then I realised that she was never coming for us; that she didn't want us. That's when I began to hate her. Now I doubt if any of my letters ever got off that island or that any letters she wrote me ever stood a chance of me receiving them.[54]

> As the years of my childhood went by a son's love for his mother turned to hatred that destroys any feeling of love for anyone.[55]

Pattie Lees spoke about the impact of discovering letters written by her mother on the family's welfare files many years after her mother had died, telling her children how much she loved them and demonstrating that she had attempted to maintain contact with them after their removal:

> She wrote that in 1958 and the first time we saw those words was in 1996 or '95 when we accessed them for the Inquiry. But they had a good effect really, in a way, because the words reached out through the years to say to my brothers, who were really very unforgiving about her behaviour and blamed, really put all the blame on Mum, that she was a horrible mother and that she was a bad mother and she sacrificed all of us so that she could pursue this life of drinking and things like that. Maybe girls have a different way of looking at it, but I kind of just felt sorry for her, and the boys were, even when we buried her—that's the sad part, that's the useless waste of life on regret—my mother died on first January 1977, and she died virtually with angry sons who never actually forgave her. They came out to participate in her burial and things like that, but not because they felt some connection with her. They came out to support me, because they knew that I loved her.[56]

A number of interviewees also indicated that their foster and adoptive parents criticized their birth families to them, and particularly their mothers, for their lack of care for their children, possibly in a misguided attempt to make the removed children feel grateful for being adopted or fostered. Instead of inducing feelings of gratitude, such criticisms had a highly negative impact on the children's sense of identity and self-es-teem:

I knew I was Aboriginal but my foster mother used to say, "Oh your mother is nothing but a black slut and she's an alcoholic and she doesn't want you. Blah, blah, blah." And so I had that feeling, "well she doesn't want me, I'm not going to say that I'm black to anyone," but I always knew that I was.[57]

I was always told Mum gave me away and that, "She didn't want you" and "You're lucky that you've got us, because your mum was no good and she gave you away," which really doesn't give you a good image about yourself either.[58]

Julie Wilson, commenting on her work at Link-Up, spoke about how her clients sometimes got locked into feeling and behaving like an abandoned child; they remained fixed in their perspective of what had happened to them in their childhood, and were unable to make adult judgments about the past:

It's easy—because I see it in my clients—to get locked into the rejected child, is what we call it, the abandoned child. I could sit there and go, well, what a lot of people do is, "Well, if she didn't try and come and look for me, well, bugger her, I'm not looking for her either." I think we get caught up in our own sense of it perhaps. The fact that I've studied the whole policy, I've understood the social context. Perhaps the job that I'm working in now makes me see it, because not only do I work on behalf of the children but I work on behalf of the mothers and the adoptive parents. I cannot do my work with such a one-eyed vision that it's all their fault, and so I need to have a look. I think the other thing that has helped me is that I'm a parent now myself. I wondered if circumstances had placed me in the position like my mum, what would I have done? Would I have handled it as well as they did, you know?[59]

Sharon Kinchela related her experience of nearly having one of her own children removed when she gave birth as a single teenage mum; this experience gave her a new appreciation of what had happened to her own mother:

I know when we come out of the homes I hated my mother. I really hated my mother, because I blamed her, but it wasn't until that happened to me and my mother was there that I saw things differently, and being a mum now, I see things differently. So I say that since getting those reports, I realise the pain . . . that's what makes me angry after getting that information, because it really puts down my mother in my eyes, and someone passing judgment that wasn't a standard in their eyes.[60]

In common with a number of other Aboriginal women who were removed as children, it was her own experiences as a mother which enabled her to feel empathy for the challenges and difficult choices her own mother faced.

THE IMPACT OF SHAME AND SELF-BLAME

Feminist psychologist Carol Gilligan argued that women define themselves in the context of their relationships with others and judge themselves in terms of their ability to care.[61] This seems particularly true for
mothers; Adrienne Rich has observed that "the mother's very character,
her status as a woman, are in question if she has 'failed' her children."[62]

There was a tendency amongst the parents of victims of apartheid in
South Africa who testified at the South African Truth and Reconciliation
Commission to blame themselves for the harms done to their children; as
Antjie Krog observed, "Although the killer should be blamed for the
death, the families of victims are often plagued by their own guilt. . . .
Parents are torn by self-doubt. Aren't parents supposed to keep their
children safe from harm at any cost?"[63] Fiona Ross has also highlighted
the need to be aware of the enduring pain that might result from a family's failure to keep harm at bay despite all their efforts to do so.[64] In the
context of his work reuniting Aboriginal families who experienced child
removal, Peter Read observed that "To grieving parents separation im-
plied a lack of their own care."[65]

It is possible that Aboriginal mothers' perceptions of having "failed"
in their responsibilities to care for their children may have acted as a
barrier to their participation in the *Bringing Them Home* Inquiry. The two
testimonial extracts from mothers separated from their children that are
included in the *Bringing Them Home* Report highlight the intergenerational impact of child removal; both mothers were themselves removed as
children, and they attributed the subsequent removal of their own children to in one case a lack of effective parental role modelling,[66] and in the
other to the psychological impact of the sexual and emotional abuse they
experienced as a child.[67] In a classic statement of self-blame, one of these
mothers states "I'm a rotten mother."[68] That both of these mothers were
also themselves removed as children is an important point; there is no
testimony in the *Bringing Them Home* Report from Aboriginal mothers
whose children were removed who were not also themselves the victims
of child removal policies and practices. This may be due in part to the
inter-generational impact of child removal (people who were removed
were more likely to have their own children removed), but also is likely
to reflect the Inquiry's almost exclusive focus on child victims.

Some mothers described the crippling impact of self-blame which has
plagued them; even in circumstances where they knew they had very
little choice they still felt responsible for the removal of their children.
Others have journeyed through self-blame to realize the impact of the
lack of support available to them and the inherent failings of the system
of child removal.

SILENCE AND "SORRY BUSINESS"

Within Aboriginal culture, "sorry business" is observed as a period of mourning or grieving due to the death of a person; it can also be observed in other cases of significant loss impacting on individuals and/or a community.[69] The exact protocols observed during "sorry business" may differ significantly from community to community but can include not making reference to or using the name of a person who has passed away.[70]

Marjorie Harris described her mother's silence about the removal of an older child:

> In Aboriginal fashion, the one that's been taken from you, you usually don't mention their name . . . [Mum] never talked about her at all because she said it was too sad to mention her name . . . That's their custom, yeah. Just like a dead person, they don't mention your name.[71]

Others identified mothers, grandmothers, aunties and other women of the community engaging in ritualistic grieving, cutting or other forms of self-harm after the removal of their children.[72]

Cultural protocols and practices relating to "sorry business" may have contributed to the reluctance of some Aboriginal parents to speak about their experiences of child removal, and have also led to cross-cultural misunderstandings, with Aboriginal parents' silence due to their deeply-felt grief being wrongly attributed to a lack of depth of feeling.[73]

A comment from Trudy McMahon, a white interviewee, highlights the different cultural values that are attributed to silence in white and Aboriginal cultures. For Trudy, the initial silence of the victims contributed to her disbelief of their stories and led her to questioning their motivations in now speaking out: "At the time of being stolen, why wasn't there anything said about it? It's only later on when there was a financial advantage in it that they start shouting. This is how I feel."[74]

Silence, typically stigmatized as a negative in Western conversation (for example, an "awkward pause"), has been described by Eades as a positive feature in Aboriginal English, used to allow people time to think things through and become comfortable with a situation, or to draw out further information.[75]

Silence that is due to cultural observations clearly poses a significant challenge for human rights inquiry processes, which are based on the model that injured parties need to testify about their experiences in order to have any hope of redress. There are practical consequences to remaining silent, particularly within Western legal mechanisms that link payment of damages to proof of harm.[76]

NAVIGATING COMPLEX FAMILY RELATIONSHIPS

Another issue that has emerged as limiting Aboriginal mothers' ability to speak of their experiences of child removal is the complexity of post-removal families and the fear of upsetting reestablished relationships with adult children, or of disturbing the delicate balance between birth and adoptive/foster family members. Ruby discussed her ambivalent feelings towards her daughter's foster mother, ranging from feelings of respect for this woman's care for her daughter, to jealousy at the closeness of their relationship. As the following extract highlights, Ruby clearly respected the mothering work undertaken by the white foster mother in caring for her removed child. Ruby and her daughter's foster mother met regularly at family functions due to their shared relationship with Ruby's daughter, and Ruby was acutely aware of the need to preserve the relationship, at least on a surface level, for the sake of her daughter, and to avoid offending her daughter's foster mother or making her feel threatened by her presence:

> [My daughter] was like her baby. I mean, she was there when [my daughter] was sick, and [my daughter] needed her. She walked the floor with [my daughter], and I understood all that, you know. But she was sort of like, she was always on tenterhooks when I was round there as though I was going to take her, you know. And, when [my daughter] started getting close to me as well, she was worried about the relationship, you know. So I'd go there and I'd include her into whatever we did as well, so she didn't feel so . . . So threatened. So I tried, I understood the position she was coming through. But it broke my heart to see, you know, the totality of their relationship, where I was a bit excluded, you know? . . . And so, at [a family function], they were all there . . . So I went over, I always go over and give her a big hug and ask how she's going, and sit down and have a yarn to her, and you know, to make her feel comfortable, but I didn't want her to feel that [my daughter] was putting me ahead of her at her, at a special day for her, you know.[77]

The difficulties of successfully maintaining relationships with adult children who were separated from their mothers in their infancy emerges as a strong theme in a number of interviews—particularly the issue of navigating complex family structures that incorporate both foster families and birth families, children that were removed and children that remained with the birth mother, and extended families including step-siblings, cousins, and more. In many ways we do not even have the terminology to talk about the diverse range of relationships involved in these complex post-removal families, as this extract from Dawn Brown's interview highlights:

Interviewer: Can you tell us about your parents?

Dawn: What parents? Like the ones I lived with when I was taken, brought up, the white people that brought me up, they were good. They looked after me, they treated me like their own daughter. I called 'em Mum and Dad 'cause that's the only Mum I knew, 'cause at that time I didn't know I had a Mum and Dad. I thought they were my Mum and Dad until I found out later on, ten years old that they weren't my Mum and Dad . . . I was equal living with them, um, my Mum and Dad that brought me up. I keep saying my Mum and Dad who brought me up, because they're the only ones I know as my Mum and Dad. Even when I talk to my father, my real Dad, I even say to him, "Oh Mum and Dad," and he looks at me, "Who are you talking about Mum and Dad?" "The ones that brought me up, you know, that's my only Mum and Dad. It's gonna take me a long time to get them outta my head."[78]

Although Ruby's was the only account I identified that addressed the issue of navigating complex family relationships from the perspective of a birth mother, a number of interviewees who were removed as children spoke about their heightened sensitivity to the feelings of their adoptive parents, who often strongly opposed any attempt by them to be reunited with their birth families, as well as the challenges they themselves faced in reintegrating into their birth families.

SILENCE AS RESISTANCE?

Rather than assuming that Aboriginal women's silence is evidence of their exclusion or being silenced, the possibility needs to be considered that remaining silent may have been an active choice for some, a form of agency or resistance. Refusal to engage can in fact be a political act, and one which denies those in power access to those who remain aloof.[79]

An important point to recognize is that the benefit to the victim in speaking may be negligible, and as we have seen in some cases speaking can have more negative consequences than positive ones. Bearing witness can therefore be seen by some to be a futile exercise. There are not always direct benefits to the victim in testifying at a human rights inquiry; such processes can be exploitative, because victims already know the truth. Vasuki Nesiah highlights that it is the privileged who receive the benefit of the truths elucidated through such processes and give them "the imprimatur of official acknowledgement."[80] Bird Rose argues that where Aboriginal people are called upon to justify themselves and their traditions and beliefs but where the decisions about the validity of these beliefs are made by others, silence "may be the better option . . . because it may be less destructive in the long run than speech."[81] This concern about the potentially destructive impact of speech is clearly evident in the comments of a number of interviewees.

Perhaps in refusing to speak some mothers are resisting the impetus of human rights processes to construct them as the "victim" of their life experiences and refusing to accept the conceptualization of the state as the arbiter of justice, rather than as the party which has inflicted their injury.[82]

This chapter has identified a number of the factors that may have contributed to the ongoing silence of the mothers of the Stolen Generations and prevented them from speaking about their experiences of the removal of their children. The social stigma attached to disclosing sexual assault and rape has a silencing impact, particularly for mothers whose children are the product of sexual assault or incest. Mothers who "fail" in their duty of care for their children frequently blame themselves and are sometimes blamed by their children (and others), making them feel that attempts to explain their actions are futile. In their attempt to rebuild shattered and fragile bonds with their now adult children, some mothers are silenced by the fear of the impact of what they might say on their ongoing relationships with their children. The incredibly complex family structures of removed children, involving birth and adoptive/foster parents, siblings, half-siblings and others, can also make it more difficult for mothers to speak frankly about the past. Silence is self-perpetuating—as people do not speak, so others' speech is not enabled, and the possibility of developing a community of interest or support is diminished.[83]

In the following chapter I begin to examine some of the structural barriers to Aboriginal mothering in the Stolen Generations era though an exploration of the impact of Aboriginal Protection legislation on Aboriginal mothers, highlighting the impact of this legislation on their legal status as guardians of their children, and their lack of legal recourse in the event of child removal.

NOTES

1. Ross, *Bearing Witness*, 163.
2. Foucault, *The History of Sexuality*, 101.
3. Bird Rose, "The Silence and Power of Women," 99.
4. See, for example, Mertus, "Truth in a Box," 142.
5. Brounéus, "Truth-Telling as Talking Cure?," 59.
6. Brounéus, "Truth-Telling as Talking Cure?," 55.
7. Goodall, "Too Early Yet or Not Soon Enough?," 5.
8. Gelder, "Aboriginal Narrative and Property," 357.
9. Brewster, *Reading Aboriginal Women's Autobiography*, 24.
10. Eades, *Courtroom Talk and Neocolonial Control*, 107.
11. Bird Rose, "The Silence and Power of Women," 99.
12. See, for example, Nesiah, "Gender and Truth Commission Mandates," 1–2.
13. Aolain and Turner, "Gender, Truth & Transition," 277.
14. Butalia, *The Other Side of Silence*, 284.

15. A pseudonym has been used for this interviewee, who asked not to be identified.

16. "Ruby," interviewed by Anne Maree Payne, 16–17.

17. "Ruby," interviewed by Anne Maree Payne, 25.

18. Morgan, *My Place*, 428.

19. Windschuttle, *The Fabrication of Aboriginal History*, 304–321.

20. Docker 1998, 19.

21. Carol Kendall interviewed by John Maynard, 5 April 2001, ORAL TRC 5000/246, National Library of Australia, 39.

22. Peter Read, interviewed by Anne Maree Payne, 24 October 2013, The University of Sydney, 17–18.

23. Docker 1998, 11.

24. Morgan, *My Place*, 431.

25. Morgan, *My Place*, 118.

26. Morgan, *My Place*, 173.

27. Morgan, *My Place*, 430.

28. Ross, *Bearing Witness*, 59.

29. Morgan, *My Place*, 398.

30. Morgan, *My Place*, 429.

31. Morgan, *My Place*, 420.

32. Morgan, *My Place*, 215.

33. Morgan, *My Place*, 299.

34. Commonwealth of Australia, "Find & Connect."

35. Nearly every aspect of Morgan's account of the relationship between Daisy and the Drake-Brockmans has been disputed by Alice's daughter Judith Drake-Brockman, who has written her own account of the family's relationship with Daisy and Gladys. Despite a criticism in the Foreword about the invalidity of "hearsay evidence," a barb clearly aimed at Morgan, in Drake-Brockman's own account she describes the appearance of Daisy's ghost on two separate occasions to validate her own version of the story. Drake-Brockman, *Wongi Wongi: To Speak*, 138–139.

36. Ross, *Bearing Witness*, 3.

37. Lesley McLennon interviewed by Helen Belle Curzon-Siggers, 11 Dec 1999, ORAL TRC 5000/77, National Library of Australia, 45–46.

38. Yvonne Mills interviewed by Colleen Hattersley, 15 August 1999, ORAL TRC 5000/37, National Library of Australia, 8.

39. Sue Gordon interviewed by John Bannister, 12 October 1999, ORAL TRC 5000/52, National Library of Australia, 36.

40. Ruth Hegarty interviewed by Helen Belle Curzon Siggers, 14 Dec 1999, ORAL TRC 5000/79, National Library of Australia, 18.

41. Jackie Frail interviewed by Rob Willis, 6 July 2000, ORAL TRC 5000/162, National Library of Australia, 15.

42. Julie Wilson interviewed by Frank Heimans, 30 January 2001, ORAL TRC 5000/226, National Library of Australia, 16.

43. Julie Wilson interviewed by Frank Heimans, 30 January 2001, ORAL TRC 5000/226, National Library of Australia, 45.

44. John Alexander, interviewed by John Bannister, 8 & 15 June 1999, ORAL TRC 5000/30, National Library of Australia, 40–42.

45. John Alexander, interviewed by John Bannister, 8 & 15 June 1999, ORAL TRC 5000/30, National Library of Australia, 43.

46. Judith Stubbs interviewed by Ann-Mari Jordens, 22 October 2000, ORAL TRC 5000/175, National Library of Australia, 43.

47. Huggins and Huggins, *Auntie Rita*, 36 (italics in original).

48. Cuthbert, "Stolen Children, Invisible Mothers and Unspeakable Stories," 141.

49. Sanger, "Mother from Child," 28 (my emphasis).

50. Darren Perry interviewed by Karen George, 12 May 2000, ORAL TRC 5000/115, National Library of Australia, 34.

51. Quoted in Bird, *The Stolen Children*, 40–41 (my emphasis).

52. Lesley McLennon interviewed by Helen Belle Curzon-Siggers, 11 December 1999, ORAL TRC 5000/77, National Library of Australia, 52.

53. Julie Wilson interviewed by Frank Heimans, 30 January 2001, ORAL TRC 5000/226, National Library of Australia, 39.

54. Quoted in Bird, *The Stolen Children*, 44.

55. Quoted in Bird, *The Stolen Children*, 49.

56. Pattie Lees interviewed by Colleen Hattersley, 13 June 2001, ORAL TRC 5000/300, National Library of Australia, 19.

57. Kathy Donovan interviewed by John Maynard, 3 April 2001, ORAL TRC 5000/264, National Library of Australia, 6.

58. Deirdre Heitmeyer interviewed by John Maynard, 4 March 1999, ORAL TRC 5000/11, National Library of Australia, 4.

59. Julie Wilson interviewed by Frank Heimans, 30 January 2001, ORAL TRC 5000/226, National Library of Australia, 45–46.

60. Sharon Kinchela, in Sharon Kinchela, Rosie Matthews & Debbie Kinchela interviewed by Colleen Hattersley, 28 March 2001, ORAL TRC 5000/248, National Library of Australia, 25.

61. Gilligan 1982, 164.

62. Rich, *Of Woman Born*, 52.

63. Krog, *Country of My Skull*, 301.

64. Ross, *Bearing Witness*, 43.

65. Read, *A Rape of the Soul So Profound*, 172.

66. Human Rights and Equal Opportunity Commission, *Bringing Them Home*, 226.

67. Human Rights and Equal Opportunity Commission, *Bringing Them Home*, 228.

68. Human Rights and Equal Opportunity Commission, *Bringing Them Home*, 226.

69. The Secretariat of National Aboriginal and Islander Child Care noted that some Aboriginal communities have observed formal mourning periods after significant events such as the loss of a Native Title claim. Secretariat of National Aboriginal and Islander Child Care, "Sorry Business."

70. Secretariat of National Aboriginal and Islander Child Care, *Sorry Business*.

71. Marjorie Harris interviewed by Glenys Dimond, 15 June 2001, ORAL TRC 5000/313, National Library of Australia, 15.

72. See for example Les Penhall interviewed by Francis Good, 25 January & 1 Feb 2000, ORAL TRC 5000/105, National Library of Australia, 22.

73. Mellor and Haebich, *Many Voices*, 8.

74. Trudy (Gertrude) McMahon interviewed by Ann-Mari Jordens, 19 May 2000, ORAL TRC 5000/116, National Library of Australia, 36.

75. Eades, *Courtroom Talk and Neocolonial Control*, 108.

76. Rubio-Marín, "What Happened to the Women," 34.

77. "Ruby," interviewed by Anne Maree Payne, 31.

78. Dawn Brown interviewed by Peter Bertani, 29 July 2000, ORAL TRC 5000/157, National Library of Australia, 1–3.

79. Janeway, *Powers of the Weak*, 172.

80. Nesiah, "Discussion Lines on Gender and Transitional Justice," 803.

81. Bird Rose, "The Silence and Power of Women," 115–116.

82. I am reminded here of Wendy Brown's analysis that well-intentioned political projects can inadvertently redraw the very configurations and effects of power that they seek to vanquish (*States of Injury*, 3). Drawing on the work of Foucault, and his insight that subjects and practices are always at risk of being re-subordinated by the discourses naming and politicizing them, as well as Nietzsche's concept of *ressentiment*, Brown theorizes about "wounded attachments," arguing that victim identification is deeply invested in its own impotence and can result in fixing the identities of the injured and the injurers as social positions (27). Brown is particularly concerned by the turn to the state as a source of support for minority rights, which she sees as legitimatizing state power and subverting the potential for more radical and emanci-

patory agendas (28). As Jan Pettman has also observed, "mobilising a constituency or community along boundaries drawn in and for dominance may reinforce those boundaries and so continue to trap people within them. It may also make the category an easy target for state management." Pettman, *Living in the Margins*, 125.

83. Elizabeth Janeway argued that "coming together" is important for disempowered people, as they need validation "that one's doubts are realistic and are shared by others." Janeway, *Powers of the Weak*, 168.

THREE

"To the Exclusion of the Rights of the Mother"

The Impact of Aboriginal "Protection" Legislation

In 2001, the circumstances of the removal of Lowitja O'Donoghue from her mother in 1934 became the basis of a national debate after commentator Andrew Bolt reported her "admission" that she had "misled Australians by claiming she was a stolen child."[1] The complex childhood removal narrative relayed by O'Donoghue, former chairperson of the Aboriginal and Torres Strait Islander Commission and a lifelong advocate for Indigenous issues, did not fit neatly within the categories of what Bolt saw as a "legitimate" Stolen Generations experience; he noted "that her white father might have given her and her four sisters and brother to the missionary-run Colebrook Home in South Australia, with her Aboriginal mother's possibly uninformed consent."[2] Then Prime Minister John Howard quickly weighed in on the debate, using Bolt's article to justify his argument that the present generation of Australians should not be forced to accept responsibility for what had happened in the past, and that there was a need "to stop navel gazing and get on with the future."[3] The attack on O'Donoghue's credibility in discussing her childhood experiences is a significant example of what historian Heather Goodall has described as the politicization of debates about Australia's past which has led to adversarial approaches, polarized understandings and simplistic polemics, at the expense of more varied, complex, "messy and ambiguous" accounts.[4]

In his essay "The Dispossession of Lowitja O'Donoghue," Stuart Rintoul provides a detailed and nuanced account of what was actually known of the circumstances of O'Donoghue's childhood removal from her mother, noting that there was nothing in the official documentation held by the United Aboriginal Mission (UAM) to answer the many questions O'Donoghue had about who had authorized her admission to the Colebrook Home and whether her mother Lily's consent to her removal was ever sought.[5] It should also be noted that all of the oral evidence collected by Rintoul, including accounts from local Aboriginal community members, from other family members, and the account of a local policeman who had worked in the area some years after Lily's children were removed, suggested that Lily could not have prevented her children's removal and was devastated by their loss. While the issue of her mother's consent or otherwise to her removal may for obvious reasons be of profound personal significance to O'Donoghue, what was missing from the public commentary by Bolt and Howard about this incident was an acknowledgment that Lily's "consent" or otherwise was irrelevant under South Australian legislation at this time, as she was not the legal guardian of her children.

In debates such as this which took place within the wider community following the publication of the *Bringing Them Home* Report about the "consent" or otherwise of Aboriginal parents to child removal, surprisingly little mention was made of the impact of Aboriginal "protection" legislation, which meant that Indigenous parents did not have the same legal rights in relation to their children as other Australian parents.[6] Under this legislation, a state-appointed Aboriginal Protector was the legal guardian of all Indigenous children until they were up to twenty-one years old in a number of Australian states and territories; all Indigenous children in these jurisdictions were deemed wards of the state, which limited their parents' ability to legally challenge state decisions about their removal.

Examining the intricacies of legislation may seem a dry approach to such an emotive issue as child removal, however I believe such an exercise is critical to understanding the constraints on Aboriginal parenting in the Stolen Generations era. Debates about whether Aboriginal children were stolen or surrendered, or whether mothers "consented" to their children's removal, need to be informed by greater appreciation of the context of the Aboriginal "protection" legislation regime, which this chapter will explore in detail, with a focus on the impact of this legislation on the rights of Indigenous parents, particularly mothers.

OVERVIEW OF STATE AND FEDERAL LAWS RELATING TO ABORIGINAL PARENTS

The *Bringing Them Home* Report detailed state laws applying to Indigenous children in its appendices.[7] This information provided the basis for an online exhibition compiled by the Australian Institute of Aboriginal and Torres Strait Islander Studies (AIATSIS), *To Remove and Protect: Laws That Changed Aboriginal Lives*, which detailed all state and territory laws applying specifically to Indigenous children, as well as general child welfare/adoption laws.[8] Reflecting the common understanding of the removal of Indigenous children as a violation of the rights of the child, the focus of *To Remove and Protect* is on legislation applying to Indigenous *children* rather than the impact of this legislation on Indigenous parents.

The *Bringing Them Home* Report traced the legislative framework under which Indigenous child removal was authorized, and argued that these separations were unlawful even by the legal standards of the time in which they happened:

> The Australian practice of Indigenous child removal involved both systematic racial discrimination and genocide as defined by international law. Yet it continued to be practised as official policy long after being clearly prohibited by treaties to which Australia had voluntarily subscribed.[9]

While Australia might have had a moral obligation to abide by the terms of the international human rights treaties it was a signatory to, Australia's commitments to such treaties do not take immediate effect on ratification but require specific domestic legislation to be legally enforceable.[10] Such domestic legislation is needed for Australian courts to ensure that "the rights in any international human rights treaty will take precedence over any state or territory legislation that is inconsistent with the treaty."[11] Australia ratified the *Convention for the Prevention of the Crime of Genocide* in 1949 and the *Convention on the Elimination of All Forms of Racial Discrimination* in 1975; the federal *Racial Discrimination Act* was passed in 1975, however genocide was not made a crime punishable under Australian law until the *International Criminal Court Act* was adopted in 2002.[12] This has contributed to the legal difficulties facing many Stolen Generations compensation cases, as racially discriminatory laws were not prohibited in Australia until the passage of the *Racial Discrimination Act* in 1975.[13]

Frank Gare, a white Australian who worked as a senior bureaucrat in the Department of Native Welfare in Western Australia during the Stolen Generations era, observed that the constitutional exclusion of the federal government from legislating in relation to Indigenous people prior to the 1967 Referendum limited the capacity of the federal government to ensure treaty compliance:

> The Australian government at that time didn't have any say in Aboriginal affairs really, it didn't step into the business until the referendum of 1967. . . . Now, the states wouldn't take much notice of a United Nations resolutions (sic), they would say, That's not binding on us. We know how to do the job and we'll carry on.[14]

A section within the *Bringing Them Home* Report headed "Deprivation of parental rights" notes that Indigenous parents were stripped of their parental rights contrary to established common law principles in Western Australia from 1905 to 1963; the Northern Territory from 1910 to 1964; South Australia from 1911 to 1962; and in Queensland from 1939 to 1965.[15]

In Victoria, while Aboriginal parents theoretically retained custody rights in relation to their children, from 1890 the Board of Protection oversaw arrangements for the care of Aboriginal children and had the power to remove Aboriginal children without the need of a court process.[16] Similarly, in NSW from 1915 onwards the Aboriginal Protection Board had the power to remove all Aboriginal children without parental consent or court process, a clear distinction between the rights of Aboriginal and non-Aboriginal children[17] — and, I would also note, the rights of their parents. The Australian Capital Territory was covered by the provisions of the *NSW Aboriginal Protection Act* until 1954, when the *Aborigines Welfare Ordinance* was passed into legislation; it included among its provisions authorization for the Minister to "provide for the maintenance, welfare and training" of Aboriginal children, though it differed from most other state and territory legislation by stipulating that this was "*on the application of their parent or guardian.*" In Tasmania, legislation relating to the removal of Aboriginal children was not passed, apparently because the state refused to acknowledge that Aboriginal people still resided there;[18] therefore unlike all the other states Aboriginal child removals in Tasmania were governed by mainstream child welfare legislation.

The *Bringing Them Home* Report noted two approaches to child removal from the 1940s onwards, with some states (NSW, Tasmania and Victoria) applying the same laws and standards to Aboriginal as to non-Aboriginal families although in a discriminatory and unfair manner, while the other states (WA, NT, SA, QLD) continued to operate separate Indigenous administrations and legislative frameworks, eventually dismantling these from the 1950s onwards.[19]

The *Bringing Them Home* Report also made the important point that while any person's parental rights have always been subject to suspension or termination by legal process, the rights of Indigenous parents were removed purely on the basis of their status as Indigenous people, and not because of individual findings of parental misconduct or judgments made on a case-by-case basis about what would be in the best interests of the child/children under their care.[20] Clearly, the legislation that appointed the Protector of Aborigines (or equivalent position) the legal guardian of *all* Indigenous children in Queensland, South Australian, Western Australia and the Northern Territory was based on the assumption that in *every* case, Indigenous parents were incapable of performing their parental duties themselves. Such legislation reflected the belief of white officials, as one Aboriginal mother I spoke to categorized it, "that they could do better at raising our kids."[21]

The sense of powerlessness engendered in Aboriginal mothers by their lack of legal rights is expressed in a number of accounts of their experiences of child removal. Ruby spoke about her sense of hopelessness and the lack of avenues for her to seek redress after her baby daughter was taken from her in the 1960s and removed to an unknown location: "I was just devastated that I . . . came back to find my baby missing. But who could I go to, you know? . . . There was no one to go to about it."[22]

Even in child removals that happened late in the Stolen Generations era when the guardianship status of Indigenous parents had notionally been restored, Aboriginal mothers still faced huge disadvantages within the legal system. Heather Vicenti, an Aboriginal mother who experienced the removal of five of her children, has written in her autobiography about the legal inequities she faced in Western Australia in 1965. She was without legal representation on the day the court passed judgment on her capacity to care for her children: "I was not notified of my rights, there was no adjournment to obtain legal advice, and I had no assistance with what was in fact a contested hearing or trial. What happened was, to my mind, a gross miscarriage of justice, a travesty."[23]

"THE CHILD OF ANY ABORIGINE": THE IMPACT OF "PROTECTION" LEGISLATION ON INDIGENOUS PARENTAL RIGHTS

State-based Aboriginal "protection" legislation in Australia imposed constraints on many aspects of the lives of Indigenous people, including restrictions on their freedom of association, freedom of movement, the right to marry, freedom from arbitrary interference in family and home, property ownership rights, freedom of religion, the right to vote and to participate in government, the right to social security, the right to work and to just and favorable conditions of work, the right to education, the right to an adequate standard of living, breaches of the principles of nondiscrimination and equality before the law, and so on. These curtailments were specifically targeted to Indigenous Australians and did not operate to limit the rights and freedoms enjoyed by other Australians, except in their interactions with Indigenous Australians. However, some of the clauses within the various state and territory protection acts that make specific reference to Indigenous parents are not highlighted in either the *Bringing Them Home* Report appendices or the AIATSIS summaries, as these aimed to highlight "laws applying specifically to Australian *children*."[24]

Of course, Aboriginal protection legislation did not develop in a vacuum—it reflected the broader societal concerns and interests that the legis-

lation was designed to implement or guard against. Historians have demonstrated how in NSW in the early twentieth century, concern about the
declining (white) birth rate led to a focus on the removal and detention of
Aboriginal girls, in an attempt to control their sexuality and reproduction.[25] Similarly, increasing interest in eugenics and concerns about the
rising "half-caste" population in the 1920s and 1930s led to the introduction of "anti-miscegenation" clauses in the protection legislation of a
number of states during this era.[26] Changes to Aboriginal Protection legislation over time reflected changing white priorities in relation to Aboriginal people; the relationship between Aboriginal "welfare" legislation
and the concerns of white Australians has long been noted.[27]

THE IMPACT OF LIMITATIONS ON ABORIGINAL MOTHERS' GUARDIANSHIP STATUS

With regard to the legal guardianship of Indigenous children, initially
"protection" legislation in a number of states did not apply in a blanket
fashion to every Indigenous child. South Australian legislation originally
gave Aboriginal parents the right to consent to apprenticeship arrangements made in relation to their children "if living and within the Prov-
ince," and limited the Protector of Aborigines' legal guardianship of Aboriginal children to those "whose parents are dead or unknown, or either
of whose parents may signify before a magistrate his or her willingness in
this behalf."[28] Similarly, Queensland's initial legislation only applied to
"half-caste" children who were orphaned or "deserted" by their parents.[29] In both of these states as well as in the Northern Territory and
Western Australia, the legal guardianship provisions were eventually extended to encompass "the child of any Aborigine." Describing her work
at the South Australian Department of Aboriginal Affairs in the mid-to-
late 1960s, Una Clarke commented, "Many children placed in Homes or
institutions were not under any court order but fostered under old legislation. This made the Minister of Aboriginal Affairs the guardian of Aboriginal people, so children were fostered without being wards of the
state . . . without the consent of the parents or without a court proving
neglect."[30]

It is also possible to trace the gradual emergence in Aboriginal Protection legislation of provisions bringing Indigenous child removal more in
keeping with mainstream child welfare processes, including the requirement for Aboriginal children who were declared neglected or uncontrol-
lable to appear before a court in NSW from 1940 onwards;[31] and the *NT
Welfare Ordinance* requirement from 1953 for the removal of a "ward"
under fourteen years to be authorized in writing by the Administrator.[32]

It is important to acknowledge the aspects of Aboriginal protection
legislation that distinguished Indigenous child removals from those of

non-Indigenous children under general child protection laws. The most significant of these was the appointment of a designated state official as the legal guardian of *all* Indigenous minors (and in some cases Indigenous women up to the age of twenty-one years) in Western Australia, South Australia, Queensland and the Northern Territory, "notwithstanding that the child has a parent or other relative living." The West Australian legislation made specific reference to mothers; the *WA Aborigines Amendment Act* 1911 specified that the Chief Protector was the legal guardian "of every aboriginal and half-caste child . . . to the exclusion of the rights of the mother of an illegitimate half-caste child."[33] The Northern Territory took legal guardianship one step further and from 1918 applied similar powers in relation to Aboriginal adults; the Chief Protector had the power "to undertake the care, custody, or control of any aboriginal or half-caste, if in his opinion it is necessary or desirable in the interests of the aboriginal or half-caste for him to do so."[34] As late as 1953 the NT Director of Native Welfare was appointed "the legal guardian of all aboriginals."[35] This legislation was replaced with a supposedly "mainstream" piece of legislation, the *NT Welfare Ordinance* 1953, which made no direct reference to Aboriginal people and was aimed at "state wards"; however, as no one who was eligible for registration on an electoral roll could be declared a "ward" under this legislation, this Ordinance "could only apply to Aboriginal people."[36] Under Clause 24. (1) of this Ordinance, the Director of Welfare was appointed the guardian of all wards "as if that ward were an infant," except under specified exemptions.

In NSW, although Aboriginal parents were not stripped of their legal guardianship status, the Aboriginal Protection Board (APB) had the power to "assume full control and custody of the child of any aborigine," on the grounds that such a removal would be in the interests of the "moral or physical welfare" of the child.[37]

Aboriginal mothers did not have standard custody rights until the 1970s;[38] this is in contrast to white mothers who gained equal custody rights with their husbands in 1934.[39] Challenging the perception that Aboriginal child removal reflected the "standards of the day," awareness existed during the Stolen Generations era of the disparity in the rights of Aboriginal parents, and there were contemporary campaigns by white feminists attempting to change the discriminatory provisions in Aboriginal protection legislation. The Australian Women's Charter 1946–1949 recommended:

> that legislative amendments be made to recognise Aboriginal parents' custody rights; that the law controlling the guardianship of Aboriginal children contain the same provisions as the law controlling other children; that Aboriginal people not be removed to, or held in, institutions except by a magistrate's order, after they have appeared before a court; and that Aboriginal parents be given the same opportunity as other

parents to appear before a court to offer evidence that they are suitable persons to have care and control of their children. [40]

However, it would be almost two decades before these changes were actually implemented in many states and in the Northern Territory.

LACK OF JUDICIAL REVIEW

Protection legislation gave authorities the blanket power to support the removal of "the child of any aboriginal," often without the requirement for removals to be considered and justified on an individual or case-by-case basis. Even in jurisdictions where authorities were required to satisfy themselves that removal was in the interests of the child, there were few opportunities to dispute such a determination, as another distinguishing feature of Aboriginal protection legislation was the lack of in-built checks and balances such as judicial monitoring and review for decisions involving Indigenous children. [41] The only specific reference to the right of appeal in early protection legislation is in the *NSW Aborigines Protection Amending Act* 1915, which gave parents the right of appeal against actions of the Aboriginal Protection Board; however, such appeals could only be made on a ground involving a question of law, or on the basis that insufficient evidence existed to support the original conviction, order or sentence. [42] Only in Victoria were the provisions of Aboriginal protection legislation explicitly made subject to mainstream child welfare legislation. [43] In Queensland in the 1930s with the passage of the *Aboriginals Preservation and Protection Act* 1939, the legislation was specifically worded to override "mainstream" adoption legislation; the Director of Native Affairs was given the power to make arrangements for the "legal custody" of Aboriginal children to any person "deemed suitable to be given legal custody of such children," irrespective of the provisions of *The Adoption of Children Act* 1935. [44] In all states except Tasmania and Victoria, Indigenous child welfare was separated from mainstream welfare provision and separate institutions were developed to house removed Indigenous children. These features of the protection legislation in place in every state and territory except Tasmania highlight the legal impediments that Indigenous parents faced in retaining custody of their children in the face of attempts to remove them, and in attempting to secure the return of their children subsequent to their removal; they literally had no legal grounds to challenge the decisions being made about their children in most Australian states and territories, let alone the resources needed to mount such a legal challenge.

Although the overwhelming majority of interviewees described Aboriginal parents' powerlessness to prevent child removal, it is also important to acknowledge that in some instances authorities actually assisted Aboriginal parents to regain custody of their children. Heather Vicenti's autobiography *Too Many Tears* includes copies of correspondence she sent to the Native Welfare Department in WA requesting the return of her child, who had been placed for adoption with his paternal grandmother soon after his birth in 1956. Vicenti successfully argued that she now had the financial means to support her child and had a carer to look after him while she was working; her letter stated "I do not wish to have my baby adopted by anyone else as I can look after him myself. I am appealing to you to help me get my baby back."[45]

A letter is reproduced from the Commissioner of Native Welfare, written in his capacity as Heather's legal guardian (as she was then aged under twenty-one years) to object on her behalf to this adoption.[46] This seems to align with the account of Frank Gare, a senior bureaucrat in Native Welfare in WA in the 1960s who had worked as a patrol officer in the Stolen Generations era; he describes a cultural shift in the Department following the appointment of a new Commissioner in 1948, and states that child removal on anything other than welfare grounds would have been "anathema" to the new commissioner.[47] Vicenti's application to have her child returned was successful, and he was returned to her care when he was six months old.[48]

Historian Anna Haebich discusses a similar legal case to that of Heather Vicenti's, which took place in the Northern Territory in 1958 and involved the return of three Aboriginal children to their parents after they had been discharged from a leprosarium. Haebich highlights that in situations such as these where Aboriginal parents were classified as wards, the state official appointed as their legal guardian had a duty to pursue their legal interests.[49] These examples highlight the importance of the legislative framework; where laws existed that protected or supported the parental rights of Indigenous people, they could be used to challenge and overturn child removal. Unfortunately, such examples of successful legal challenges to child removal by Indigenous parents appear to have been rare.

OTHER IMPACTS OF PROTECTION LEGISLATION ON ABORIGINAL PARENTS

Protection legislation impacted on Aboriginal parents in a number of other ways. In New South Wales, communication with removed children was only possible with the authorization of the Board or equivalent. A number of interviews in the NLA Oral History Project described the interviewees' discovery of letters held in their welfare files that had been sent to them by their parents but which they never received.[50] Removal of children from "Aboriginal institutions" was an offense in a number of states (including New South Wales, the Northern Territory, South Australia and Western Australia); obstructing officers performing their duties relating to the legislation, which would have included any attempts to "obstruct" child removal, was also an offense in some states (the Northern Territory, Queensland, South Australia and Victoria).[51] Aboriginal parents could be compelled to pay maintenance for the support of their removed children in the Australian Capital Territory, New South Wales, the Northern Territory, Queensland, South Australia and Western Australia; this included the states where Aboriginal parents were not in fact the legal guardians of their children, but nonetheless were still expected to contribute financially towards their upkeep after their removal.

Although there were undoubtedly national patterns detectable in the waves of state and territory Aboriginal protection legislation, with very similar acts and clauses often being adopted in different states and territories within similar timeframes, there are also regional variations, with some clauses tailored to what were obviously seen to be particular problems or issues experienced in a specific state or territory. In NSW and the ACT, clauses appear from the 1940s in protection legislation allowing Aboriginal parents or the child's guardian to apply to admit their children to the control of the Aboriginal Protection Board.[52] The type of scenario that this legislation might have been aimed at is mentioned in several Aboriginal women's autobiographies. Mum Shirl discussed a number of Aboriginal families living in Redfern forced by circumstances to place their children in homes.[53] In Ruby Langford's autobiography *Don't Take Your Love to Town*, Langford spoke about her anguish when she considered placing her children in care on her return to Sydney after the death of her father. She was unemployed, broke and without a partner, with a number of young children to care for. She made arrangements to place the children in temporary care so she could find work and get back on her feet:

> I thought if I could put the kids in the Church of England homes and go back to machining I'd manage better. I think I must have decided this in the numbness of shock over Dad's death. . . . I went up in the lift, my heart sinking as the lift rose, wondering how long it would be before I could afford to get the kids out again. I told him [the head of the homes] I was a qualified machinist and wanted to place my kids in the homes till I got settled. I'd give him the endowment and what I could afford out of my wages. He asked all sorts of personal questions and I told him everything. He said he'd give me a date, and that someone would come and pick the kids up. . . . At night my mind was in turmoil and I came slowly to the realisation of what I was doing. The people would be picking the kids up in a few days and I couldn't bear it. . . . In my anguish I tossed and turned and was weeping as though my heart would break.[54]

The next day the family was granted a reprieve at the last moment when Langford's former partner returned and they were married; Langford comments with relief, "I didn't have to put my children in the homes after all."[55]

Again in NSW, from 1943 the *Aborigines Protection (Amendment) Act* authorized the Aboriginal Protection Board to make payments to foster parents, reflecting the shift in NSW from segregation of Aboriginal children in training institutions towards assimilation into white families.[56] The bitter irony of such payments being authorized to white foster parents while Aboriginal mothers were denied access to state support must also be noted; racial discrimination in access to parenting payments is discussed in detail in chapter 4.

In the Northern Territory, the passage of the 1918 *Ordinance* allowed for Aboriginal children to be removed interstate; a number of interviewees from the Northern Territory related their experience of being sent interstate, some were wartime evacuees but there were also a number who were sent to Victoria, South Australia and even Tasmania simply to attend high school.[57] The United Aboriginal Mission's newsletter, *The United Aborigines Messenger*, indicates that some institutions deliberately sought to place great physical distance between removed children and their families:

> The Mission desired to give the half-caste children such a training as would help them merge into the white population. This they were unable to do so long as the home was in close proximity to an Aboriginal camp . . . After much prayer for guidance, it was decided to remove the children to a place further south, where there were no Aborigines.[58]

The *WA Native Administration Act* 1936 included a clause which appears to have been aimed at preventing Aboriginal parents from prostituting their children to pearlers. Clause 44 of the Act made it an offense for "Any native who, being the parent or having custody of any female child apparently under the age of sixteen years, allows that child to be within two miles of any creek or inlet used by the boats of pearlers or other sea boats." While some have argued that protecting Aboriginal girls from sexual intercourse was a "major motive" behind efforts to remove Aboriginal children believed to be at risk in Western Australia,[59] Liz Conor highlights white discomfort in the years immediately preceding the second world war with racial "miscegenation," particularly between Aboriginal women and Asian men (many pearling luggers were operated by Japanese crew). She argues that "it was Aboriginal women's sexual activity with 'alien' men, particularly 'Asiatics,' which finally prompted dramatically contrasting government interventions and media exposure."[60] Irrespective of the real motivations of legislators, the perceived need to explicitly legislate for this scenario is very revealing of white attitudes towards Aboriginal parents as fit carers for their children.

"UPON THE EVIDENCE OF THE MOTHER": LIMITATIONS ON ACCEPTING ABORIGINAL WOMEN'S TESTIMONY ABOUT THE PATERNITY OF THEIR CHILDREN

There was a clause in the protection legislation of all states (with the exception of Tasmania, which had no such legislation, and Victoria) which made specific reference to Aboriginal mothers. In relation to the enforcement of white fathers contributing towards child maintenance payments, the legislation stipulated that Aboriginal women's testimony as to the paternity of their "half-caste" child would not be accepted "upon the evidence of the mother, unless her evidence be corroborated in some material particular." The wording of this clause is almost identical in New South Wales, the Northern Territory, South Australia and Western Australia, with the Queensland legislation instead stipulating "no man shall be taken to be the father of any such child which is illegitimate upon the oath of the mother only." Apart from reflecting a deep-seated contempt toward the veracity of Aboriginal women, such clauses in Aboriginal "protection" legislation perhaps also reflected that the interests of the white legislators lay with protecting the white fathers of "half-caste" children, rather than the Aboriginal mothers left to raise these children without financial support.

Having identified a range of legal restrictions impacting on Aboriginal mothering, the focus of the next chapter is on the impact of racial discrimination on Aboriginal mothers' access to social security benefits in the Stolen Generations era.

NOTES

1. Bolt, "I Wasn't Stolen." Robert Manne reports that O'Donoghue used the term "uninformed consent" to describe her mother's actions. Manne, *In Denial*, 2.

2. Bolt, "I Wasn't Stolen." For further analysis of debates about who can claim the status of being "stolen," see Payne, "Untold Suffering," "Appendix 4: Who Can Claim the Status of Being 'Stolen'?," 338–345. Further discussion of the issue of "consent" can be found in chapter 7.

3. Simkin, "Debate Rages over Stolen Generations Phrase." For further discussion about the Howard era response to the issue of the Stolen Generations see Payne, "'For All of Us, for None of You': Practical Reconciliation."

4. Goodall, "Too Early Yet or Not Soon Enough?," 13–16.

5. Rintoul, "The Dispossession of Lowitja O'Donoghue," 110.

6. See Payne "'To the Exclusion of the Rights of the Mother': Legal Barriers to Aboriginal Mothering in the Stolen Generations Era."

7. Human Rights and Equal Opportunity Commission, *Bringing Them Home*, Appendices 1–7.

8. Australian Institute for Aboriginal and Torres Strait Islander Studies, "To Remove and Protect."

9. Human Rights and Equal Opportunity Commission, *Bringing Them Home*, 266.

10. Oguro, Payne & Varnham, "Integrating Human Rights Education into Schools: Legislation, Curriculum and Practice," 8.

11. Australian Human Rights Commission, "Voices of Australia."

12. Scott, "Why Wasn't Genocide a Crime in Australia?"

13. Marchetti & Ransley, "Unconscious Racism," 542–543.

14. Frank Gare, interviewed by W. J. E. Bannister, 11 March 1999, ORAL TRC 5000/14, National Library of Australia, Session 3, 00:36:12.

15. Human Rights and Equal Opportunity Commission, *Bringing Them Home*, 255.

16. Swain, "History of Child Protection Legislation," 18.

17. Swain, "History of Child Protection Legislation," 18.

18. Swain, "History of Child Protection Legislation," 19.

19. Human Rights and Equal Opportunity Commission, *Bringing Them Home*, 250.

20. Human Rights and Equal Opportunity Commission, *Bringing Them Home*, 255.

21. "Ruby," interviewed by Anne Maree Payne, 49.

22. "Ruby," interviewed by Anne Maree Payne, 48.

23. Vicenti and Dickman, "Too Many Tears," 111.

24. Human Rights and Equal Opportunity Commission, *Bringing Them Home*, 600. My emphasis.

25. Goodall, "Assimilation Begins in the Home," 79–80.

26. Brock, "Aboriginal Families and the Law in the Era of Segregation and Assimilation," 136.

27. Rowley, *Outcasts in White Australia*, 22.

28. *SA Ordinance for the Protection, Maintenance and Upbringing of Orphans and other Destitute Children and Aborigines Act* 1844.

29. *Qld Aboriginal Protection and Restriction of the Sale of Opium Act* 1897.

30. Clarke, *Things are so much better than they used to be*, 190–191.

31. *NSW Aborigines Protection (Amendment) Act* 1940 13A. (5) and (6).

32. *NT Welfare Ordinance 1953* 17. (1.).

33. *WA Aborigines Amendment Act* 1911 (3).

34. *NT Aboriginals Ordinance, 1918*, 6. (1.).

35. *NT Aboriginals Ordinance* 1953, Clause 7.

36. Australian Institute of Aboriginal and Torres Strait Islander Studies, "To Remove and Protect."

37. *NSW Aborigines Protection Amending Act* 1915, 13A.

38. Lake, *Getting Equal*, 83.

39. Lake, *Getting Equal*, 86.

40. Quoted in Lake, *Getting Equal*, 195–196.

41. Human Rights and Equal Opportunity Commission, "The National Inquiry into the Separation of Aboriginal and Torres Strait Islander Children from Their Families, Bringing Them Home," para. 6.7.

42. As outlined in Part V of the *NSW Justices Act* 1902.

43. see *Vic Aborigines Act* 1915, 6. (x).

44. Clause 18 (3).

45. Vicenti and Dickman, "Too Many Tears," 79–80.

46. Vicenti and Dickman, "Too Many Tears," 80.

47. Frank Gare, interviewed by W. J. E. Bannister, 11 March 1999, ORAL TRC 5000/14, National Library of Australia, Session 1, 00:35:47.

48. Vicenti and Dickman, "Too Many Tears," 80.

49. Haebich, *Broken Circles*, 544.

50. See, for example, Jackie Frail interviewed by Rob Willis, 6 July 2000, ORAL TRC 5000/162, National Library of Australia; Debra (Chandler) Hocking interviewed by Lyn McCleavy, 16 May 2000 and 22 & 29 May 2001, ORAL TRC 5000/279, National Library of Australia; Ryan Kelly interviewed by John Maynard, 1 April 2001, ORAL TRC 5000/240, National Library of Australia; Pattie Lees interviewed by Colleen Hattersley, 13 June 2001, ORAL TRC 5000/300, National Library of Australia; Yvonne Mills interviewed by Colleen Hattersley, 15 August 1999, ORAL TRC 5000/37, National Library of Australia; Vince Wenberg interviewed by Frank Heimans, 6 September 2001, ORAL TRC 5000/319, National Library of Australia.

51. Ella Simon's autobiography recounts an incident which took place on Purfleet Mission, where one of her cousins was arrested for using threatening language when he complained to a Board representative about the removal of Aboriginal children. Simon, *Through My Eyes*, 90.

52. *NSW Aborigines Protection (Amendment) Act* 1940 7 (2); *ACT Aborigines Welfare Ordinance* 1954 (5.) (1) (e).

53. Mum Shirl, *Mum Shirl. An Autobiography*.

54. Langford, *Don't Take Your Love to Town*, 102–103

55. Langford, *Don't Take Your Love to Town*, 103.

56. Goodall, "Assimilation Begins in the Home," 85.

57. See, for example, Clair Andersen & Jaye Clair interviewed by Lyn McLeavy, 20 July, 24 August & 15 September 2000 and 25 May 2001, ORAL TRC 5000/287, National Library of Australia.

58. Quoted in Rintoul, "The Dispossession of Lowitja O'Donoghue," 110–111.

59. Windschuttle, *The Fabrication of Aboriginal History*, 443.

60. Conor, "'Black Velvet' and 'Purple Indignation,'" para. 12.

FOUR

"Strange Anomalies"

Limitations on Aboriginal Mothers' Access to Social Security

Another major structural barrier facing Aboriginal mothers in the Stolen Generations era was their exclusion from or differential access to social security benefits because of racial discrimination in the determination of their eligibility to receive such payments. This chapter focuses on family-based payments such as the maternity allowance and child endowment, identifying the impact these discriminatory measures had on Aboriginal mothers and families. This chapter also includes material drawn from the oral history interviews and other autobiographical sources about Aboriginal mothers' experiences of receiving (or being denied) social security payments, highlighting the often-severe impact that racial discrimination in access to social security had on an individual and family level.

Despite being more likely to live in poverty and most in need of the safety net provided by access to social security, Aboriginal mothers in the Stolen Generations era faced racially discriminatory provisions limiting their access to social security payments that were provided by state and federal governments to support white Australian mothers, children and families. Peggy Brock argues that these restrictions on Commonwealth welfare payments impacted more severely on Aboriginal women than on Aboriginal men; Aboriginal women who married white men could also be left in limbo due to legally-created ambiguities between white and Aboriginal identities.[1] As historian Fiona Paisley has noted,

> childhood, motherhood and womanhood under White Australia, cannot be viewed outside of racial constructions of difference. The experience of the child, the qualities of the mother and the morality of the

woman were shaped in relation to racial classification, and exclusion
from or access to, enfranchised representation in the modern nation
state.[2]

While the reproductive and child-rearing efforts of white mothers were
supported by state and federal social security payments, those of Aboriginal mothers in the Stolen Generations era (and other "non-desirable"
mothers) were discouraged by the withholding of payments that would
have provided invaluable support and had the potential to prevent families from falling into the extreme poverty that then led to child removal
on the grounds of "neglect." Anna Haebich has noted that Indigenous
child removal was a preferred policy in some states and territories because as a policy option it was less costly and easier to administer than
the significant expenditure and effort that would have been required to
address Aboriginal disadvantage.[3]

From as early as 1905 onwards,[4] state-based Aboriginal protection
legislation began to include clauses enabling Aboriginal people to be
exempted from the provisions of the legislation, subject to a range of
conditions being met. While Aboriginal Australians who were "primitive," "nomadic" or "dependent" on government welfare were routinely
excluded from receiving social security payments, exceptions were made
for Aboriginal people who had received certificates of exemption.[5] The
lure of an exemption in return for benefits impacted particularly on extended Aboriginal families; in order to qualify, exempted Aboriginal people had to move away from the reserve or mission where extended family members resided, whereas non-Aboriginal people received such payment irrespective of their circumstances.[6]

MATERNITY PAYMENTS

Anxieties in the new Australian nation about the declining white birth
rate linked to fears about the growth in nonwhite population groups
have been well documented.[7] The controls placed on Aboriginal people
through protection legislation, limiting their access to major centers of
population and their interactions with other Australians, have been
linked with the development and implementation of other measures designed to limit, control or deport other "undesirable" population
groups.[8]

Maternity was central to population debates and ideas about the future of the new Commonwealth. In addition to discouraging the growth
of "undesirable" groups, measures were also put in place to promote an
increase in the white population. This led the federal government to
introduce a Maternity Allowance in 1912, but to deny payment of the
allowance to "women who were Asiatics, Aboriginal natives of Australia,
Papua or the islands of the Pacific."[9]

"Half-caste" Aboriginal mothers who had "a preponderance of white blood" were deemed eligible to receive the Commonwealth maternity allowance. However, analysis of the management of Aboriginal affairs in Queensland undertaken by Rosalind Kidd provides a useful case study of the interrelationship between Commonwealth and state "welfare" payments and how these were (mis)managed in relation to Aboriginal people. Federal maternity allowance funds were co-opted by some state-based Aboriginal agencies rather than payments going directly to Aboriginal families. This payment was specifically targeted by authorities in Queensland, with the Chief Protector advising mission authorities how to "tap into the windfall."[10] Kidd states:

> This cash bonus was routinely and unlawfully usurped since 1928 on missions and settlements, and used to cover clothing and medical expenses which were legally an institutional cost. Mothers of dormitory children received only 20 per cent of the allowance, and only 50 per cent was paid to mothers with children at home. Altered qualifications in 1942 enabled all "full blood" women to claim the maternity allowance, provided they were not living on state-controlled communities.[11]

In her autobiography Heather Vicenti reproduces documentation relating to her aunty, Ida Calgaret, highlighting the real-life impact of restrictions to maternity payments on Aboriginal families. A Native Welfare Officer interviewed Ida and her husband in 1949, reporting "They have four children and all appear well cared for and are very light coloured. The parents are concerned by the fact that they were not permitted Baby Bonus and request that their caste be examined and that they be advised of the result."[12] The official determination of the "caste review" was that Ida was deemed to possess five-eighths "native blood," and her application to receive the allowance was unsuccessful; a document reproduced by Vicenti notes "The Commonwealth Social Services laws preclude the grant of a maternity allowance to a person possessing more than half native blood, unless such person possesses a Certificate of Citizenship or Exemption. This condition has disqualified Mrs Horace Calgaret from receiving a maternity allowance."[13] All of Ida's children were eventually removed by authorities and sent to Roelands Mission, despite the assessment of the Native Welfare Officer that they were "well cared for"; Vicenti states that Ida and her husband were threatened that the children would be split up and sent to separate institutions unless they were "sent willingly."[14]

In 1942 the maternity allowance was extended to "Aboriginal natives" who were exempted from state-based Aboriginal protection laws. It was not until 1959 that all Aboriginal people—except those classed as "nomadic or primitive"—were granted entitlement to Commonwealth pensions and maternity allowances, with full equality in the payment of Commonwealth social security benefits not gained until 1966.[15] The exclusion of payment of maternity benefits to "nomadic or primitive" Aboriginal people as late as 1959 highlights the racist underpinning of such policies; if they had been based on an assessment of need rather than racially-based motivations, these groups would surely have been a high priority to receive these payments.

In addition to being denied maternity payments offered to promote white motherhood, Anna Haebich has identified the "shocking neglect" of Aboriginal mothers' maternal health at this time,[16] with Central Australia also reporting one of the highest incidences of infant mortality in the world as late as the 1960s.[17] Haebich describes the "anti-natalist" strategies put in place in Australia to minimize further growth of the "half-caste" population as having direct equivalence to the measures put in place by some European countries in the 1930s to manage the reproduction of unwanted racial groups.[18] In its most extreme form, anti-natalism in Nazi Germany led from forced sterilization (1933) to involuntary abortion and marriage restrictions (1935), and ultimately to genocide.[19] Two-thirds of German Jews deported to and killed in the death camps were female, with pregnant women or mothers accompanied by young children most likely of adults who were otherwise fit to work to be immediately selected for death upon arrival at the camps.[20] While in no way suggesting a direct parallel between the experiences of Aboriginal mothers in the Stolen Generations era and those of Jewish mothers during the Holocaust, the over-representation of Jewish mothers and children as victims in the Holocaust highlights the vulnerability of women because of their status as mothers or potential mothers or the carers of children when states make racially-based decisions to "manage" populations that are identified as undesirable.

CHILD ENDOWMENT

Another family payment that was initially withheld and then eventually paid on a discriminatory basis to Aboriginal families during the Stolen Generations era was the child endowment. The child endowment was first introduced in NSW in 1927 "for the benefit of children by means of endowment payable to mothers";[21] this Act has been described as pioneering in that it no longer imposed a blanket exclusion on people classified as "Aboriginal."[22] The child endowment was paid for a brief time directly to Aboriginal families but then payments were made instead to the NSW Aboriginal Protection Board, with Aboriginal families not receiving the payment on the same basis as non-Aboriginal families until the 1960s.[23] In a similar fashion to the grab for federal maternity allowance payments by the Queensland Aboriginal Affairs organizations outlined by Rosalind Kidd, Heather Goodall has described how the NSW Aboriginal Protection Board co-opted federal child endowment payments with the aim of supplementing dwindling state-based funding for Aboriginal welfare after its rations budget was cut during the Depression era. The NSW Treasury then cut the APB budget again so there was no net gain for Aboriginal welfare funding and a loss of control of precious funds by individual Aboriginal mothers. Goodall notes:

> The Board justified its assumption of control over Family Endowment payments by suggesting that Aboriginal women had "squandered" this benefit, an assertion which was in complete contradiction to the actual concerns held by Commissioner. The Board argued that if a woman was judged to be "competent" she might receive direct cash payments of the state Endowment, but this occurred for only a few families before the 1940s.[24]

In her autobiography Ella Simon described the personal impact of this policy approach:

> My endowment went to the Board which sent this pink slip of paper to the Manager who would pass it on to me and supervise how it was spent. You could only take it to a big store to be cashed as they had to send it to the Board to get their money. There was one time I had to wait six months before I got it, because the second Manager, that Scotsman, had just simply decided he would cut me out of regular child endowment. It was as simple as that. I had to fight six months to get it back.[25]

Kidd similarly identified that in Queensland, Aboriginal settlements applied for and received federal child endowment funds as a bulk monthly payment, a move justified by the argument that Aboriginal mothers might not expend the funds appropriately to benefit their children; Kidd notes "Only a fraction was paid to the parents."[26] Again, rather than federal funds being seen as a valuable increase in much-needed funding for Aboriginal welfare in Queensland, "the department slashed mission subsidies in 1942."[27] Likewise, child endowment payments were co-opted by authorities in "most states and the Northern Territory," with funding being used to expand Aboriginal institutions; Haebich notes that such funding thus ironically "contributed to the continued removal and institutionalisation of Aboriginal children—in express contradiction to stated policies of keeping children with their families,"[28] a policy goal that apparently only applied to non-Indigenous families.

The federal government first introduced a national child endowment scheme in 1941, and extended the scope of the scheme in 1950.[29] Initially, "nomadic" or "dependent" Aboriginal people were not eligible to receive the payment.[30] While "Nomadic" persons were disqualified from receiving child endowment payments, there was no precise definition of "nomadic"; an anomaly meant "that while a full-blood mother could not receive a maternity allowance, she could receive child endowment after the child was born."[31] Children living in institutions were also initially excluded from receiving the endowment;[32] this was amended in 1942. Subsidies provided by the state government for the support of institutionalized children in Queensland were paid differentially on the basis of race; the rate for white children living in institutional care was set at seven shillings per week and came from the Home Department budget, whereas the rate for Aboriginal children was about one third of this and came from general funding for Aboriginal relief.[33] This racially discriminatory approach to state funding for the care of Aboriginal children may help us to better understand the many accounts provided by Aboriginal people of the poor standards of housing and nutrition they received in institutional care.

Many sources highlight the importance of child endowment payments to Aboriginal mothers, which were for many the first regular income they had received.[34] In her autobiography Alice Nannup described the personal impact of the extension of the child endowment to struggling Aboriginal mothers.[35] Nannup was confronted one day in the main street by an Aboriginal Affairs officer who accused her of misspending her child endowment money;[36] eventually she satisfied the officer that she had not spent her endowment funds inappropriately by producing the parcel of goods she had purchased. Nannup commented, "Getting a bad report about you was something to worry about, in case they got it into their heads to take your children away from you. That was something I was never, ever threatened with, but the worry was always there."[37] Nannup's comments highlight the interconnectedness of poverty, access to welfare payments, and child removal for Aboriginal families.

PENSIONS

The new federal government passed "groundbreaking" social security legislation in the *Invalid and Old-Age Pensions Act* 1908;[38] however "Asiatics (except those born in Australia), or aboriginal natives of Australia, Africa, the Islands of the Pacific, or New Zealand" were disqualified from receiving these pensions.[39] In 1937 the Commonwealth Conference on Aboriginal Welfare resolved "That all natives of less than full blood be eligible to receive invalid and old-age pensions and maternity allowance on the recommendation of the State authority, to whom the grant should be made in trust for the individual,"[40] clearly highlighting the differential basis in which these payments were made to Indigenous Australians. In 1942 Aboriginal people who were exempted from state protection laws became eligible for the first time to receive federal pensions and benefits; in 1959 the *Social Services Act* was amended to remove the disqualification of Aboriginal people, except for those deemed "nomadic" or "primitive"; and it was not until 1966 that all specific references to Aborigines were removed from the Act.[41]

When the Widows' Pension was introduced nationally in 1942, "aboriginal natives of Australia" were again specifically excluded, along with "aliens" and "aboriginal natives of Africa, the Islands of the Pacific, and New Zealand."[42]

One benefit that Aboriginal women were not excluded from on racially discriminatory grounds was the War Widows' Pension (*Commonwealth War Pensions Act* 1914*)*. Rita Huggins described the importance of the small but regular war widows' pension payments she received after the death of her husband:

> He had contributed to a superannuation fund from which I received a small fortnightly cheque, as well as a war widow's pension from Veterans' Affairs. This money was a godsend and enabled my family to have shelter, food and clothing.[43]

Similarly, Sally Morgan described her mother receiving a war widow's pension after her father's suicide was attributed to his war service; "It was regular money at a time when we needed it."[44] Tellingly, although struggling financially neither Rita Huggins nor Gladys Corunna (Sally Morgan's mother) experienced the removal of their children; the small but regular pension payments they received were vital in maintaining the integrity of their families.

The Single Mothers' pension was not introduced in Australia until 1974, outside of the scope of the Stolen Generations era. Of the interviews I have analyzed from the NLA collection, over half of the Aboriginal interviewees who were removed from their families as children came from single parent families, highlighting the extreme difficulties facing single Aboriginal parents, the overwhelming majority of whom were mothers.

RATIONING OUT WELFARE

In addition to being specifically excluded from receiving family payments such as child endowment and the maternity allowance, some state-based Aboriginal welfare administrations "paid" benefits to Aboriginal people in the form of food rations rather than cash payments, presumably on the basis of assumptions that Aboriginal people could not be trusted to make wise choices about how they would expend cash funds.

Alice Nannup described the indignity of being forced to go to the police station and ask for assistance in the form of rations:

> It was terrible going down to the station to ask for help. It was a really hard thing for me to do, to go asking for things, but we were left with no other choice. . . . They'd ask you everything under the sun, and they'd say things like, "Why haven't you got a job, plenty of jobs

around." Well, this just wasn't true, and besides, I had four children to look after. How was I going to manage another job as well?[45]

Heather Vicenti's autobiography also described her experience of being given food rations when what she most desperately needed was money to pay the rent for housing for herself and her children.[46]

Ruth Hegarty's autobiography detailed the differential basis on which Aboriginal families were allocated the maternity allowance (Baby Bonus) and child endowment funds even after they became eligible to receive them:

> The Baby Bonus, which was a Government payment of seventeen pounds for boys and fifteen pounds for girls, was useful for purchasing things from the Mission Store as well as other goods, unlike the Child Endowment. We purchased a cabinet and table and chairs for the kitchen. The Child Endowment, though introduced in about 1941 and payable to all Australian families, was now available to Aboriginal people living on Missions. However, it was not readily made available to us as cash, but could be used to purchase goods, on Order Forms, to the value of whatever you were entitled to.[47]

THE IMPACT OF "RACIAL CLASSIFICATION" SYSTEMS ON ACCESS TO SOCIAL SECURITY

Aboriginal mothers also experienced bizarre problems due to convoluted racially-based state welfare systems, which arose when their children had a different "racial classification" to their own, and so had different entitlements to welfare. Heather Vicenti's autobiography details correspondence written by a white friend to the Minister for Native Affairs complaining on Vicenti's behalf about the discrepancy between welfare assistance paid to Aboriginal and non-Aboriginal women (as noted above, Vicenti had received rations rather than money when she approached Native Welfare for relief after her marriage ended). The response from the Minister for Native Welfare dated 22 February 1962 advised that "native applicants" had to apply for relief to the Native Welfare Department irrespective of the caste status of their children, while "non-native" applicants "including quadroons or less" applied to the Child Welfare Department.[48] But by 1963 the Department had apparently changed its policy; a letter from the Commissioner of Native Welfare dated 17 June 1963 stated "the children concerned are quadroons and, therefore, outside the jurisdiction of the Native Welfare Act."[49] Because of her "half-caste" status, Vicenti was entitled to rations and not money:

> This situation meant I was unable to pay rent. My children, though, were classed as "quadroons," so they came within the jurisdiction of the Child Welfare Act. Monies were distributed through the Child Welfare Department. It was a very strange anomaly.[50]

The ludicrousness of attempting to administer family welfare along racial lines recalls Charles Rowley's insight that "prejudice creates its own special problems": noting that state Aboriginal Affairs departments undoubtedly contributed significantly to the problems they were meant to be solving, Crowley commented, "There is something reminiscent of Lilliputian politics, in both the scale and in the degree of logical absurdity, in the administration of Aboriginal Affairs at this time."[51]

This chapter has highlighted the impact of racial discrimination in limiting Aboriginal mothers' access to social security benefits, resulting in more Aboriginal families living in poverty and more children being at risk of removal on the grounds of "neglect." In the next chapter the impact of the requirement of Aboriginal mothers to return to work on their carers' responsibilities will be explored.

NOTES

1. Brock, "Aboriginal Families and the Law in the Era of Segregation and Assimilation," 147, 149.
2. Paisley, "Feminist Challenges to White Australia, 1900–1930s," 269.
3. Haebich, *Broken Circles,* 34–35.
4. WA 1905; QLD 1934; SA 1939; NSW 1943; ACT 1954.
5. Goodall, "Assimilation Begins in the Home," 85.
6. Brock, "Aboriginal Families and the Law in the Era of Segregation and Assimilation," 147.
7. See for example Goodall, "'Saving the Children.' Gender and the Colonisation of Aboriginal Children in NSW, 1788 to 1990"; Markus, "Legislating White Australia, 1900–1970."
8. Markus, "Legislating White Australia, 1900–1970," 242–243.
9. Lake, "A Revolution in the Family," 379.
10. Kidd, *The Way We Civilise,* 86.
11. Kidd, *The Way We Civilise,* 166.
12. Vicenti and Dickman, "Too Many Tears," 39.
13. Vicenti and Dickman, "Too Many Tears," 40.
14. Vicenti and Dickman, "Too Many Tears," 40.
15. Markus, "Legislating White Australia, 1900–1970," 250.
16. Haebich, *Broken Circles,* 204.
17. Haebich reports the infant mortality figure at 25 percent. Haebich, *Broken Circles,* 29.
18. Haebich, *Broken Circles,* 205.
19. Bock, "Antinatalism, Maternity and Paternity in National Socialist Racism," 234.
20. Bock, "Antinatalism, Maternity and Paternity in National Socialist Racism," 249.
21. *NSW Family Endowment Act* 1927 preamble.
22. Bock, "Antinatalism, Maternity and Paternity in National Socialist Racism," 249.
23. Goodall, "Assimilation Begins in the Home," 93.
24. Goodall, "Assimilation Begins in the Home," 93.
25. Simon, *Through My Eyes,* 98–99.
26. Kidd, *The Way We Civilise,* 167.
27. Kidd, *The Way We Civilise,* 167.
28. Haebich, *Broken Circles,* 451.
29. Lake, "A Revolution in the Family," 392.
30. Rowley, *Outcasts in White Australia,* 38.
31. Rowley, *Outcasts in White Australia,* 396.

32. O'Neill, "Child Endowment Act 1941."

33. Kidd, *The Way We Civilise*, 58.

34. Brock, "Aboriginal Families and the Law in the Era of Segregation and Assimilation," 146.

35. Nannup, Marsh & Kinnane, *When the Pelican Laughed*, 180.

36. Nannup, Marsh & Kinnane, *When the Pelican Laughed*, 188.

37. Nannup, Marsh & Kinnane, *When the Pelican Laughed*, 188–189.

38. National Museum of Australia, "1908: Legislation Introduction National Age and Invalid Pensions."

39. Shaw, "Myths and Facts about Aborigines and Social Security."

40. Commonwealth of Australia, "Aboriginal Welfare. Initial Conference of Commonwealth and State Aboriginal Authorities," 4.

41. Shaw, "Myths and Facts about Aborigines and Social Security."

42. *Commonwealth Widows' Pensions Act* 1942.

43. Huggins and Huggins, *Auntie Rita*, 66.

44. Morgan, *My Place*, 60.

45. Nannup, Marsh & Kinnane, *When the Pelican Laughed*, 173.

46. Vicenti and Dickman, "Too Many Tears," 96.

47. Hegarty, *Bittersweet Journey*, 68.

48. Vicenti and Dickman, "Too Many Tears," 96.

49. Vicenti and Dickman, "Too Many Tears," 97.

50. Vicenti and Dickman, "Too Many Tears," 97.

51. Rowley, *Outcasts in White Australia*, 8.

FIVE

"Forcible Removal Through Employment"

The Impact of the Requirement to Work on Aboriginal Mothers

An issue many Aboriginal mothers faced during the Stolen Generations era was the requirement that they return to work irrespective of their carers' responsibilities for their babies and young children. The *Bringing Them Home* Report described Aboriginal children being sent out to work as "forcible removal through employment," although only briefly acknowledged that this practice also impacted on mothers.[1] The requirement to work particularly impacted on young Aboriginal mothers living on missions, who were often sent on domestic service placements within twelve months of the birth of a child, resulting in the removal of their child or children to be raised in mission dormitories, or necessitating other care arrangements to be put in place. Even Aboriginal mothers who were not living on missions often faced the necessity of seeking paid work to support themselves and their children, impacting on their carer's responsibilities.

Aboriginal protection legislation contained clauses relating to apprenticeship and licensing as well as the placement in domestic service of Aboriginal minors and, in the case of the Northern Territory, all Aboriginal people who were not exempted from the legislation. It was an offense under these Acts to leave employment without permission, and in those states where state authorities were the legal guardians of Aboriginal children, they had the power to approve apprenticeship, licensing and domestic service arrangements for them, sometimes in the case of Aboriginal women until they turned twenty-one. This led to the situation experienced by a number of Aboriginal mothers living on missions, who were sent on work placements as domestic servants, returned to the Mission pregnant, and subsequently were sent on another domestic service placement after the birth of their child, with no consideration being given by authorities to these women's primary care commitments for their own child or children.

Mervyn Pattemore, a white missionary who worked in the Northern Territory, described the establishment of the Retta Dixon Home in Alice Springs specifically to provide care for the children of Aboriginal mothers who were required to return to work: "mothers had these children and had to go out to work. There was no single parents' benefit and things like that. No social services for them. They had to go out to work."[2]

Annie Mullins, an Aboriginal mother whose three children were removed to a mission dormitory in Queensland when she was sent out on work placements as a domestic servant, described the impact of work commitments on Aboriginal mothers' ability to care for their children:

> And when I had my children, my girls had to be taken into the mission too . . . we had to leave them when we had to go to employment. . . . We had to go and work on all the cattle stations. And hand them in when they turned six. . . . I had the three girls. And when they grew up, the station people didn't want them women with children going out to the station. They wanted us to leave the children behind. . . . And we knew how to take care of our children. . . . But they still took the children off us, and told us it was the government orders, to take the children off their parents while they went out to employment. . . . You weren't allowed to see your children till twelve months were up.[3]

Annie described her attempts to reclaim wages from the Queensland government for years of unpaid domestic work and was bitter that she was forced to leave her children behind but was not even appropriately recompensed for her work: "I used to go, I worked there for nothing, we worked there for nothing. Leaving a little tiny baby."[4]

The types of work undertaken by many Aboriginal women during the Stolen Generations era, such as domestic service or station work, were more likely to be in remote areas, requiring people to live-in and spend lengthy periods away from home. Some mothers were allowed to take their children with them on work placements, particularly younger children, however white employers did not always welcome the presence of children. Annie attributed this to the belief that the children's presence "used to hinder the mothers from working."[5] She described being forced to leave her daughter outside in a pram as her mistress would not allow her to bring the child inside the house:

I had to leave [her daughter] under the tree in a pram. The poor little girl used to cry her little head off. Yeah. While she had the mother inside crawling on hands and knees polishing the floors and all that."[6]
Well, it was tough now. All of us went out of the mission and left all of the kids behind. We had to go out and work. If you came back, if you broke your agreement, they'd make you go back to do it again . . . we didn't have any choices.[7]

Ruby spoke about her experience growing up on a mission and being raised by her grandparents and extended family because of her mother's work commitments:

My mum didn't raise me all the time, I mean I knew my mum. I'd seen her intermittently from time to time. Other times she was with me and other times she wasn't. Most of the time I was raised by my grandparents . . . [the Mission] used Aboriginal people as itinerant workers. And they couldn't get enough people to work on the farms and on the properties, you know the sheep stations and cattle stations and so any available bodies they would send out to work, and if they had children they were placed with grandparents or others that were able to look after them in the community. If there wasn't anyone [like] that, family, they were then put into dormitories.[8]

When Ruby herself had a baby as a single parent in her teens, she was sent out on a work placement by the mission after her son's birth and had to make alternative arrangements for the care of her baby:

I was put in the babies quarters . . . I stayed there until [my son] was about 12 months old . . . And in the end they ended up sending me out to work . . . I had to then find somebody else to look after [my son]—I was still breastfeeding. And I said to, I said "Oh, I can't." They wouldn't let you take him with you. So my aunt said to me, "I'll take him." . . . And, I hated the thought of leaving him, you know, but it was either that or he was going to be put . . . with someone else to raise him in the baby dormitory.[9]

In her autobiography Rita Huggins described the care arrangements she put in place for her eldest child, conceived while she was working as a domestic servant as a young woman:

During my domestic service my first-born . . . was born in Cherbourg on 18 May 1942. Due to my young age and domestic service duties I left her in my parents' care. It was a hard thing for me to do but with being sent out to work all the time I had no choice.[10]

Ruth Hegarty's autobiographical account of her experiences as a "Dormitory Girl" at Cherbourg details her institutionalization in the dormitory system as a six-month-old baby, and removal from her mother's care as a four-and-a-half-year-old girl:

> When the children of dormitory mums reached school age, they were removed from their mother's care. . . . Worse was to come. Because Mum was no longer responsible for me in the government's eyes, she was free to go out to work. Most of the mothers who no longer had children to care for were required to go away to work. Often they would be sent a long way off, their children would not see or hear from them for many months. This happened to us only six months after I started school, I was just five years old and already I was to experience a second separation from my mum.[11]

Hegarty was to lose two of her own children to the dorm system, after becoming pregnant as a young domestic worker, before eventually marrying and leaving the mission. Hegarty's account focused on the institutionalization of the dormitory system, which eventually sent young Aboriginal girls out as domestic workers with no life skills or experience to help them deal with the lack of institutional framework. Not surprisingly many of them became pregnant and Hegarty emphasized the cycle of early pregnancy, child removal and subsequent loss of parent-child bonds, as a pattern that was repeated throughout several generations. Hegarty also highlighted the lack of options available to Aboriginal women living on Cherbourg Mission, who were powerless to control many aspects of their lives and who had no other model of "normal" family life to compare their own experiences to.

Aboriginal mothers graphically described the physical and emotional impact of being separated from their children to work as domestic servants, highlighted in this comment by Ruby: "So they sent me out to [station name], out 200 km from the nearest town. I fretted, I was having trouble with the breast milk. . . . And, I was, it was heartbreaking, because I was Nanny to twins and four kids."[12] There is a terrible irony evident in these accounts by Aboriginal mothers, who were deprived of the opportunity to mother their own children while they worked in other people's homes caring for white children.

MOTHERING AS RESISTANCE

White feminist analysis has often focused on women's exclusion from the public domain and confinement to the home, with equal opportunity to access employment being an important focus of their campaigns for gender equality. However, for many Aboriginal and migrant women in Australia, work outside the home—usually of low status and poorly paid—has always been a significant feature of their lives.[13] The concept that women are oppressed in the private sphere and are liberated by participating in the public sphere has been challenged by black feminists, who argue that work was often a site of racism and oppression for black women, whereas their homes were a source of comfort and sites of resistance to a racist society.[14]

The ideal of the all-sacrificing mother who places her child's needs before her own has endured despite massive changes to women's legal, political, economic and social status. Mothers who are seen to fail to subsume their own needs or to fail in their responsibilities of care for their children are subjected to harsh judgment by society. However, the mothering work undertaken by some mothers may be primarily focused on the physical survival of their children; their priorities as mothers may revolve around securing food and shelter, cultural affirmation and building safe neighborhoods, both for their own children and other children in the community.[15] This type of mothering, which has been described as "motherhood as preservation,"[16] stands in stark contrast to the style of nurturing mothering that is seen by white society to constitute "good" mothering. At the same time, the role of the state in policing the family, and the role of race, class and other social differences in society's judgments about motherhood, are rarely acknowledged or challenged in community debates about motherhood.

Possibly due to the importance of the home in many women's lives, loss of security and violation of the home and family are acutely felt by women, as such incursions emphasize their powerlessness to protect their loved ones.[17] Rather than their homes being "a domestic space separate from the public world,"[18] Aboriginal families in Australia experienced an extremely high level of state intervention in almost every aspect of their day-to-day life.[19] Child removal policies and practices in the Stolen Generations era clearly highlight these interrelationships and connections between the public and private domains in the lives of Aboriginal families.

In her autobiography, prominent Aboriginal activist and foster mother Mum Shirl described her grandmother as

> a traditional woman who kept a lookout for everything; the welfare of all children, the men, other women, the countryside. In her own way, I guess she was very attached to me and cared about me, but it seemed that she was very attached to and cared about everybody.[20]

The role Mum Shirl described her grandmother fulfilling resembles the "community mothering" role that has been recognized as an aspect of black mothering.[21] In her lifelong struggle for Aboriginal social justice, Mum Shirl's own motherwork[22] was by necessity also primarily focused on motherhood as preservation; she described her thought processes when meeting young, needy Aboriginal mothers:

> The young girl with three or four children who hasn't got anywhere to live; she needs bond money, key money, money to have the electricity and gas turned on, money to buy food for the children and something to cook it in, like a saucepan or frying pan. So straight away when I

meet this girl and I'm talking to her, and she is telling me how she got into this state of having nowhere to live, I am thinking, "How can I get some money?"[23]

bell hooks has described the importance of black women's role in home making as an important strategy of resistance in an environment of extreme racism.[24] hooks argues that insufficient acknowledgment has been given to the work undertaken by black mothers to create "homeplaces" that could operate as sites of resistance and liberation struggle.[25] hooks emphasizes the love and commitment of black mothers, who were unable to care for their children due to the demands of work or the brutal realities of a racist system in which their motherhood and the very humanity of themselves and their children were devalued.[26] An act of love in an environment in which one's humanity is denied is indeed an act of political resistance, particularly within a racist system which demonized Aboriginal mothers and characterized them as incapable of the same depth of feeling for their children that white mothers had.

hooks' powerful account of the enduring dedication and love of absent black mothers resonates strongly with the experiences of the mothers of the Stolen Generations, who while they may have been denied the opportunity to "mother" their children, never forgot them and never ceased hoping to one day be reunited with them. Doris Pilkington poignantly described her mother Molly's wish to see her youngest daughter one more time, "All she wanted was 'to put my arms around her just once and hold her to me.' One time."[27] Sadly, Molly died without this wish being realized.[28]

The following chapter explores the impact of increased surveillance of and intervention in Aboriginal families, as well as the impact of the pervasive fear of child removal on Aboriginal mothers in the Stolen Generations era.

NOTES

1. Human Rights and Equal Opportunity Commission, *Bringing Them Home*, 75.

2. Mervyn Pattemore interviewed by Glenys Dimond, 1 November 2000, ORAL TRC 5000/195, National Library of Australia, 36–37.

3. Annie Mullins interviewed by Lyn McLeavy, 30 September 2000, ORAL TRC 5000/280, National Library of Australia, 19–20.

4. Annie Mullins interviewed by Lyn McLeavy, 30 September 2000, ORAL TRC 5000/280, National Library of Australia, 30–31.

5. Annie Mullins interviewed by Lyn McLeavy, 30 September 2000, ORAL TRC 5000/280, National Library of Australia, 36.

6. Annie Mullins interviewed by Lyn McLeavy, 30 September 2000, ORAL TRC 5000/280, National Library of Australia, 32.

7. Annie Mullins interviewed by Lyn McLeavy, 30 September 2000, ORAL TRC 5000/280, National Library of Australia, 34.

8. "Ruby," interviewed by Anne Maree Payne, 1–2.

9. "Ruby," interviewed by Anne Maree Payne, 19–21.

10. Huggins and Huggins, *Auntie Rita*, 42.

11. Hegarty, *Is That You, Ruthie?*, 22 and 29.

12. "Ruby," interviewed by Anne Maree Payne, 21.

13. Pettman, *Living in the Margins*, 64.

14. Roberts, "Racism and Patriarchy in the Meaning of Motherhood," 235–236.

15. O'Reilly, *Toni Morrison and Motherhood: A Politics of the Heart*, 32.

16. O'Reilly, *Toni Morrison and Motherhood: A Politics of the Heart*, 32.

17. Aolain and Turner, "Gender, Truth & Transition," 271–272.

18. Blunt and Rose, "Introduction: Women's Colonial and Postcolonial Geographies," 4.

19. Goodall 1990, 3; Goodall, "Assimilation Begins in the Home"; Pettman 1991, 94.

20. Mum Shirl, *Mum Shirl. An Autobiography*, 1

21. O'Reilly, *Toni Morrison and Motherhood: A Politics of the Heart*, 5.

22. Motherhood researcher Andrea O'Reilly defines "motherwork" as the tasks of preservation, nurturance, cultural bearing, and healing that makes survival and resistance possible for African American people. See O'Reilly, "Toni Morrison and Motherhood: A Politics of the Heart," 29.

23. Mum Shirl, *Mum Shirl. An Autobiography*, 43.

24. hooks, *Yearning: Race, Gender, and Cultural Politics*, 42.

25. hooks, *Yearning: Race, Gender, and Cultural Politics*, 43.

26. hooks, *Yearning: Race, Gender, and Cultural Politics*, 44.

27. Pilkington interviewed by Anne Brewster, "The Stolen Generations: Rites of Passage," 156.

28. Stephens, "Mother's Regret Carried to Grave."

SIX

Monitored Motherhood

The Impact of State Surveillance and the Threat of Intervention in Aboriginal Families

Aboriginal families living on missions and reserves were subjected to a heightened degree of supervision and surveillance by white authorities, which contributed to an increased risk of child removal. This chapter explores the impact of white surveillance on Aboriginal families, child removals which took place as a consequence of mission policy, as well as the pervasive fear of child removal that affected many Aboriginal mothers in the Stolen Generations era, irrespective of whether or not their own children were removed.

In *Maternal Thinking*, feminist philosopher Sarah Ruddick identified how children's perceptions about the power held by their mothers are highly out of kilter with the reality of mothers' relative powerlessness and social impotence.[1] While mothers are typically seen as having failed whenever something goes wrong with a child, Ruddick emphasized that in many cases, a mother's ability to determine her own and her children's lives "depends on economic and social policies over which she has minimal control."[2] Ruddick highlighted the "cruel and bitter work" of mothering in an environment where children suffer the effects of preventable social ills that are beyond the scope of an individual mother to address,[3] a description very pertinent to the highly monitored Aboriginal mothers of the Stolen Generations era.

Peter Read has contrasted child removals from two Aboriginal communities in NSW between 1945 and 1969; nineteen children were removed from Erambie Aboriginal reserve in this period, but none from the large Aboriginal community living in Narrandera where there was no reserve,[4] highlighting the impact that increased surveillance could have on child removal. Read's oral history of the Erambie Reserve in Cowra documents the diverse circumstances that led to child removal, including parental ill-health, neglect arising from alcoholism, and the removal of children as a form of social control to punish dissenting adults who did not cooperate with the white manager. One interviewee in Read's anthology highlights an example of what she saw as child removal as payback for noncompliant behavior:

> I think they sent [Name's] children away because they reckoned she was drinking too much. She was the only one that stuck up for herself, I think. He [the manager] just done that for spite, I reckon. They had her up for neglect I think . . . I think that was him [the manager] taking it out on [Name], getting at the kids. That's the only way he could get her.[5]

Aboriginal mothers were often targeted by welfare agencies in the era of assimilation policies, because these agencies recognized the pivotal role that mothers played in transmitting cultural values. The NSW Aboriginal Protection Board has been described by Heather Goodall as using Aboriginal women's care for and commitment to their families "as a weapon" in an effort to impose nuclear family structures and white values on Aboriginal families.[6] Regular home inspections paid close attention to Aboriginal women's housekeeping and monitored families' living arrangements, income levels, the amount of time spent in the home, hygiene practices, sleeping arrangements and the number of people living in a house.[7] In Queensland, white nursing staff from the Baby Welfare Centre on Palm Island reported on the cleanliness and hygiene of homes they visited, checking bedding, cutlery, crockery, food storage and washing facilities; mothers had to attend weekly classes if they were seen to be lacking in domestic skills.[8] Rosalind Kidd notes that failures in child health were primarily attributed to mothers, and the poverty and deprivation of Aboriginal communities was rarely recorded.[9]

REMOVAL DUE TO MISSION POLICY

A number of interviewees described their experiences growing up on Aboriginal missions and stated that a requirement of living on some missions was that all children were sent to live in the mission dormitory when they reached a certain age. Haebich has argued that this was particularly the case in Queensland.[10] The *Bringing Them Home* Report describes this as "forcible separation through the dormitory system," and notes that in Queensland almost all of more than two thousand children sent to missions and settlements between 1908 and 1971 would have ended up in dormitories.[11]

Aboriginal mother Wilma Walker described the removal of her children to the Daintree Mission dormitory in the 1950s:

Wilma: I couldn't say [anything] because I was frightened thinking about that police all the time, you know, whether they were grabbing 'em and sending 'em away. I was thinking of that what's they're gonna keep 'em there for a while and send him back afternoon like that, you know. But they keeping it for good. They take 'em away there, them three.

Interviewer: When did you realise that they weren't going to come back?

Wilma: We thinking all when they gonna come back and then we used to talk together. Be thinking about it all the time and talk, "When them kids gonna come back here to us?" but they never tell us they'd gone for good. [12]

At first Wilma was able to visit her children in the dormitory on a regular basis, even though parental visits were limited to Sundays only. However, when the local mission closed her children were relocated without her knowledge or consent to another mission some distance away. [13]

Annie Mullins spoke about her removal from her mother when she was sent to the Doomadgee Mission dormitory: "she [Annie's mother] grew them [her children] up until they were six years old, that is when they'd take the children into the dormitory. Government orders." [14]

Jean Sibley, who gave birth to twelve children and also raised four step-children, spoke about her children being placed in the mission dormitory when her husband was away due to work:

When Jack went cane-cutting. They put me and the children in the dormitory, but they separate the boys from me, put 'em in the boys' dormitory . . . they were only small . . . they used to sing out to me, you know, from outside. [15]

Stuart Rintoul's oral history collection *The Wailing* includes one man's account of his removal at age ten to the mission dormitory on Yarrabah Mission in Queensland:

There was a dormitory set up—one for girls, one for boys, when we were ten years of age. I remember going there, till we were sixteen. We had to do that. We were taken off our parents, forcibly. It was a very sad day. I cried for about a week after. No one actually came to get me. It was a known thing that as soon as your sons or daughters reached the age of ten you were to take them up to the dormitory and place them in the dormitory. This had happened on that day. My mother took me up and left me there. [16]

Evelyn Crawford's autobiography mentioned Aboriginal parents living on Brewarrina Mission in New South Wales being powerless to prevent their daughters being sent to the dormitory, "whether [they] wanted it or not"; she believed this was a factor in her parents' eventual decision to leave the Mission.[17] In *Under the Wintamarra Tree*, Doris Pilkington describes being housed separately from her mother and baby sister (who was still being breastfed) when arriving at the Moore River Settlement in Western Australia in 1940; Doris was sent to the kindergarten section while Molly and Anna were placed in the dormitory for working girls.[18]

Removal due to mission policy is another example of a significant structural barrier to Aboriginal mothering in the Stolen Generations era; all children of a certain age on some missions were institutionalized, irrespective of their parents' wishes or the quality of care they provided to their children.

THE "UBIQUITOUS SHADOW": THE IMPACT OF THE THREAT OF CHILD REMOVAL

In their reflections on experiences of Indigenous child separation, Mellor and Haebich identified the "ubiquitous shadow" of the threat of removal hanging over Aboriginal families in the Stolen Generations era. Aboriginal parents adopted a range of strategies to minimize this threat, including frequent moves, avoiding population centers and Missions, and ensuring that their children were always immaculately presented, no mean feat when living in what were often the most basic conditions such as bush camps lacking any water and sanitation facilities.[19] A number of NLA interviewees identified the impact on their families of living in constant fear of child removal, particularly the ways in which this fear dominated the lives of their mothers. Acutely aware of the monitoring of their parenting by various authorities, Aboriginal mothers often went to great lengths to attempt to maintain the integrity of their families. Bill Rutter commented:

> It was always there, yeah, [the fear] of being taken by the welfare. She kept us kind of spick and span all the time because she was afraid of losing us if she didn't look after us and so on.[20]

A number of interviewees described their mothers' desperate attempts to hide them from welfare authorities to prevent their removal. Some of Daphne Doney's only recollections of her life before her removal were her vivid early memories of hiding in the bush:

> Mum used to take me off into the bush on quite a few occasions, and I used to have to sit there, and she'd go, "Shhh, don't make a noise, don't make a noise! Be very, very quiet." . . . So this went on for quite a while and, until eventually the Welfare ended up taking me. Mum got caught

unawares, because they kept coming back and coming back to try and get me and she was never there. So, we were hiding in the bush.[21]

Audrey Kinnear described light-skinned Aboriginal children in South Australia being hidden from authorities:

> When the authorities were coming, the police or welfare officers, they used to hide the kids. You know, have holes in the ground and dig holes and children in there, put the rugs over and the dogs over them. Or they hid them in hollow trees, hid us in hollow trees and all that used to happen. So it was just enormous disruption to our people's lives . . . So it was all around Australia really where parents were, you know, mothers were hiding their children away from the authorities.[22]

Mothers who had previously experienced child removal spoke of their fear that other children would also be taken from them. Ruby described moving interstate after the removal of her two eldest children, and keeping a very low profile to avoid coming to the attention of authorities:

> Interviewer: So when you came to [City], and you know, you met your husband, and you had your children here, did you, were you afraid when you had your children here that something would happen?
> Ruby: Yes, I did—and that's one of the reasons I never mixed with the Aboriginal community, because I knew that they [the Government] would be looking for me, because I did abscond.[23]

Heather Vicenti, who had previously experienced the removal of five of her children, described her dread when welfare authorities learned of the existence of two more children she had subsequently given birth to: "Every knock on the door, every strange voice, and every official letter that I received filled me with an absolute terror. My life would not be the same again for many years."[24]

A number of other Aboriginal interviewees spoke about the impact on their mothers of the constant threat of child removal. Jaye and her sister Clair described their mother being obsessed with her children being clean and well presented, as she was fearful of the consequences if they did not appear well cared for:

> Jaye: there was always this real ritual about looking nice and clean and being respectful you know and I guess that all comes from her sort of upbringing that if you are clean and tidy you'll go unnoticed but if you are dirty and disrespectful and all of that sort of stuff well then you know you are going to be punished for that sort of thing . . . But if we ever went to town or church, God forbid if you went you know, with your hair untidy or your clothes not right. She [her mother] was always, she was always scared that something was going to happen.

Clair: I think, yes she had a real thing about "The Welfare." She always had this thing that "The Welfare" would get you and take you
away from her even though she was doing the best she could. She
lived in fear that the kids would be taken.[25]

Clair described a time when the family was living on a rural block out of
town in very basic accommodation with a dirt floor and no running
water or electricity: "it was like a bomb site, you know, like it was a really
dirty environment, and yet if we were going somewhere . . . we'd come
out of that caravan or that humpy and we would be immaculate."[26] Her
mother's fears intensified when the family moved into town and came
under the closer scrutiny of welfare officials:

> When we moved to town she became almost neurotic about the house
> being tidy in case we got kicked out and worrying about "The Welfare"
> coming to check up about how clean she was keeping the house. And
> that you know if it wasn't right then we would be taken away, so she
> had this sort of real compulsion all of the time and an awareness that
> she thought someone would be coming to check up. I don't think she
> could really perceive that we would get this house and we could just
> live our own life there. She always felt that someone was coming to
> check up. And I mean in the neighbourhood there were people who
> were checked up on and children were removed, so it wasn't an abso-
> lutely unrealistic belief to have.[27]

Interviewees also highlighted the vulnerability of Aboriginal mothers to
welfare intervention when their husbands were absent due to work commitments, often of an itinerant or seasonal nature.

Heather Goodall's research has identified the "turmoil of movement"
Aboriginal families were forced into in an effort to keep their children;
families faced difficult choices:

> Escaping from the managed stations, they tried to gain access to town
> public schools, only to be rejected as the schools were segregated one
> by one. They then had to decide whether to try another town or seek
> asylum on a pastoral camp at the cost of no schooling at all and so an
> increased risk of accusations of neglect.[28]

The fear and trauma of child removal has also impacted intergenerationally. Deirdre Heitmeyer, who was removed as a child, described the extreme anxiety she experienced when she went into hospital for the birth
of her own children: "I was just a wreck, and I had to leave the hospital,
had to get out and take my kids with me, because I just could not bear to
be in there and have that fear that I might lose them."[29]

The structural barriers to Aboriginal mothering in the Stolen Generations era resulted in Aboriginal mothers being subjected to discriminatory and inequitable constraints on their parenting, placing them at en-
hanced risk of having their children removed. Many of these issues were

interrelated and combined to result in more Aboriginal families living in poverty, subject to state surveillance and intervention and therefore at increased risk of child removal. As this chapter has highlighted, even for many Aboriginal families which did not directly experience child removal, the threat of removal remained an ever-present fear.

In chapter 7, the analysis moves from the structural barriers to Aboriginal mothering to focus on the attitudinal barriers, examining perceptions of culture and mothering, views about Aboriginal mothers and debates around the issue of what it means to be "stolen," consent and the concept of forcible removal. Chapters 7 and 8 will highlight how characterizations of Aboriginal mothers as neglectful, uncaring and disinterested parents were integral to the justification of child removal policies and processes in the Stolen Generations era and continue to be used to justify these past practices today.

NOTES

1. Ruddick, *Maternal Thinking*, 34.
2. Ruddick, *Maternal Thinking*, 35.
3. Ruddick, *Maternal Thinking*, 29.
4. Read, *Down There with Me on the Cowra Mission*, 9.
5. Quoted in Read, *Down There with Me on the Cowra Mission*, 117–118.
6. Goodall, "Assimilation Begins in the Home," 88.
7. Goodall, "Assimilation Begins in the Home," 87.
8. Kidd, *The Way We Civilise*, 176.
9. Kidd, *The Way We Civilise*, 258–259.
10. Haebich, *Broken Circles*, 174.
11. Human Rights and Equal Opportunity Commission, *Bringing Them Home*, 75.
12. Wilma Walker interviewed by Deborah Somersall, 14 August 1999, ORAL TRC 5000/36, National Library of Australia, 18–19.
13. Wilma Walker interviewed by Deborah Somersall, 14 August 1999, ORAL TRC 5000/36, National Library of Australia, 22.
14. Annie Mullins interviewed by Lyn McLeavy, 30 September 2000, ORAL TRC 5000/280, National Library of Australia, 3.
15. Jean Sibley interviewed by Phillip Connors, 16 November 1999, ORAL TRC 5000/148, National Library of Australia, 36–37.
16. Quoted in Rintoul 1993, 114.
17. Crawford, *Over My Tracks*, 80.
18. Pilkington, *Under the Wintamarra Tree*, 58.
19. Mellor and Haebich, *Many Voices*, 46.
20. Bill Rutter interviewed by Rob Willis, 12 April 1999, ORAL TRC 5000/18, National Library of Australia, 2.
21. Daphne Doney interviewed by Marnie Richardson, 2 September 2000, ORAL TRC 5000/177, National Library of Australia, 2.
22. Audrey Ngingali Kinnear interviewed by Francine George, 25 February 1999, ORAL TRC 5000/7, National Library of Australia, 6.
23. "Ruby," interviewed by Anne Maree Payne.
24. Vicenti and Dickman, "Too Many Tears," 129.
25. Clair Andersen & Jaye Clair interviewed by Lyn McLeavy, 20 July, 24 August & 15 September 2000 and 25 May 2001, ORAL TRC 5000/287, National Library of Australia, 44–45.

26. Clair Andersen & Jaye Clair interviewed by Lyn McLeavy, 20 July, 24 August & 15 September 2000, and 25 May 2001, ORAL TRC 5000/287, National Library of Australia, 45.

27. Clair Andersen & Jaye Clair interviewed by Lyn McLeavy, 20 July, 24 August & 15 September 2000, and 25 May 2001, ORAL TRC 5000/287, National Library of Australia, 46.

28. Goodall, *Invasion to Embassy*, 131–132.

29. Deirdre Heitmeyer interviewed by John Maynard, 4 March 1999, ORAL TRC 5000/11, National Library of Australia, 12.

SEVEN

Sitting in Judgment? Views about Aboriginal Mothering

This chapter analyzes the attitudes and perceptions expressed by interviewees about the Aboriginal mothers of Stolen Generations children. Aboriginal mothering was seen by both Aboriginal and white interviewees as something that was distinct from white mothering and culturally based; however, there was little recognition amongst white people who were involved in child removal that their own values about what constitutes "good" or "normal" mothering were also culturally based, and limited recognition of how poverty, racism and the other structural barriers discussed in the preceding chapters impacted on the mothering of Aboriginal women in the Stolen Generations era.

CULTURE AND MOTHERING

European studies of Aboriginal families and parenting have a long history in the academic literature. White views of Aboriginal parents have ranged from seeing them as "extremely indulgent and loving" to "extremely neglectful and cruel"; anthropologist Gillian Cowlishaw suggests that European views on Aboriginal parenting provide more insight into European values on parenting than Aboriginal ones.[1]

A renowned early study by anthropologist Bronislaw Malinowski published in 1913 strongly denounced previous theories that had suggested that no family unit existed in "traditional" Aboriginal culture; Malinowski stated that "the evidence affirms beyond any doubt the existence of strong feelings of affection and attachment between parents and children."[2] But Aboriginal parental affection and attachment was questioned by some white authorities during the Stolen Generations era, as will be explored in more detail below.

There is a belief expressed by both Aboriginal and white interviewees in the NLA *Bringing Them Home* collection that Aboriginal mothering is distinctly different from white approaches to child rearing. Do Aboriginal women mother differently, and were these differences stigmatized and equated with poor mothering by white interviewees? The National Collaborating Centre for Aboriginal Health in Canada describes Indigenous mothering as "a social and cultural act that occurs between multiple configurations of people of many generations—individually and communally."[3] Research undertaken in Australia by Atkinson and Swain has also highlighted "the social and emotional strengths" provided by Indigenous extended family networks and the role of kinship in sustaining and reproducing Indigenous identity;[4] however it is clear that such strengths were not always recognised by non-Indigenous observers of Aboriginal families.

Pettman has identified some key demographic differences in the lives of Aboriginal mothers, including that they

> have children earlier, have more children, have more of their children die young, bring those surviving up differently, have supportive kin, live under threat of welfare and the police, have more health problems, are more likely to go to gaol or be otherwise institutionalised, and die younger than other Australian women.[5]

White interviewees expressed both positive and negative perceptions of Aboriginal parenting. Aboriginal babies and children were seen to be much-indulged, particularly those living in "traditional" Aboriginal communities, where they were rarely admonished, and never physically disciplined. Una Clarke, who wrote in her memoir about her experiences working as a cottage mother on Croker Island in the 1950s and 1960s, commented

> Aboriginal children are very much loved and never out of somebody's arms. Occasionally the adults raised their voices in their own language to the children. But I have never seen an Aboriginal smack a child, not even a two year old having a temper tantrum. They simply ignore the kicking, screaming child. Smacking as a form of punishment belongs only to our Western culture.[6]

Clarke's memoir acknowledged that Aboriginal children who were brought to the mission must have perceived the differences between Aboriginal and white approaches to child rearing. She described a five-year-old boy who "whined and grizzled all day" as "a typical example of children deprived in babyhood of their mothers. Aboriginal mothers carry their babies all day."[7]

This observation is paralleled in the account of Doris Pilkington, well-known author of *Follow the Rabbit Proof Fence*, who was removed as a child. In her autobiographical narrative *Under the Wintamarra Tree*, Doris described the traumatic memory of being institutionalized, sleeping behind the bars of a cot for the first time and having to become accustomed to sleeping alone:

> Routinely a child would wake up in the early hours of the morning soaking wet, cold and anxious for the comforting body of the mother who once was always there beside them . . . the most recent arrivals would wake and feel around the confines of the cot only to discover no-one there, and when their tiny fingers jarred against the cold steel rods the child would cry out, "Mummy, Mummy."[8]

The availability of extended family members to care for children was recognized by some white interviewees as placing Aboriginal families at an advantage in comparison to white nuclear-style families. Trudy McMahon, who worked with Aboriginal mothers at a baby health center in the 1970s, described Aboriginal extended families as a positive factor in caring for children: "there was very little problems with them because babies were never left behind in the house by themselves. There was always somebody there because there was usually two or three women with their children. There were quite a few children there."[9]

However, not all saw extended kinship networks as a positive feature of Indigenous families, and there is evidence to suggest that one key point of differentiation between Aboriginal and non-Aboriginal children placed in care in the Stolen Generations era was the reluctance of authorities to place removed Aboriginal children with other family members. The most common reason identified by Aboriginal interviewees for their removal from their families in the more than one hundred accounts of child removal I analyzed from the NLA Oral History Project was the death or illness of a parent.[10] Due to the high proportion of single parent families amongst the interviews I analyzed (over half of the Aboriginal interviewees who had been removed as children were from single parent families), and the welfare authorities' apparent unwillingness to consider placing children with other Aboriginal relatives, Aboriginal children were at a particularly high risk of removal and institutionalization in the event of a parent's death or illness.

According to Aboriginal interviewee Japarta Ryan, the idea of being orphaned is foreign to Aboriginal culture, because extended family members would always step in to care for a child or children:

> Now, there's no such thing as an orphan in Aboriginal society, because what happens is I have other mothers, brothers and sisters who look after me. My mother's sisters, ever since my mother died, become my mother.[11]

A number of Aboriginal interviewees who were orphaned or whose primary parent was deemed to be unable to care for them questioned the failure of the welfare system to take into account their extended family's willingness and capacity to care for them, if there was indeed a genuine concern that their parents were incapable of doing so; they saw this as further evidence of their removal being racially-based rather than it being based on legitimate welfare grounds. Some indicated that their extended family attempted to take them in but were rejected as suitable carers by welfare authorities: "They had a big family but they were willing to take these three extra mouths in to feed but the courts said, 'No, they've got to go.'" [12]

This appears to be a clear point of distinction between the removals of Indigenous and non-Indigenous children in this era and undermines the argument that such removals were undertaken according to "the standards of the time"; in the case of non-Indigenous children, an effort was made to place the children with relatives before the last resort of institutionalization, whereas for many Indigenous children institutionalization appears to have been the preferred option. [13]

It was the strong perception of a number of Aboriginal interviewees that their removal to institutions was the first step in a deliberate and sustained attempt to break their ties to their Aboriginal families and to assimilate them into white culture. An extract from a letter on Syd Jackson's welfare file, written by the Superintendent of the Moore River Native Settlement and dated 19th September 1941 about the establishment of Roelands in WA, confirms that parents and other Aboriginal relatives were seen by some involved in Aboriginal child removals as an obstacle to the successful assimilation of Aboriginal "half-caste" children:

> Mr Bell is anxious to secure orphan children or children with no near family affiliations. He realizes, and so does Sister Kate, that the presence of relatives is harmful in the rearing of coloured children to white standards. He knows, as well as we have known for many years, that parents undo much of our good work, especially when they are of the nomad type or live under camping conditions. [14]

SEGREGATED MOTHERS

Trudy McMahon, who worked as a nurse in New South Wales in the Stolen Generations era as well as a baby health worker, saw Aboriginal mothers as having "different attitudes" towards their children and not seeming to really want to have children. She described Aboriginal women self-segregating into a separate ward of the Peak Hill hospital in New South Wales in the late 1940s because they had their "own ideas" about being a mother: "I think they didn't want to be with the others. I think they had their own ideas, they wanted to be separate." [15]

A far more likely scenario is that these Aboriginal women were segregated not by their personal choice but because white patients and white hospital staff felt uncomfortable about Aboriginal women sharing a maternity ward with white women. Mabel Edmund's autobiography describes her being galvanized by her experiences of being segregated into a separate ward for black mothers at the maternity hospital in Rockhampton.[16] In her autobiography, Alice Nannup powerfully described her feelings of isolation on being excluded from the main maternity ward after the birth of her first baby: "We weren't allowed in the main ward where all the other women would be, we had to be kept separate in a little place that was just like a meat-house."[17] Nannup related gradual changes in the practice of segregating Aboriginal mothers in maternity wards over time, however racist attitudes persisted:

> Another Aboriginal lady who'd had a baby and I were in a little room together. We were kept separate from the other ladies—that's the white ladies—and in some ways we didn't mind, because it was privacy for us not being stared at or talked about. But in another way we did mind, and although we used to have a good laugh about it, it still hurt that they thought they were better than we were.
>
> When I went into hospital the next time, when my son Noel was born, we were accepted into the general ward. But even though we were allowed in there we had to be screened off.[18]

"KEEPERS OF THE FAMILY": ABORIGINAL WOMEN'S MOTHERWORK

While there is not an extensive amount of theoretical literature written by Indigenous Australian women about motherhood, Judy Atkinson has described the importance of women's status as mothers or potential mothers in Aboriginal culture.[19] Drawing on Aboriginal women's autobiographical writings, Aileen Moreton-Robinson has emphasized the importance of relational ties to Aboriginal women:

> The most important relationships for Aboriginal women in their narratives are with either their surrogate or extended families. Aboriginal mothers and grandmothers demonstrate a spirit of generosity to their families and communities and, for children who have no experience of their families in the mission dormitories, it is the older children from whom they learn about the ethics of relationality. Aboriginal women's relationality is based on giving priority to personal relations based on principles of generosity, empathy and care which connote ideals of respect, consideration, understanding, politeness and nurturing. All of these women sought to impart such ethics to their own children and grandchildren later in life.[20]

Interestingly, white feminists such as Carol Gilligan have also argued that [white] women's identity is defined in a context of relationship and judged by a standard of responsibility and care.[21] However, for Moreton-

Robinson these relationships for Aboriginal women are deeper and provide a link to their identity, country, spirituality and cultural knowledge:

> The narratives of Aboriginal women reveal that they are embodied,
> and embedded in a network of social relationships in Aboriginal do-
> mains. The body for Aboriginal women is the link to people, country,
> spirits, herstory and the future and is a positive site of value and affir-
> mation as well as a site of resistance. As keepers of the family, Aborigi-
> nal women are the bearers of subjugated knowledge. [22]

White historian Margaret Somerville, who collaborated with Aboriginal
elder Patsy Cohen to write a unique history of the Ingelba region in
Northern NSW based on the community's memories of five Aboriginal
"matriarchs," describes the importance of kinship knowledge in Aboriginal communities:

> Aboriginal people here have related to their past through their collec-
> tive kin. . . . The network of individual and collective kin is maintained
> by the women in their kin work . . . kin networks provided a mecha-
> nism for relating people to the landscape and drawing new people into
> a sense of identity in place. Knowledge about kin and the everyday
> social knowledge associated with the construction of these kin net-
> works made the cultural work of the day possible. [23]

Somerville described her inability to participate in the early stages of the
Ingelba project as she did not have the necessary knowledge and understanding of the complex social relations of the community, maintained by
Aboriginal women through their "kin talk," an oral knowledge-base essential to the effective functioning of kin networks. [24] Of course, one of the
effects of Aboriginal child removal was to disrupt the transmission of this
knowledge base, with significant implications for the removed child's
identity, relationship to country and cultural understanding, an issue
addressed by a number of interviewees who had been removed as children in the NLA's *Bringing Them Home* Oral History Project.

    In her study of Aboriginal women's autobiographical writing, Anne
Brewster identified the importance of the extended family network in
sustaining Aboriginal families;[25] the role of the Aboriginal family in resisting "the pressure to conform to a white culture" and in providing "a
site of power and consolidation for Aboriginal women";[26] the description
of "strategies of resistance";[27] the role of Aboriginal women as custodians
of their family history;[28] as well as the political critique of the injustices
Aboriginal people have faced and continue to face in Australia. [29]

    Some white interviewees who were the adoptive or foster parents of
removed Aboriginal children spoke about their emerging awareness of
the importance to Aboriginal children of having culturally-appropriate
parenting. This was something that they became aware of in the process
of attempting to parent Aboriginal children, and not something that they
believed was widely recognized at the time. Keith McEwan described

how he and his wife were not equipped culturally to adopt an Aboriginal child and were not even aware of the identity issues that might emerge.[30] Margaret Meyer, who worked as a cottage mother in Victoria, also commented on this issue in relation to the Aboriginal children in her care: "but I really did feel quite a sorrow that they didn't have Aboriginal cottage parents. I felt that that would have been more appropriate."[31]

Describing this issue from the perspective of a removed child, Jackie Frail highlighted the cultural dislocation she experienced after her removal from Lightning Ridge to a white foster family as "like sending someone to the moon"; she was cut off from her extended family and sent to a new place which she had "nothing in common with."[32]

It was not until the 1980s with the emergence of the Aboriginal Child Placement Principle that there was widespread recognition amongst the non-Indigenous community of the importance of Aboriginal carers for removed Aboriginal children, and a formal process put in place to ensure that where possible, Aboriginal children remained in culturally appropriate care.[33] At the same time there was emerging recognition of the rights of adopted people to have access to information about their birth families, which had previously been denied to them.[34]

"SITTING IN JUDGMENT": PERCEPTIONS OF NEGLECT

It is notable that only a small number of Aboriginal interviewees who were removed as children attributed the primary reason for their removal as "neglect." The concept of "neglect," particularly child neglect, has a great deal of stigma attached to it, so it is probably not surprising that it is not a term that was widely used by Aboriginal interviewees; for example, one interviewee described his feelings of shame when reading his welfare record: "It was very sad. Parts of it I feel real ashamed, why I don't know. Excuse me."[35] Much of the debate around the Stolen Generations, and in particular the findings of the *Bringing Them Home* Inquiry, has centered around issues such as "neglect," and disputes about the *Bringing Them Home* Inquiry's categorization of "forcible removals," a categorization necessary to the genocide finding of the Inquiry; with the countervailing viewpoint being that children were removed in their best interests and/or that their parents consented to their removal. In outlining the origins of what he calls "the myth" of the Stolen Generations, Keith Windschuttle describes Aboriginal Australians taking comfort from the idea that their removal could be attributed to "faceless white bureaucrats driven by racism" rather than "the failings of their families."[36] The counter argument, that child removal should only ever be a last resort because of the harm it causes, was powerfully expressed by Deirdre Heitmeyer:

> People say they thought [removing children] was in their best interests, they did it for everyone's best interests, but I'm just not believing that. I

mean, how can someone think taking a kid off their mother is in your best interest? I just wonder and shake my head.[37]

Some Aboriginal interviewees described the desperate circumstances their mothers faced. In one case an Aboriginal mother went to the police seeking help for domestic violence, but when she eventually fled the family home she was charged with abandoning her children; the children were ultimately removed and institutionalized and she never saw them again.[38] Other interviewees challenged the construction of "neglect" that was used by white authorities to remove them, and suggested that different social and cultural values around parenting, raising children and particularly the role of the extended family in child rearing could have been at play. Sharon Kinchela commented on Aboriginal parenting being judged by white standards and found wanting:

> When you look at it, to have non-Aboriginal people sitting in judgement, because they would not have a clue, even back in the seventies, have any kind of cultural understanding that that may have been normal practice for child-rearing, learning by experience and things like that. . . . That doesn't mean that we were neglected, and I guess that's what makes me angry. And they were talking about my mother and how she would have neglected us. I to this day do not believe that, but the pain that my mother carries, she won't even talk about it to us.[39]

Perhaps the "failure" of some Aboriginal families was their failure to conform to white expectations of a nuclear family and a certain standard of living. As outlined in chapter 4, racial discrimination in access to social security payments, leading to a lack of support for struggling Indigenous families, could be seen as being as much or more of a factor in children's removal in these circumstances as "neglect" by their parents.

Relating her mother's experience of having five children removed in the early 1970s after her marriage broke up, Sharon Kinchela described her mother, rather than being neglectful, as a revered figure in the local Aboriginal community, widely known for her caring nature and for taking in upwards of sixty young Aboriginal people who at various stages were in need of a home and a meal:

> All these people who really just needed love and a family, and that's what my mum provided. . . . And fed them all. . . . And that was just like a normal life how it used to be when we were little. My mother, even today she would give her last to anybody.[40]

In contrast to Aboriginal interviewees, white interviewees involved in child removal were much more likely to identify neglect as a key factor leading to the removal of Aboriginal children. Neglect was primarily seen by this group as something that was the fault of the individual parent or parents, not a product of systemic issues such as poverty and homelessness. Contemporary legal processes reflected this conceptualization, with the parent or parents being "charged" with neglect, or even the child being charged with being neglected.[41]

Dorothy Pyatt, a retired female police officer, described the living conditions at Umeewarra Mission at the time of her first being posted to Port Augusta in the early 1950s:

> Ah six pretty dreadful old huts where the natives camped. They camped out in the sand hills or in the mission huts and they were very, very dirty and very smelly. I was pretty horrified when I first went there, I'd seen some dirt and filth around the west end but I'd never seen anything as bad as that. So I went and talked to the ladies in the huts and I said, "Look you've got to clean these places up, this is dreadful. You've got to keep it clean and tidy." . . . Because they still reverted, I never bothered again, it was a waste of time.[42]

Although the "dreadful old huts" are provided by the Mission as accommodation for Aboriginal people, it is seen by Dorothy as the fault of the female Aboriginal occupants that they were "very dirty and very smelly," because they were not keeping the huts "clean and tidy;" her attempts to enforce better housekeeping standards were "a waste of time" because the occupants "reverted" to failing to maintain the huts to an acceptable (white) standard. Rosalind Kidd has identified how contemporary white officials involved in monitoring Aboriginal missions also routinely overlooked systemic issues, and blamed Aboriginal people for the appalling conditions they were forced to live in. She describes a visiting doctor complaining of conditions at Cherbourg in 1947:

> Huts were filthy and overcrowded, kitchens dirt encrusted, toilets leaking and smelling, clothing and bedding unwashed. . . . His recommendation? Regular house inspections and fines for negligence. But a survey of housing conditions revealed a chronic absence of bedding, cooking and eating utensils, weatherproof shelter, toilets and water. The dormitory kitchen was filthy, no condensed milk was available, and neither milk nor fresh produce was available at the store.[43]

Una Clarke's memoir describes her work caring for multiple children within the cottage system then in place on Croker Island in the 1940s and 1950s; ninety-five children were initially cared for by only three women missionaries.[44] Highlighting the substandard living conditions on the Mission, Clarke commented, "nothing could have prepared me for the shock of the living conditions at Croker Island";[45] later she states, "I think had I gone to Africa I may have expected the conditions to be appalling, but because I was in Australia I found it difficult to accept."[46] She believed that the intention to relocate the mission may have led to the chronic lack of spending on facilities and infrastructure.[47]

Alice Marbach, a dorm matron at Daintree Mission and later a foster mother to Aboriginal children, described her role in the period 1957–1962 in the removal of twins from a large Aboriginal family who were living in a "branch humpy" on a beach; the children were described by Alice as "very, very neglected."[48] These twins ended up being fostered by Alice, and she described how eventually she received the twins' child endowment payments and a foster parenting payment:

> I had to try and manage, which was not easy. But a lot of people sort of sent me money and helped . . . the Department of Children's Services — or the Department of Family Services as it is now, I think — they pay so much per child if you foster a child. The twins had not been put on that, I'd just been managing with their endowment and a little bit that a friend sent to me every month, but they were willing to put the boys on support.[49]

It is important to note here that as a white foster parent, Alice was in receipt of payments, both charitable and welfare, that may not have been readily available to the twins' Aboriginal parents, particularly if they were still judged to be living a "nomadic" lifestyle; nondiscriminatory access to social security payments was not fully achieved in Australia until 1966.[50]

When asked what kind of things were seen to constitute child neglect, a former police officer replied:

> Because they weren't fed properly. Parents were drinking and neglectful, especially those who had come from a pretty primitive background and they were, they were drifters. They'd drift around from place to place, they were always travelling somewhere.[51]

Neglect by this definition included living a nomadic lifestyle, something that was reflected in child welfare legislation during the Stolen Generations era, where neglect encompassed failure to provide food and lodging and to enforce regular school attendance,[52] amongst other grounds. As we have seen in chapter 4, Aboriginal people deemed to be living a "nomadic lifestyle" were also amongst the last to receive full equity in access to social security payments,[53] despite arguably having the greatest need for support.

Frank Gare, a former patrol officer and Aboriginal administrator, discussed changes in child removal practices in Western Australia in the late 1940s/early 1950s, claiming that arbitrary removals of Aboriginal children ceased, to be instead replaced by the application of a child welfare framework.[54] However, it should be noted here that the Commissioner of Native Welfare's status as the legal guardian of all Aboriginal children in WA did not in fact cease until the passage of the WA *Native Welfare* Act in 1963. In terms of his specific experience as a patrol officer and traveling inspector in Western Australia in the 1940s and 1950s, Frank stated that there was recognition that "children were better off with their parents," and that patrol officers were very reluctant to use the provisions of the Child Welfare Act "for the simple reason that we didn't want to separate kids from their parents."[55] When pushed by the interviewer as to whether Aboriginal child removals in West Australia stopped or just continued under a different guise, he argued that there was "no continuity" between the era of arbitrary removals and that of child welfare-related removals:

> The Child Welfare Act was used only if a child's life was in jeopardy, or it's welfare, it's physical welfare. . . . It's been often alleged it was just a subterfuge, cutting it out, because the same policy continued under the guise of the Child Welfare Act. I'm sure Middleton didn't see it that way—we certainly didn't out in the field.[56]

Anna Haebich, however, has identified the endurance of "an obstinate culture of removal" within the Western Australian Department of Native Welfare; she argues that substandard housing was primarily used as a justification for child removal or for the ongoing refusal to allow Aboriginal children to return to their families.[57] This was acknowledged by Frank Gare, who indicated that removed Aboriginal children were sometimes allowed to go home for visits during school holidays if they had a "suitable home" to go to—"they wouldn't be allowed willingly to go home to just camp conditions, that is living in a bush humpy."[58]

There is a sense of indignation expressed by some white interviewees who were involved in child removal; they feel betrayed, that their past actions have been unfairly judged, and they ask what they should have done when faced with the situation of Aboriginal children living in conditions of deprivation and abuse:

> Sir Ronald [Wilson] can't have it both ways. He can't have horrible things happening, and welfare people not having to take notice of the horrible things that are happening. That is one of the defects in Sir Ronald's report.[59]

I am not attempting to argue here that no Aboriginal child was ever neglected, or that white officials were wrong to be concerned about Aboriginal children (and their parents) living in circumstances of poverty, homelessness and extreme social deprivation. What I am highlighting, however, is the construction of child neglect by white interviewees as a parental responsibility, irrespective of the broader systemic issues that were often directly imposed on Aboriginal families by white legislation and policy. Limiting access to welfare payments that other families were eligible for; limiting employment opportunities; withholding payment for work; forcing families to live in cramped and deprived conditions on missions and reserves—these factors contributed significantly to the socio-economic status of Aboriginal families during the Stolen Generations era, but were not identified by most white people involved in Aboriginal child removals as major contributing factors to Aboriginal children's living circumstances.

ALCOHOLISM AS A FACTOR IN NEGLECT

Alcohol was frequently mentioned by white interviewees in conjunction with neglect as a factor contributing to Aboriginal child removal; for example, Dorothy Pyatt's comment, "A child would be neglected because the parents were drinking too much and neglectful."[60]

Some Aboriginal interviewees who were removed as children also spoke about alcohol abuse by their parent or parents. While acknowledging her mother's alcoholism, Oomera Edwards commented that there was an extended family support structure in place, so even though her parents were drinking she did not believe the children were neglected:

> From what I understand Mum was drinking and we were removed on reasons of being neglected. . . . The reality of that is that we were living with other aunts, uncles, and grandparents in a family group. So the reality of being neglected wasn't true because this support network and the support system that held us was in place, which meant that even if Mum and Dad drank, we were still held. So one part of that is true; the other isn't.[61]

In her autobiography Mum Shirl paid tribute to a number of women in the Redfern community who were renowned for the care they had extended to others. One of these, "'Mother' to so many kids," began to drink after the tragic death of her husband; Mum Shirl comments, "She is still a wonderful person, even if she drinks, and so many people owe her so much."[62] George Bloomfield spoke very movingly about his mother, the challenges she faced, her struggles with alcoholism, the broader circumstances that made it impossible for his mum to care for him and his siblings and the need to avoid simplistic criticisms of Aboriginal parents. He argued that just because his mother was an alcoholic did not automatically make her a bad mother:

> I see mothers are not really bad mums . . . being an alcoholic doesn't make you a bad mum . . . I mean, she's an alcoholic, let's deal with the alcoholism, because I know my mother was a good mother even though she was an alcoholic.[63]

For George, his mother's alcoholism was a result of child removal, and not the cause of it, "it was because of what happened to her. Like I found out her lifestyle, us being taken away, she lost all of us."[64]

In her autobiography Ella Simon reminded readers that alcohol abuse was not an issue confined to the Aboriginal community: "It is true that people turn to drink as a way of escape from hopelessness and the Aboriginal is doing that—but so are the whites."[65] Simon's observations are reinforced by a major national study of the experiences of both Indigenous and non-Indigenous adults who had spent their childhoods in out-of-home care, in which 24.2 percent of respondents listed their parents' drug and alcohol problems as a major reason for their entry into care;[66]

this study also emphasized that the risk of addictions developing in adulthood is increased for people who have themselves experienced extreme levels of childhood trauma.[67]

ABANDONMENT OR VOLUNTARY RELINQUISHMENT OF CHILDREN

A number of white interviewees involved in child removals described Aboriginal parents voluntarily relinquishing their children; for example, this statement from Mervyn, a missionary who was Superintendent of the Retta Dixon Home for eighteen years:

> Half of my time, a lot of my time anyway, was spent trying to dissuade people from putting kids in the home. That's what they wanted to do . . . But, uh, I had to sit down and counsel them and tell them, "No, it's your responsibility to look after your children."[68]

Others described the abandonment of Aboriginal children by their parents:

> I remember a child that, a part-Aboriginal child I had to go and arrest. . . . The parents had just gone off and left the child and it'd been left in the hospital, they'd be left in the hospital and they'd never come back for it. So um, it had to be taken and put in the care of the State. I don't know what happened to it.[69]

Being abandoned or "voluntarily" relinquished by their parents was not raised as a reason for their removal from their birth families by any Aboriginal interviewees in the *Bringing Them Home* oral history collection whose interviews I analyzed, although there are some references to this occurring in Aboriginal women's autobiographies. As outlined in chapter 3, Ruby Langford discussed being in a position of severe financial distress and initiating discussions with authorities to relinquish her children into state care, a situation luckily avoided by the unexpected return of her partner;[70] and Mum Shirl's autobiography also mentioned some Aboriginal families living in Redfern who had been forced by circumstances to place their children in homes.[71] These situations are described as the desperate measures of parents who have no other alternatives, and hardly equated to some white interviewees' descriptions of Aboriginal parents "going off" and abandoning their child or children.

Trudy McMahon, who worked as a nurse at a hospital in western NSW in the late 1940s, described Aboriginal mothers having different attitudes towards their children, as not being committed to mothering:

> Well, I think they had different attitudes to their children. I don't think, it didn't seem to me as if they were so anxious to have the children. Because the ones that were left behind, they certainly weren't wanted. . . . The girls [the other white nurses] used to say, "Watch out,

she's ready to run off." In the morning you come to the ward and they're gone.[72]

She spoke about Aboriginal mothers just disappearing, running off from the hospital, sometimes taking their child and sometimes leaving them behind. Despite describing the "different attitudes" of Aboriginal mothers towards their children, the circumstances seemed very similar to her earlier descriptions of young white mothers relinquishing their children for adoption; however, all white mothers were not therefore assumed by McMahon to be disinterested in their children. She went on to acknowledge that it was virtually impossible for a single mother at the time (her nursing career started in 1948) to keep her baby, unless she had support from her parents or the father of the baby.[73]

Discussing the lack of parental follow-up on removed children by Aboriginal parents, Barbara Lange commented, "In fact, it used to really upset, I can remember, Miss [one of the Inspectors], the fact that sometimes the parents were only too glad that the children should be taken down to Adelaide and cared for."[74] Barbara did not recall any Aboriginal parents ever coming to the records to try and trace their children: "No. Not in my time they didn't, which really amazed me because I would've thought with those dear little children somebody would've been inquiring about them."[75] However, later in her interview Barbara acknowledged that issues such as lack of money, transport and the knowledge required to navigate the welfare system would have been significant barriers to Aboriginal parents living in remote areas of South Australia trying to stay in contact with their children who had been relocated to Adelaide.[76]

Mum Shirl, describing her work for the Child Welfare Department in the Redfern community, discussed why some parents might have stayed away:

> Sometimes I would be asked to locate the parents of a child and again I often found that the parents were afraid of this Government institution, which was why they were staying away from it and not coming forward and claiming their child. The welfare department had a terrible name amongst the Aboriginal people for coming and taking children away. It was like a punishment that happened to people when they were already having a hard time because they had no money.[77]

From the perspective of the Aboriginal interviewees, some believed that they were deliberately removed as far away from their parent or parents as possible, to make it impossible for their families to remain in contact with them.[78]

THE ISSUE OF INFANTICIDE

Some white interviewees went further than stating that "half-caste" children were unwanted or the particular focus of neglect and abuse within Aboriginal communities and claimed that they were at risk of infanticide. These claims were not based on these interviewees' direct experience of instances of infanticide, but rather on rumor and perception. For example, Colin Macleod, a former patrol officer, stated in the context of explaining why Aboriginal girls were targeted for removal, that pregnant Aboriginal girls were murdered: "if she happened to get pregnant, I don't doubt many were hit on the head and killed. I don't have specific demonstrations of that, but girls did disappear."[79]

Justifying the removal of Aboriginal children as something that was a necessary measure, Mervyn Pattemore commented:

> It's hard to say what might have happened to some of those little kids. To put it bluntly, I was riding in the truck with the Superintendent down at, down at Phillip Creek. We were driving to the camp, through the mulga, the bushes and the anthills, and the Superintendent said to me, he said uh, "I wonder what story these anthills can tell." You know what he was referring to? . . . Infanticide. Yeah. Little coloured kids, often times, were not wanted. Well this one, Peter Gunner, his mother stuffed him in a rabbit warren, rabbit burrow. But that's what was happening.[80]

The reference to Peter Gunner relates to the *Cubillo and Gunner v Commonwealth* case brought before the Federal Court in 2000; during proceedings it was alleged that Gunner's mother had left him to die after being ostracized by her "tribe" because of his birth.[81]

Marjorie Harris, an Aboriginal interviewee who was removed as a child, spoke about her mother attempting to kill her shortly after her birth; she stated she was rescued by her grandmother who raised her, and that she was eventually accepted by her mother.[82] She was the only Aboriginal interviewee to raise the issue of infanticide. This case of attempted infanticide challenges simplistic notions that infanticide took place because "traditional" Aboriginal people rejected "half-caste" children; in this case it was her "full-blood" grandmother who saved her life and raised her. This suggests that motivations for mothers committing or attempting infanticide were complex, and it cannot be readily extrapolated from these cases that all "half-caste" Aboriginal children were at risk of harm from "full-blood" mothers or extended family members.

Reports of Aboriginal women's infanticide of "lighter-skinned children" date back to the early days of colonization in Australia.[83] As late as the Commonwealth Conference of Commonwealth and State Aboriginal Authorities in 1937, A. O. Neville argued that "In a bad season in the north practically no children are reared. . . . Infanticide and abortion are extensively practiced amongst the bush people . . . they just knock them on the head if they cannot feed them."[84] Theorists have argued that the problematizing of motherhood was part of a broader historical shift towards regulating reproduction that took place from the late eighteenth century onwards, as maternity was "increasingly associated with problems of infanticide, population control, poverty, and colonial, national and racial instability."[85] Distinctions between "civilized" and "barbaric" mothers were a vital part of colonial narratives and were used to bolster beliefs about white racial superiority;[86] and as we see here, have also been employed to justify Aboriginal child removal. Judith Allen's study of women and crime in Australia challenges any construction of infanticide as a practice limited to "barbaric" Aboriginal mothers; she argues that infanticide was "the familiar, if desperate, resort of unmarried and married women in a range of circumstances" in nineteenth century Australia.[87] Noting that there was a degree of "fatalism" surrounding the death of babies in the nineteenth century, Allen comments that the lack of successful prosecutions of mothers who murdered their babies, combined with the lack of state regulation of infant births and deaths, highlight the prevalent social attitude of the time, that "this was women's business, to be managed by them as best they could."[88] In her analysis of the representation of "half-caste" characters in Australian novels of the 1930s, Mickey Dewar highlighted that claims of infanticide and even cannibalism among Aboriginal people were widespread but were "never narrated by an eye-witness, but only on hearsay evidence,"[89] reminding us that such arguments helped "to maintain an ideology which removed children of mixed descent from their Aboriginal families."[90]

An Aboriginal perspective on the issue of the infanticide of "half-caste" children was provided by Theresa Clements in her brief autobiography written in the 1930s. Clements noted that in the early days of white settlement Aboriginal people did not let "Little white strangers" born to Aboriginal mothers live;[91] she did not attribute this to rejection or infanticide by their mothers, however, and described the care her grandmother lavished on her son (Clements's father) to ensure his survival—"she never let him out of her sight."[92] Ella Simon's 1978 autobiography also discussed the infanticide of "half-caste" children in "old Aboriginal tribes," although the story Simon's recounted about her grandmother was that she was "abandoned" and raised by white station people only after the death of her own mother.[93]

Anna Haebich discusses the development of an image of a "primordial model" of Aboriginal mothers and their "half-caste" children, seen to consist of

> "a black woman living in comparative savagery" with her abandoned child, "the offspring of a white man," rejected by both white and black and living in a cultural limbo of disease, immorality and squalor. The

potent mix of Aboriginality, poverty, illegitimacy and the absence of a protective patriarchal figure, positioned "half-caste" children automatically as being "children in need" and made them the inevitable target of special state intervention.[94]

An anthropological study of infanticide in Aboriginal Australia undertaken by Gillian Cowlishaw highlighted the unreliability of the sources and made absolutely no reference to the murder of "half-caste" children, which presumably it would have addressed if the infanticide of half-caste children had indeed been a widespread practice or problem.[95] Rather than infanticide being racially motivated, this study identified that the mother's situation at the time of the child's birth was the key factor.[96] As historian Lynette Russell has argued,

> Any discussion of infanticide needs to be conducted within a framework that acknowledges that Australia has a lengthy history of denigrating Aboriginal motherhood, most notably when that motherhood involves mixed-race children.[97]

Identifying the impact of extreme poverty, poor living conditions and the resultant health problems on Aboriginal families, Anna Haebich points out that in the 1960s "Central Australia reportedly had the highest infant mortality rate in the world—one in four Aboriginal infants died."[98]

THE IMPACT OF WHITE VIEWS ABOUT ABORIGINAL MOTHERS

The accounts of some white people involved in child removal in the Stolen Generations era highlight the extent to which they legitimate their past actions on the basis that the positive benefits accruing to removed children outweighed any negatives. It is this reasoning that leads many of the white interviewees who were involved in child removals to strongly challenge any suggestion made today that removed Aboriginal children suffered any form of mistreatment after their removal, to contest that conditions in missions were poor, or that standards of care were in many cases inadequate, despite overwhelming testimony from removed Aboriginal children to the contrary.

Aboriginal mothers were judged by "European eyes" and seen as failing to meet white standards:

> What was the mind-set? I think I've already said that I think a lot of them, both missionaries and public servants, really believed that they were doing the best for these children. They saw them in the deplorable conditions in their camps, quite away from the poverty of those camps—poverty to our European eyes. But the problem of having a drunken father and a mother who may not seem to be caring for them, I can quite see why they would feel that they had to take these children off to help them.[99]

It has been well documented that some of the proponents of Aboriginal child removal during the Stolen Generations era viewed Aboriginal mothers as incapable of having the depth of feeling for their children that a white mother would have had.[100] Frank Gare commented on A. O. Neville's lack of empathy for Aboriginal mothers:

> [Neville's approach] certainly lacked feeling. He believed that when you take a child away from the mother, the mother might act up for a while but would soon forget the child, which is just nonsense. He did everything with the best of intentions of course, which is quite common in many of these moves.[101]

Alice Marbach, who had worked on a mission and subsequently as a foster mother to Aboriginal children, described the paternalistic attitude towards Aboriginal people prevalent at the time: "Well, the government's attitude obviously was that they weren't able to care for themselves in this society and they needed someone to supervise them."[102]

Colin Macleod, who worked as a patrol officer in the Northern Territory from 1955 to 1958, described himself as being "very cognisant of the hurt to mother and child" that child removal could cause; he quoted from a report he wrote in November 1957 recommending the removal of three Aboriginal girls from their mother as evidence of this awareness:

> If we could remove her from her present environment without too much suffering on the part of [child's name] or her mother, much good could be done, possibly leading to an adoption.[103]

The fact that he was aware of the pain the child's removal would cause both the child and her mother, but still made the recommendation to remove her, highlights the extent to which white people involved in child removals convinced themselves that the positive benefits accruing to the removed child would outweigh any negatives.

In the view of some white interviewees, the powerlessness of Aboriginal parents to prevent child removal was somehow seen as the parents' fault. Aboriginal parents were described as passively accepting their children's fate and not fighting to prevent their removal:

> Looking back on it today, if anybody'd come to take my kids, I'd, it'd been over the barrel of a gun. They wouldn't have taken them. But those people, in those days, it was a different situation. They were prepared to accept the situation as far as I see it, that uh, that kiddies would benefit, and that's what they wanted.[104]

As the detailed examination of Aboriginal protection legislation in chapter 3 revealed, parental interference with child removal was an offense, so rather than being "prepared to accept the situation" Aboriginal parents were explicitly disempowered from resisting child removal. Other white interviewees expressed empathy for Aboriginal mothers and contrasted their treatment with that which white mothers would have received in similar circumstances:

> The disrespect and the cold-heartedness of not seeing the welfare of the mother and the effect on her and on the child, the baby, to be separated. There's this feeling, it's so difficult to comprehend now but there was a feeling that we were taking a baby away from an inferior person and giving it to superior people. And that's underlying it and that's a racist concept . . . there was the whole prevailing concept that people like [his adoptive son's birth mother], they were classified, branded, they were put in a certain group and not looked upon as the white mother next door or down the street or over the road who would be . . . there would be an outcry if that happened. But it didn't in these cases with Aboriginal mothers.[105]

As the adoptive father of an Aboriginal child, Keith McEwan acknowledged in his interview both the lack of options available to Aboriginal mothers and the lack of support to help them retain their children:

> The realisation for our son to know that there was a mother there, who didn't willingly and lightheartedly abandon him or give him up, but under the circumstances there was no other course of action. There was no facilities to help her get a house, to live with relatives, no concern about that.[106]

In reflecting on their involvement in Aboriginal child removal, some white interviewees remained adamant that removal was the best and only option; however Frank Gare described an emerging awareness amongst white administrators in Western Australia that child removal may not in fact have been in the best interests of the child, and that the role of the mother was critical to children's healthy development, based on influential child development psychologist John Bowlby's research finding "that separating children from their mothers was a calamitous thing to do."[107] In fact, Bowlby's advice was that a child needed "a warm, intimate, and continuous relationship with his mother (or permanent mother-substitute) in which both find satisfaction and enjoyment."[108] This relationship did not necessarily have to be with the birth mother; Bowlby in fact strongly endorsed early adoption as a preference to children being left "in limbo" in temporary or institutional care arrangements, as he felt that continuity of mothering was critical to the healthy development of the child.[109] Bowlby was however a strong advocate for parental care, even that provided by supposedly "bad parents," in preference to the institutionalization of children:

> It must never be forgotten that even the bad parent who neglects her child is none the less providing for him. Except in the worst cases, she is giving him food and shelter, comforting him in distress, teaching him simple skills, and above all is providing him with that continuity of human care on which his sense of security rests. He may be ill-fed

and ill-sheltered, he may be very dirty and suffering from disease, he may be ill-treated, but, unless his parents have wholly rejected him, he is secure in the knowledge that there is someone to whom he is of value and who will strive, even though inadequately, to provide for him until such time as he can fend for himself.[110]

In the following chapter, the reasons provided by both white and Aboriginal interviewees to explain the removal of Aboriginal children from their families in the Stolen Generations era are explored in detail, with a particular focus on perceptions of Aboriginal mothers.

NOTES

1. Cowlishaw, "Infanticide in Aboriginal Australia," 270.
2. Malinowski, *The Family among the Australian Aborigines*, 249.
3. Charbonneau et al., "Storying the Untold," 164–165.
4. Atkinson and Swain, "A Network of Support."
5. McConnochie, Hollinsworth & Pettman, *Race and Racism in Australia*, 205.
6. Clarke, *Things Are So Much Better than They Used to Be*, 160.
7. Clarke, *Things Are So Much Better than They Used to Be*, 127.
8. Pilkington, *Under the Wintamarra Tree*, 74.
9. Trudy (Gertrude) McMahon interviewed by Ann-Mari Jordens, 19 May 2000, ORAL TRC 5000/116, National Library of Australia, 32.
10. See Payne, "Untold Suffering," 159–160.
11. Japarta Maurie Ryan, interviewed by Glenys Dimond, 29 December 2000, ORAL TRC 5000/233, National Library of Australia, 3.
12. Eunice Wright interviewed by Roderic Lacey, 26 July 2000, ORAL TRC 5000/152, National Library of Australia, 17.
13. Haebich, *Broken Circles*, 154; Parry, "'Such a Longing,'" 327–328; Read, *The Stolen Generations: The Removal of Aboriginal Children in New South Wales 1883 to 1969*, 7.
14. Extract from a document quoted from during interview, Syd Jackson interviewed by Helen Belle Curzon-Siggers, 26 July–7 September 2000, ORAL TRC 5000/184, National Library of Australia, 12.
15. Trudy (Gertrude) McMahon interviewed by Ann-Mari Jordens, 19 May 2000, ORAL TRC 5000/116, National Library of Australia, 11.
16. Edmund, *No Regrets*, 49.
17. Nannup, Marsh & Kinnane, *When the Pelican Laughed*, 155.
18. Nannup, Marsh & Kinnane, *When the Pelican Laughed*, 187.
19. Atkinson, *Trauma Trails*, 3.
20. Moreton-Robinson, "When the Object Speaks," 279.
21. Gilligan, *In a Different Voice.*
22. Moreton-Robinson, "When the Object Speaks," 285.
23. Cohen and Somerville, *Ingelba and the Five Black Matriarchs*, 52.
24. Cohen and Somerville, *Ingelba and the Five Black Matriarchs*, 141.
25. Brewster, "Reading Aboriginal Women's Autobiography," 32.
26. Brewster, "Reading Aboriginal Women's Autobiography," 30.
27. Brewster, "Reading Aboriginal Women's Autobiography," 50.
28. Brewster, "Reading Aboriginal Women's Autobiography," 53.
29. Brewster, "Reading Aboriginal Women's Autobiography," 56.
30. Keith McEwan interviewed by Gordon Dowell, 19 May 2000, ORAL TRC 5000/137, National Library of Australia, 15.
31. Margaret Meyer interviewed by Gordon Dowell, 19 April 2000, ORAL TRC 5000/110, National Library of Australia, 11.

32. Jackie Frail interviewed by Rob Willis, 6 July 2000, ORAL TRC 5000/162, National Library of Australia, 5.

33. Although a 2016 press release issued by the Grandmothers Against Removals group claims that this principle is being routinely breached in contemporary welfare practices. Grandmothers Against Removals, "A Fundraiser for Grandmothers Against Removals."

34. Haebich, *Broken Circles*, 603.

35. David Mills interviewed by Karen George, 26 July 2000, ORAL TRC 5000/151, National Library of Australia, 32.

36. Windschuttle, *The Fabrication of Aboriginal History*, 30.

37. Deirdre Heitmeyer interviewed by John Maynard, 4 March 1999, ORAL TRC 5000/11, National Library of Australia, 5.

38. Vince Wenberg interviewed by Frank Heimans, 6 September 2001, ORAL TRC 5000/319, National Library of Australia.

39. Sharon Kinchela, in Sharon Kinchela, Rosie Matthews & Debbie Kinchela interviewed by Colleen Hattersley, 28 March 2001, ORAL TRC 5000/248, National Library of Australia, 23.

40. Sharon Kinchela, in Sharon Kinchela, Rosie Matthews & Debbie Kinchela interviewed by Colleen Hattersley, 28 March 2001, ORAL TRC 5000/248, National Library of Australia, 32.

41. Swain, "History of Child Protection Legislation," 7.

42. Dorothy Pyatt interviewed by Karen George, 6 December 2000, ORAL TRC 5000/222, National Library of Australia, 15.

43. Kidd, *The Way We Civilise*, 176–177.

44. Clarke, *Things Are So Much Better than They Used to Be*, 114.

45. Clarke, *Things Are So Much Better than They Used to Be*, 113.

46. Clarke, *Things Are So Much Better than They Used to Be*, 121.

47. Clarke, *Things Are So Much Better than They Used to Be*, 121.

48. Alice Marbach interviewed by Deborah Somersall, 26 February 2000, ORAL TRC 5000/95, National Library of Australia, 24.

49. Alice Marbach interviewed by Deborah Somersall, 26 February 2000, ORAL TRC 5000/95, National Library of Australia, 30.

50. Markus, "Legislating White Australia," 250.

51. Dorothy Pyatt interviewed by Karen George, 6 December 2000, ORAL TRC 5000/222, National Library of Australia, 32.

52. Swain, "History of Child Protection Legislation," 7.

53. Shaw, "Myths and Facts about Aborigines and Social Security."

54. Frank Gare, interviewed by W. J. E. Bannister, 11 March 1999, ORAL TRC 5000/14, National Library of Australia, Session 2, 00:03:33.

55. Frank Gare, interviewed by W. J. E. Bannister, 11 March 1999, ORAL TRC 5000/14, National Library of Australia, Session 2, 00:05:56.

56. Frank Gare, interviewed by W. J. E. Bannister, 11 March 1999, ORAL TRC 5000/14, National Library of Australia, Session 2, 00:37:33.

57. Haebich, *Broken Circles*, 525.

58. Frank Gare, interviewed by W. J. E. Bannister, 11 March 1999, ORAL TRC 5000/14, National Library of Australia, Session 2, 00:10:56.

59. Colin Macleod interviewed by Gordon Dowell, 16 February 2000, ORAL TRC 5000/90, National Library of Australia, 13.

60. Dorothy Pyatt interviewed by Karen George, 6 December 2000, ORAL TRC 5000/222, National Library of Australia, 19.

61. Oomera (Coral) Edwards interviewed by Ann-Mari Jordens, 5 March 2000, ORAL TRC 5000/94, National Library of Australia, 2.

62. Mum Shirl, *Mum Shirl. An Autobiography*, 41.

63. George Bloomfield interviewed by John Maynard, 7 April 2001, ORAL TRC 5000/247, National Library of Australia, 85–86.

64. George Bloomfield interviewed by John Maynard, 7 April 2001, ORAL TRC 5000/247, National Library of Australia, 46.

65. Simon, *Through My Eyes*, 144.

66. Fernandez et al, *No Child Should Grow Up Like This*, 8.

67. Fernandez et al., *No Child Should Grow Up Like This*, 14.

68. Mervyn Pattemore interviewed by Glenys Dimond, 1 November 2000, ORAL TRC 5000/195, National Library of Australia, 26.

69. Dorothy Pyatt interviewed by Karen George, 6 December 2000, ORAL TRC 5000/222, National Library of Australia, 25.

70. Langford, *Don't Take Your Love to Town*, 102–103.

71. Mum Shirl, *Mum Shirl. An Autobiography*.

72. Trudy (Gertrude) McMahon interviewed by Ann-Mari Jordens, 19 May 2000, ORAL TRC 5000/116, National Library of Australia, 11.

73. The Single Mothers' pension was not introduced in Australia until 1974.

74. Barbara Lange interviewed by David Woodgate, 30 March 2001, ORAL TRC 5000/250, National Library of Australia, 11.

75. Barbara Lange interviewed by David Woodgate, 30 March 2001, ORAL TRC 5000/250, National Library of Australia, 14.

76. Barbara Lange interviewed by David Woodgate, 30 March 2001, ORAL TRC 5000/250, National Library of Australia, 15.

77. Mum Shirl, *Mum Shirl. An Autobiography*, 67.

78. See for example Keiran Michael interviewed by Phillip Connors, 17 September 1999, ORAL TRC 5000/41, National Library of Australia.

79. Colin Macleod interviewed by Gordon Dowell, 16 February 2000, ORAL TRC 5000/90, National Library of Australia, 15.

80. Mervyn Pattemore interviewed by Glenys Dimond, 1 November 2000, ORAL TRC 5000/195, National Library of Australia, 31.

81. Guilliatt, "Their Day in Court."

82. Marjorie Harris interviewed by Glenys Dimond, 15 June 2001, ORAL TRC 5000/313, National Library of Australia, 3.

83. Grimshaw et al., *Creating a Nation*, 140.

84. Commonwealth of Australia, "Aboriginal Welfare. Initial Conference of Commonwealth and State Aboriginal Authorities," 16.

85. Greenfield, "Introduction," vii–viii.

86. Greenfield, "Introduction," 4.

87. Allen, *Sex and Secrets*, 245.

88. Allen, *Sex and Secrets*, 33.

89. Dewar, "The Literary Construction of 'Half-Caste' in the 1930s," 181.

90. Dewar, "The Literary Construction of 'Half-Caste' in the 1930s," 182.

91. Clements, *From Old Maloga*, 2.

92. Clements, *From Old Maloga*, 2.

93. Simon, *Through My Eyes*, 22.

94. Haebich, *Broken Circles*, 137.

95. See Cowlishaw, "Infanticide in Aboriginal Australia."

96. Cowlishaw, "Infanticide in Aboriginal Australia," 264.

97. Russell, "'Dirty Domestics and Worse Cooks,'" 31–32.

98. Haebich, *Broken Circles*, 29. A recent study exploring efforts to "close the gap" in life expectancy between Indigenous and non-Indigenous Australians attributed improvements in the mortality rate for zero- to four-year-old Aboriginal children in the Northern Territory between 1967 and 1971 to "improved management of maternal and child health and of infectious diseases," and also emphasized the major role of socioeconomic disadvantage in reduced life expectancy. Georges et al., "Progress in Closing the Gap in Life Expectancy at Birth for Aboriginal People in the Northern Territory, 1967–2012."

99. Barrie Dexter, in Barrie & Judith Dexter interviewed by Steven Guth, 24 March 1999, ORAL TRC 5000/21, National Library of Australia, 10.

100. There are many examples quoted in the academic literature, drawn from correspondence, submissions, parliamentary debate, reports, and other sources. See, for example, Haebich, *Broken Circles*, 233, 235, 517.

101. Frank Gare, interviewed by W. J. E. Bannister, 11 March 1999, ORAL TRC 5000/14, National Library of Australia, Session 2, 00:02:14.

102. Alice Marbach interviewed by Deborah Somersall, 26 February 2000, ORAL TRC 5000/95, National Library of Australia, 19.

103. Colin Macleod interviewed by Gordon Dowell, 16 February 2000, ORAL TRC 5000/90, National Library of Australia, 17.

104. Mervyn Pattemore interviewed by Glenys Dimond, 1 November 2000, ORAL TRC 5000/195, National Library of Australia, 32.

105. Keith McEwan interviewed by Gordon Dowell, 19 May 2000, ORAL TRC 5000/137, National Library of Australia, 28.

106. Keith McEwan interviewed by Gordon Dowell, 19 May 2000, ORAL TRC 5000/137, National Library of Australia, 26–27.

107. Frank Gare, interviewed by W. J. E. Bannister, 11 March 1999, ORAL TRC 5000/14, National Library of Australia, Session 1, 00:57:03.

108. Bowlby, *Maternal Care and Mental Health*, 11.

109. Bowlby, *Maternal Care and Mental Health*, 101.

110. Bowlby, *Maternal Care and Mental Health*, 67–68.

EIGHT

For Their Own Good? Diverse Perspectives on Aboriginal Child Removal

This chapter analyzes accounts of Aboriginal child removal in the Stolen Generations era, contrasting the perspectives of Aboriginal people who were themselves removed as children with those of white people who were involved in a variety of ways in child removal. It addresses debates around what it means to be "stolen," the issue of consent and the concept of "forcible removal" in relation to the Stolen Generations. I have deliberately defined "involvement" in child removal very broadly; interviewees in this category include people working on missions or in institutions caring for removed Aboriginal children; patrol officers who actually removed or made recommendations relating to the removal of children; medical staff who observed child removals; white foster or adoptive parents of Indigenous children; senior bureaucrats administering Aboriginal Affairs; police officers; and Welfare workers.

It is clear that a number of the white interviewees who had some level of involvement in the removals process were aware of the systemic issues facing Aboriginal families in the Stolen Generations era, such as the impact of extreme poverty, the lack of suitable housing and sanitation, the denial of family benefit payments to Aboriginal mothers, and the lack of parental custody. After all, in many cases these were people working on the ground directly with Aboriginal people and they were better informed than most non-Indigenous Australians of that time about Aboriginal issues; indeed, some had dedicated their lives to working with Aboriginal people, which made contemporary criticisms of their past actions particularly hard for them to understand and accept.[1] However, these interviewees rarely made explicit connections between these systemic

117

issues of poverty and parental powerlessness and the phenomenon of Aboriginal child removal, with nearly half attributing child removal primarily to poor parenting (child neglect or children "voluntarily" relinquished or abandoned). As Kidd has emphasized, "Poverty, derelict housing, low education and employment levels, alcoholism and domestic violence, individual despair and community upheaval are still—conveniently—interpreted as aspects of an Aboriginal, rather than a governmental, problem."[2]

In many ways, the accounts of the white interviewees highlight that negative outcomes could result even when people felt that they were acting in the "best interests" of Aboriginal children. Legal scholar Anne Orford has described "the everydayness and bureaucratization of genocide" in the case of the Stolen Generations.[3] Barrie Dexter, who was a senior official in the Department of Aboriginal Affairs from 1967 to 1972, recognized that motivations of welfare and genocide were not necessarily mutually exclusive and could coexist:

> What do I think about [the Stolen Generations]? I think that those who perpetrated it, if I can use that word, in the past thought that they were doing it for the best of the children involved, but I think there was also another stream in it which was to eliminate the Aboriginal race by creaming off the part-Aborigines and leaving the traditional full-blood Aborigines just to die off, as was thought to be the likely outcome. So there's those two strands. I've no doubt that most of the missionaries, many of whom I knew quite well, approached it with a dedication, as did a lot of public servants I think. I personally feel, in the light of hindsight, that they were all misguided in this.[4]

A majority of the white interviewees insisted that Aboriginal children were removed from their families for their own good, and only when they would benefit from removal. The accounts of many of the Aboriginal interviewees who were removed as children make a strong counter argument, describing being removed to environments where they experienced a poor standard of living and/or emotional and physical abuse.

Because the focus of this book is on Aboriginal mothers, and because these issues have been well-documented in a number of previous accounts, this book does not provide in-depth analysis of the experiences of Aboriginal interviewees who were removed as children. However, it is important to note that in contrast to the views expressed by a number of white interviewees that Aboriginal children were well cared for, only a minority of the Aboriginal interviewees who were removed as children related positive experiences of their care subsequent to their removal.[5] Pattie Lees suggested that the government should be judged by the outcomes of its actions, in the same way that Aboriginal parents had been judged:

If you did a report card on the government and what they did to our family, let alone all the other kids that were taken away, they would be no better judged that what happened to my mother.[6]

THE VEXED ISSUE OF "CONSENT"

What constitutes consent in twenty-first century Australia is a complex legal determination; valid consent is multidimensional and entails an assessment of a person's capacity to grant consent, that the consent given relates to the process which takes place, and that appropriate information was provided to allow a person to make an informed decision. The NSW Department of Communities and Justice website provides a detailed overview of the process underpinning the obtaining of parental consent to adoption today; parents considering consenting to adoption are required to seek advice from a registered adoption counsellor, and there are additional steps which Aboriginal and Torres Strait Islander parents considering adoption must undertake, no doubt initiated in response to the findings of the *Bringing Them Home* Inquiry.[7] The adoption consent advice provided by the Department services advises that "The Court cannot make an adoption order unless consent has been given by each of the child's parents and anyone who has parental responsibility for the child," and that "all reasonable attempts are made to encourage both parents to participate in decisions made about their child."[8] However Lily Arthur, NSW Coordinator of Origins Forced Adoption Support Network, advised me that in her experience,

> Mothers and families or fathers are being told—"Don't bother getting any legal advice." Which is outrageous. That [the Department of Community Services] can come into a labour ward and take a child. Or interview somebody on the pretext of . . . determining whether they're going to be fit and the child's going to be taken from them in the labour ward—without any sort of representation . . . to guard their interest.[9]

This comment highlights that even with the range of checks and measures in place to protect parental rights in adoption today, there can still be issues in obtaining informed consent. However, no such checks and measures were in place during the Stolen Generations era.

Analysis of the comments made by white interviewees in the *Bringing Them Home* Oral History archive highlights that some white people involved in Aboriginal child removals in the Stolen Generations era dispute the term "Stolen" Generation or Generations, arguing that there was never any "theft" as Aboriginal parents consented to their children's removal. For some white interviewees, consent was seen as a very clear-cut issue; if mothers signed consent forms it was because they wanted to relinquish their babies. Barbara Lange, who worked in the adoptions section of the South Australian Children's Welfare and Public Relief Board, commented,

> Well, they were virtually giving their babies out, and there was no pressure either, I might add. If they really wanted to give their babies up they consented with their signature in front of witnesses that that's what they wanted to do.[10]

Other white interviewees inferred parental consent from the lack of objections made by Aboriginal parents to white authorities about child removal. In relation to the removal of sixteen children in the Northern Territory, Mervyn Pattemore—who worked at the Phillip Creek Mission where the children were placed after their removal—stated that none of the parents of the removed children complained to him, and that he only knew of the children's removal from their families because he was later informed of it by the Superintendent: "No complaints from anyone. Mothers, fathers, foster fathers, it was, it came to me from the Superintendent. That these little kiddies had been taken away."[11] Mervyn went on to acknowledge that these removals in fact happened prior to his arrival at the Mission, and as he was at this stage working as a teacher on this Mission it is unclear why parents would have complained to him some months after their children's removal when he first arrived on the Mission, or indeed what authority he would have had to address any complaints if he had received them.

There appears to be little understanding or empathy among some of the white interviewees who were involved in child removal about the circumstances that might have led to Aboriginal children being institutionalized. When asked if she had an understanding of how Aboriginal parents on Daintree River Mission felt about their children being placed in the dormitory, Alice Marbach (who had worked on the Mission as Dormitory Matron) responded, "No, because they had put them there of their own accord, so we thought they must be quite content about that."[12]

While the issue of parental consent to removals has often been the focus of discussion in the context of the Stolen Generations, it is important to highlight here that as discussed in detail in chapter 3, Aboriginal parents were not always the legal custodians of their children, so the issue of parental consent was at times meaningless. Children in some jurisdictions could be removed irrespective of their parents' wishes, something that Aboriginal parents would have been acutely aware of. Les Penhall, who worked as a patrol officer in the Northern Territory, acknowledged this:

> The Chief Protector of Aboriginals was the legal guardian of those people, and he had the right to look after those children. So to me there was no written consent or anything like that. Whatever would've happened would have been verbal, but that was the position in those days.

> The Director of Native Affairs didn't have to have any consent. He
> could look after the children and that was it. [13]

The impact of the lack of parental legal guardianship of Aboriginal chil-
dren was also acknowledged by another former patrol officer, Frank
Gare, when discussing the powers of A. O. Neville, Chief Protector of
Aborigines in WA:

> At this time he was guardian of all native children in the state and his
> powers exceeded of those of the parents, so he was able to direct the
> police, or he gave the police authority, to pick up any of these light
> caste children they encountered in their patrols and either send them to
> the nearest mission or the nearest institution. [14]

In other instances, consent may have been given for the temporary care of
children while their parents were undergoing difficulties; however, Aboriginal parents then experienced significant obstacles or their wishes
were ignored when they later attempted to reclaim their children. Alice
Marbach described a particular instance which took place at the Daintree
River Mission, in which the parents apparently gave consent for two of
their children to go into the mission dormitory on the understanding that
they could have them back at a later stage. When the mission dormitory
closed and the parents returned to collect their children however, they
were not allowed to reclaim them:

> When they heard we were leaving they came, and they did want them
> back, but the sergeant gave the order that I was to take them with me,
> because he knew how the parents had treated them. Actually, later on
> every one of that family's children, and they had twelve or thirteen of
> them altogether, every one was taken from them. [15]

A newspaper article published in the *Gladstone News* in 2011, celebrating
Alice's lifetime of work with Aboriginal children, again included reference to the removal of these specific children. [16] In this interview Alice is
reported as stating that the Protector of Aborigines had asked her to take
the children, something she did not mention in her NLA interview; and
rather than describing the circumstances around the removal of the children she merely states, "they weren't able to go back to their parents." [17]
There is no mention in this article of any of the actions taken by others to
prevent the children's return, or that their parents wanted them back but
weren't allowed to take them. This example illustrates how people may
construct their life narrative differently by placing emphasis on different
facts in a different context and for a different audience.

For some interviewees, both Aboriginal and non-Aboriginal, the inevitability of the children's removal and the mothers' inability to prevent it
were seen to constitute a form of consent. When asked by the interviewer
whether he thought "that the Aboriginal mothers had in some way consented to this happening," Les Penhall replied:

I think that they were aware that it was going to happen. Because, again, under the old Aboriginals Ordinance that we were operating under, they knew that cohabiting, a white man cohabiting with an Aboriginal woman, was an offence that was punishable by six months in prison, a hundred pound fine or both. They were also aware that if there were any children from that liaison that there was a possibility that they would be removed. Now, I think that you've got to look at it from the point of view that they were not going to dob in the father of those children because they may have been frightened of any retaliation. They weren't going to dob in their Aboriginal male consort who'd made the liaison for the act to happen. They were in a hell of a spot. Because of that fact and the problems that the children were causing, and the domestic violence that went with them, most of them were quite happy to see the kids go. As I say, they were aware that this could happen.[18]

Similarly, Aboriginal interviewee Marjorie Harris, who was removed and sent to The Bungalow in Alice Springs in her early teens, described her mother's fatalistic acceptance of the inevitability of her removal:

She was very sad, she said, but she knew, she said, "I knew you had to be taken away. I knew that." But I wasn't stolen. My mother knew. She dreaded that the day might arrive, you know, but they all knew that the half-caste kids had to be taken away. They all knew that. They used to talk about it all the time.[19]

Here, her mother's awareness that she would be removed seems to have merged in Marjorie's perception with her mother agreeing to her removal. However, knowledge of the likelihood of your child's removal and apparent resignation to circumstances beyond your control is not the same thing as consenting to the removal.

Keith McEwan, the white adoptive father of an Aboriginal child, described how his son's adoption was delayed for ten months; they were told this was due to the child's illness but they subsequently learned it was because his mother had not consented to his adoption:

We were told that he had a chest infection or weakness and he should be kept there. . . . We learnt from the files later in the archives, that we only have read in the last two or three years, that he was held up because the mother hadn't consented to the adoption and they were trying to find her to get her consent.[20]

McEwan acknowledged how problematic the notion of consent might be from the perspective of the Aboriginal mother:

This consenting doesn't mean much. I think in [his adoptive son's birth mother's] case she didn't have other options, so you can consent to something if it's presented to you in such a way if you're not given alternatives. If there was alternatives saying that "Do you want your baby to be adopted or we can provide for you these facilities, these options, this set-up." There was none of that offered to her.[21]

Some of the white interviewees made reference to changes in legislation or policy and practice occurring from the 1960s which placed a greater onus on the need for obtaining Aboriginal parents' consent to child removal. Frank Gare, the former Commissioner for Native Welfare in Western Australia, quoted from the WA Department of Native Welfare Instruction Manual issued in 1965, which stipulated that "young mothers should not be put under any sort of pressure" to relinquish their children.[22] This of course raises the issue of what the practice was in relation to adoptions of Aboriginal children prior to the manual being issued in 1965.

THE CONCEPT OF "FORCIBLE REMOVAL"

In addition to differing interpretations of what entailed a mother's consent to child removal, the notion of Aboriginal parents being compelled or coerced to relinquish children is disputed by some white people who were involved in child removals; they place an emphasis instead on their perception that Aboriginal parents voluntarily relinquished children. An account of the Mission school at Umeewarra by Dorothy Pyatt, who visited the Mission in her role as a police officer, described the freedom of Aboriginal parents and children to come and go as they pleased:

> They ran a school for the children of the mission where the children were free to come and go. There was no compulsion. The natives, some of them were quite primitive and they camped in the sand hills which surrounded the mission and would bring their children to the mission and say, "You give them education" and they could see that their children would benefit. But it was a pretty easy sort of situation because if they'd all want to go walkabout, they'd come and take their children and off they'd go. But they were happy to leave their children there because they knew that they would get some benefit from it.[23]

It is interesting to contrast this statement with the relevant clause in the *SA Aborigines Amendment Act* 1939, which stated

> The parent of every child to whom this section applies who fails to cause the child to attend at a school on each occasion when the school is open for instruction shall be guilty of an offence against this Act and liable to a penalty.[24]

The wander-in-and-out-at-will approach described by Dorothy Pyatt is in stark contrast to many of the accounts of Aboriginal interviewees, who rather than being free to come and go as they pleased experienced a complete removal from their families and communities. Another white interviewee Mervyn Pattemore described life on the Phillip Creek Mission during the time he worked there as a near-idyllic childhood for Aboriginal children, who could do as they pleased:

> The kiddies could just ramble where they were and where they wanted to until evening time, supper-time. And the kids'd be there for supper. 'Cause they wouldn't be getting anything down in this, uh, in the camp . . . They could go back to the camp, if they wanted to, through the day. They could go rambling and hunting. They could please themselves what they did after that mid-day meal. They uh, the uh, adults, the parents were very happy about the kids being in school.[25]

When asked by the interviewer if the children were locked up, Mervyn insisted that this was done at the children's own request, implying that it was essential for their safety:

> Locked up in these dormitories. Yes they were. For their own good and at their own request . . . the girls, particularly, would come over around about nine or ten o'clock and ask the superintendent, "Will you please come over and lock the door." . . . there was no bone of contention as far as the parents were concerned, or the children. It was just one of those things that they required themselves. But, as I say, these things are lost sight of. In today's modern society, they have no conception at all of conditions fifty years back.[26]

The idea of "forcible removal" was a key aspect of the *Bringing Them Home* Inquiry, because child removals had to involve force to fit the requirements of Article II(e) of the *Genocide Convention*. However, I believe it is more meaningful to our understanding of this era to consider more broadly all aspects of Aboriginal child removal, without limiting analysis to those removals seen to entail "force." Any situation in which a parent is unable to care for their child is a personal tragedy for those involved irrespective of the circumstances; as Annie Ozies commented, "Any mother, it doesn't matter who they are, if you take their child away from them, their heart is broken, they're devastated."[27]

REMOVAL BECAUSE OF "HALF-CASTE" STATUS

Another common reason for removal provided by Aboriginal interviewees who were removed as children was that they had been removed because they were "half-caste." Anne Ronberg commented

> I think I was separated from my, um, my family due to the colour of my skin. They um, they had the um, assimilation policy where um, part-Aboriginal children were, were removed from the um, Aboriginal mothers to be uh, assimilated into the white um, white population. . . . I do believe that that was the reason why we were removed. Not because we were neglected.[28]

Sharon Kinchela distinguished between the removal of Aboriginal children and the removal of non-Aboriginal children on various grounds, highlighting the racially discriminatory nature of Aboriginal child removals:

> There is a difference between the children that were removed in the forties, fifties and sixties who are non-Aboriginal. They were taken away for various reasons, but the reasons for Aboriginal people to be removed, it was legislation, it was law in this country, that because they were mixed blood they could take Aboriginal children away . . . I don't deny or I don't look down on or begrudge any child who has been separated from their parents, because that experience needs to be acknowledged because it is painful. But the fact remains here in Australia that there was law in this country, that said that they could take us because we were mixed blood children, or because we were Aboriginal, basically.[29]

The claim that any children were removed during the Stolen Generations era on the basis of their Aboriginality has been contested, most notably by commentator Andrew Bolt, who claims that the Stolen Generations is "a myth" and that no one has been able to meet his challenge "to name even 10 children who fit *the proper definition*";[30] and historian Keith Windschuttle, who argues that there were no Stolen Generations:

> Aboriginal children were never removed from their families in order to put an end to Aboriginality or, indeed, to serve any improper government policy or program. The small numbers of Aboriginal child removals in the twentieth century were almost all based on traditional grounds of child welfare. Most children affected had been orphaned, abandoned, destitute, neglected or subject to various forms of domestic violence, sexual exploitation and sexual abuse.[31]

Such a categorical statement omits any acknowledgment that "child welfare" processes may have operated on a racially-discriminatory basis, and have had unrecognized cultural biases built-in to their application and implementation. Other scholars have emphasized that "welfare" and "genocide" are not necessarily mutually exclusive categories,[32] and that a wide range of administrative and supposed "welfare" practices can be informed by an eliminatory intent.[33] As W. E. H. Stanner commented in 1964 in relation to white Australian attitudes towards Aboriginal people, "Our intentions are now so benevolent that we find it difficult to see that they are still fundamentally dictatorial."[34]

A significant issue among Aboriginal interviewees who believe they were removed from their "full-blood" mothers because they were "half-caste" is that in a number of cases described by interviewees, only "half-caste" children were removed; their mothers were allowed to keep and raise their "full-blood" children. Some have argued that the focus on the removal of "half-caste" children is evidence that authorities' motivations in removing these children were benign and aimed at giving them a chance to be successful in white society.[35] However, I believe this evidence of the selective removal of "half-caste" children, leaving "full-blood" children to be raised by their parent or parents, casts significant doubt over claims that child removals were primarily motivated by concern for the welfare of the child and highlights instead the underlying racial motivations for child removal. It is highly suggestive that the Welfare's concern was not about children living in poverty or being "neglected," but that "white" or "near-white" children were living in appalling conditions—these same conditions were, it seems, perfectly acceptable for "full-blood" Aboriginal children to live in. As Eileen Moseley commented, "why didn't they take the tribal people, traditional children? They just took the half-caste children."[36]

This also speaks to contemporary perceptions of Aboriginal motherhood; the same mothers who were considered "neglectful" and incapable of raising a "half-caste" child were nevertheless deemed capable of raising their "full-blood" children.

White interviewees who were involved in child removals also identified the "half-caste" status of Aboriginal children as a factor contributing to their removal; however, their perception was that "half-caste" children were unwanted in "traditional" Aboriginal communities, exemplified in this comment by Trudy McMahon:

> Once they were half-castes their tribe didn't want them, and that is definite because I was told that, not only by the matron when I came and she left, but I was also told by themselves that they didn't want the children.[37]

This view was prevalent amongst white interviewees and was expressed by people who worked in a range of different roles in Aboriginal child removal—including patrol officers, a police officer, a nurse, a missionary and a cottage mother. In some instances, the belief that "half-caste" children were unwanted in Aboriginal communities was not based on personal experience but rather was described as being a widely known fact:

> It was sort of common knowledge. The old fellas, the old fellas didn't like these children. It sort of messed up the tribal situation, which was very sad for the child involved. If there was an opportunity for it to get a better life, um, well I couldn't, I couldn't see anything wrong with that. But [child removal] had to be done . . . through the proper channels.[38]

In his autobiographical account of his experiences working as a patrol officer in the NT, Colin Macleod commented:

> Full-blooded Aboriginals and part-Aboriginals did not always see themselves as one people, even if they had blood relatives. Part-coloured people often saw themselves as a cut above their full-blooded

cousins and half brothers. When young girls approached puberty, there was the prospect of them not having the protection of either culture.[39]

"Half-caste" children were described by some white interviewees as being at particular risk of being harmed or neglected:

> Part-coloured children were the butt of jokes, torment, teasing and bullying in Aboriginal communities. In many cases, of course, they were loved. In many cases, they were hated, and kicked and butted about.[40]

> Well, they didn't really fit in at all. That was one of the major problems, a lot of the fights were over the kids. The women in particular used to fight amongst themselves, and that was all usually over children, and usually over the part-Aboriginal children. You know, because quite often the woman might have one part-Aboriginal child but she'd have a number of traditional Aboriginal full blood children as well. It was always that the part-Aboriginal was the one that was neglected. I know that, you know, at that particular time there was a policy of removal of part-Aboriginal children. It was a policy. It was never enshrined in legislation. It was always taken as a guideline that the welfare of the child was paramount. It was from that attitude that most of these children were taken into care. They weren't forcibly removed.[41]

This perspective has been challenged by other research arguing that "half-caste" children were not outcasts and were accepted even by "traditional" Aboriginal communities; Shino Konishi quotes one correspondent who wrote in the *Northern Territory Times* in 1928 that "In 40 years I have never known [Aboriginal people] to despise the half caste."[42]

The inherent racism within the white concern with "half-caste" children should be noted; white sensibilities were perturbed at the idea that children of white descent could be "living like blacks":

> That outraged [O. A. Neville's] sensibilities, that these nearly white children could be living like blacks, so he devised this scheme of setting up institutions for them.[43]

> Because I've seen a fair haired child in an Aboriginal tribe, just roaming the outback and you think, "Poor little kid, what hope has he got."[44]

Whilst there is a degree of white discomfort at the thought of children of "white" or "near-white" appearance growing up in Aboriginal families, there seems to have been no thought about the discomfort these children might experience at being placed in the culturally foreign environment of white families. Keith McEwan, the white adoptive father of an Aboriginal child, commented that he and his wife were totally unprepared for the cross-cultural issues that might arise when they adopted an Aboriginal child in 1961:

> So we then proceeded [to adopt] without any advice of how we were going, or any questions on how we were going to bring up an Aborigi-

nal person, a child, in a white community with hardly another person, an Aboriginal person, around in our suburb we were going to live in or were living in, away from their communities, away from their people. . . . There was no advice about how we might proceed and what help we may get. This wasn't forthcoming.[45]

In contrast to the views expressed by a number of white interviewees, only two of over one hundred Aboriginal people whose interviews I have analyzed spoke about half-caste children being unwanted in their community of birth. One Aboriginal interviewee who was removed to Doomadgee Mission in north-west Queensland described "half-caste" children being in "no man's land."[46] The second Aboriginal interviewee who raised this issue stated that "half-caste" children were unwelcome in Northern Territory Aboriginal communities, and expressed her support for child removal practices because of this:

> I don't agree with, that we should have been left out in the bush on our own, with the Aboriginal side of the family. Because we weren't wanted. I know that for a fact. It was all over Australia. This is full-blood and half-caste child I'm speaking of. Not half-caste parents. I'm speaking of full-blood tribal people. They really didn't want us. They didn't want us. Therefore it was a good thing that we were taken away, uh, to a better life, presumably. But we did have a good life. Most of us did. And if we didn't, well, you can still say it was a good life, because we learned to read and write and go with the mainstream. You got to look at it this way too. We are also part-white, therefore, the government of those days did the right thing by taking us away. Although, in some cases it wasn't very good for some of the kids but, um, I think the majority of mission brought up kids are um, much happier being taken away than, than being left out there.[47]

Most Aboriginal interviewees who were removed as children had a very different perception about the reasons why "half-caste" children were targeted for removal: they believed it was because it was government policy to remove them, and also because their very existence and their visibility on stations or in towns was an embarrassment to the white community.[48] Far from fearing harm from their family or being rejected by their community, many spoke about attempts to hide them to protect them from removal; the trope of hiding a "fair-skinned" child away from police or "the Welfare" is a common element in many Stolen Generations narratives.[49] Many also spoke about the difficulties that their removal from their families had caused them in later attempting to reintegrate into their community, particularly the loss of cultural knowledge and the loss of traditional languages.

"MANAGING" ABORIGINAL MATERNITY

Another rationale provided by white interviewees for Aboriginal child removal was that Aboriginal girls were at particular risk of sexual abuse and / or pregnancy. It has been documented that Aboriginal girls were at a higher risk of being removed during the Stolen Generations era, particularly prior to the 1950s, because child removals at this time were in large part motivated by authorities' attempts to control the "half-caste problem."[50] Measures were implemented to limit white access to settlements and missions; however controlling the sexuality and reproduction of Aboriginal women by removing girls was a favored strategy, no doubt because there were more readily available mechanisms to police and control Aboriginal women's behavior than white male behavior. These gendered removals of Aboriginal girls and attempts to manage their reproductive choices could arguably fall within Article II (d) of the *Convention on the Prevention and Punishment of the Crime of Genocide*, which addresses "Imposing measures intended to prevent live births within the group."[51] It is interesting and reflective of the overall child-centered case being constructed that the *Bringing Them Home* Inquiry did not pursue this line of argument, but instead focused on Article II (e) of the *Genocide Convention* relating to the forcible transfer of children.

Some white people involved in child removal described Aboriginal girls being at risk primarily from Aboriginal men, who were described as either sexual predators or complicit in the sexual exploitation of girls:

> I was told, and I have no means of knowing whether this is in fact so, but it was certainly believed by the superintendent that was at Daintree at the time, that girls were not safe, morally, in the [Mission] village, once they could walk.[52]

> In the control camps, of course, there were a lot of Aboriginal men and women and, as far as I can gather, the men used to make assignations for the girls, or more or less sell them to the soldiers. These children were mainly a result of liaisons between soldiers and Aboriginal women.[53]

> Young part-coloured girls became playthings of the outback, to be used and swapped like currency.[54]

It is noteworthy here that while allegations are made about Aboriginal men "pimping" Aboriginal women and girls, there is no critique of the behavior of white men in seeking such sexual liaisons. The issue of the sexual abuse of Aboriginal children is again a significant point of difference in the accounts of Aboriginal and white interviewees; a number of Aboriginal interviewees removed as children described their experiences of sexual abuse, but it was in these instances at the hands of their white carers or employers and took place after their removal from their families.[55]

REMOVAL FOR EDUCATION

A number of white people who were involved in child removal emphasized the advantages that accrued to removed Aboriginal children as a consequence of their removal. For example, Barrie Dexter, a senior white bureaucrat who worked in the federal Office of Aboriginal Affairs, discussed the "benefit" of being from the Stolen Generations, including that the person could work across both European and Aboriginal contexts as an adult.[56]

The opportunity to have access to a Western education was seen as a major "upside" of Aboriginal child removal amongst white interviewees, that somehow compensated for the more negative aspects of their removal:

> I think some kids were taken away screaming and kicking from perfectly adequate families because that was what the law was, that they had to round them all up and take them and give them a good education, because that would give them a better chance in life. . . . I think that some of them who were brought screaming and kicking and went into, and had good educations are now champions of their community.[57]

Such views were in stark contrast to those of Aboriginal people who were removed as children; they frequently described the standard of the education they received as being minimal, designed to equip them with basic skills to undertake the menial tasks that were seen to be all they could aspire to.

As Julie Wilson commented, "education was my right in this country. So you can't tell me that something that was already my right is a gift or a trade-off for taking me away from my biological family and my cultural traditions. I don't accept that for one moment."[58]

The substandard level of the education which was provided to Aboriginal people in many homes and "training" institutions has been well documented. A modified curriculum was offered to Aboriginal children, vocational education was seen as most appropriate for Aboriginal people (although rarely provided in a meaningful way), teachers on some missions and reserves lacked educational qualifications and training, and Aboriginal parents in some states struggled to gain access to local public schools for their children.[59]

Some Aboriginal interviewees who were removed as children acknowledged the importance to them personally of receiving an education, despite the other negatives of being removed:

> You look at the disadvantages, you look at the bad experiences. But
> also you have to leave them behind and look at the good things that
> happened in life, the advantages of getting educated . . . you just can't
> live in the stone age. You have to appreciate the things that did happen
> in the areas of education, and learning how to understand another
> society and that . . .[60]

A number of white interviewees emphasized that removal to attend
school was supported by the children's parents at the time of their removal, or at least their consent was inferred by their failure to protest.
Mervyn Pattemore, former Superintendent of the Retta Dixon Home,
commented

> It was government policy that little half-caste kids would be taken for
> education. And, uh, to the best of my knowledge, all the parents were
> acquainted with the, er, policy, and were in agreement—that these chil-
> dren would go. Now, if they didn't want that, they could have just as
> easily gone bush. They could have taken the children out, away.[61]

Mervyn maintained in his interview that there were no Stolen Generations children at the Retta Dixon Home during his eighteen years in
charge, but conceded under probing by the interviewer that one group of
children were in fact removed without parental consent or on the
grounds of neglect:

> Any little coloured child, uh, was given the opportunity for education.
> Our mission decided, "yes, alright, if they're gotta be taken, uh come
> from their, uh, outback homes, we would like to help." And that's how
> we accepted sixteen children, I think, what they like to term the "Stolen
> Generation." They were the only children we had of that, in that cate-
> gory actually, the only ones we had.[62]

It is clear from the accounts of some Aboriginal people removed as children that some parents, particularly those living in remote areas with
limited options for schooling, did want their children to receive an education even if that meant them leaving home to do so. However, truancy
was grounds for neglect under state child welfare legislation across Australia,[63] so failure to comply with children being removed to attend
school may have resulted in the children's removal anyway on the
grounds of neglect. Chapter 9 discusses the concept of Aboriginal mothers facing "choiceless choices," having to decide between a limited range
of bad options, none of which allowed them to exercise their parental
authority in a meaningful manner; "choosing" to send your child away to
school knowing they would be removed anyway is a good example of
such a "choiceless choice."

In an example of the nuances in thinking about child removal apparent in some accounts, one white interviewee distinguished between children being "sent in," "taken in" and "brought in" to St Mary's (a hostel in

Alice Springs); he then shifted to emphasizing that the costs of the children's education were being subsidized by the government:

> Most of the children that went there [St Mary's] were sent in by their parents. There could've been an odd one or two, but I can't recall any, that were taken in and put there by government. But some of them were sort of brought in, there's no doubt about that. But the government subsidised their education and their accommodation and everything else. They subsidised St Mary's for operating it.[64]

Alice Nannup's autobiography *When the Pelican Laughed* described her mother agreeing to her being sent from home (a remote station in the Port Hedland region of Western Australia) to receive an education, in the belief that she would then return home to work on the station.[65] Rather than being educated, she was trained as a domestic servant at the Moore River Settlement; the Mission school only taught to Grade Three, and Nannup stated "Moore River did nothing for me by way of schooling . . . all I ever did there was work."[66] She was then sent on work placements which she believes were deliberately chosen to keep her far removed from home and family; she never saw her family again: "North girls were sent South to jobs and Sou'westers were always sent North. They were very strict about that because they meant for us to never find our way back home."[67] Ella Simon's autobiography also noted the poor quality of schooling provided to Aboriginal people living on reserves (in her case New South Wales rather than Western Australia), with Simon noting that Aboriginal people came out of school after years of schooling "scarcely being able to read."[68]

Several white interviewees mentioned that some children were allowed to return home during the school holidays in some circumstances; for example, Frank Gare stated

> The objective was to get the kids placed somewhere where the parents could see them from time to time, and they always spent their holidays with their parents, unless their parents were absolutely hopeless, but in such cases the parents usually didn't turn up to pick them up anyway.[69]

However very few of the Aboriginal interviewees who were removed as children spoke about being allowed to go home for the holidays; some talked about being distributed amongst white people who volunteered to have them, with very little or no quality control in the vetting of their host families. Others from the Northern Territory were sent interstate to Victoria, South Australia, or even in one instance to Tasmania to attend high school; it is hard to imagine what educational need impelled sending children so far away from their families.

Glynn Pritchard, who was the foster mother to two Aboriginal children sent from the Northern Territory to Victoria to attend school, commented that alternative approaches to interstate child removal could have been implemented:

> I think there should have been a way that the children could have been educated without them having to be separated from their parents. If they'd been able to set up a camp near the school or something like that so that the children could still have the constant contact with their parents but be educated at the same time. Either that or the school taken into the camp.[70]

Mona Tur appeared to have experienced, as her interviewer commented, "the best of the situation" of child removal. She was placed in the United Aborigines Mission Home at Oodnadatta in 1948 when she was aged around twelve years "for safekeeping" by her mother; the couple who ran the mission "were absolutely marvellous . . . they really treated us like their own children" rather than as institutional inmates; she was allowed to maintain contact with her mother and to continue to speak her traditional language. When she was eventually sent to Adelaide to work, she was allowed to return home regularly for visits. Although commenting that she didn't appreciate it at the time as a fourteen-year-old girl sent to work in Adelaide and homesick for her family,

> in my case it was the best thing that could have happened to me, looking back now. I did miss my family but I went home and lived with them, you know, I was able to go back and live with them, and I didn't miss out on anything, because I was always getting that education as well. . . . I was very lucky.[71]

This account highlights that it was possible for Aboriginal children whose parents were working or living in remote locations to receive an education but also maintain their family and cultural ties, where the policies and practices of the mission or home they were in were supportive of this happening.

REMOVAL FOR REASONS UNKNOWN

For some Aboriginal interviewees who were removed as children, the reasons for their removal were unknown to them, and they have had to accept that they will never know the exact circumstances leading to their removal. In some instances, this is because the "official" records do not provide any details, and in other cases it is because their mother or other surviving relatives refused to talk about their removal. Christine commented:

> I don't know. But I guess I'll never know. No one has ever told me. It's just in the records. It doesn't even say it. She just signed away. Her signature's on the paper. I reckon it was just forced. . . . I don't know what the situation is, because no-one will talk.[72]

As we have seen in this chapter, Aboriginal mothers of Stolen Generations children have been and continue to be primarily characterized by
some as neglectful and inadequate parents; their characterization as such
is central to claims that the removal of Aboriginal children was "for their
own good." Mothers' own actions were seen to have contributed to the
removal of their children, and they are seen therefore as less deserving of
sympathy or redress, and as having abrogated the right to raise their
children.

The diverse perspectives on Aboriginal child removal outlined in this
chapter highlight that for many, the Stolen Generations era remains a
period of contested history, where there seems little common ground
between the main parties who were directly involved as to what actually
happened and who, if anyone, was to blame.

Can we find "the truth" amongst such differing accounts of the past?
Peter Read has described history as a series of "big truths" and "little
truths"; there are always "qualifications and anomalies and differences
within the larger story,"[73] and this is certainly true of the accounts analyzed in this book. There are, however, also conflicting accounts that
challenge the "big truth" about the removal of Aboriginal children, with
sometimes very marked differences in the "facts" as described by Aboriginal and white people.

The issue of the Stolen Generations has become highly politicized in
Australia, with nearly every aspect of the history of child removals contested and scrutinized. As discussed in chapter 2, it is highly likely that
this contestation over the history of the Stolen Generations has contributed to the reluctance of Aboriginal mothers to speak publicly about their
experiences. In chapter 9, the complex experiences of some Aboriginal
mothers of Stolen Generations children are analyzed, highlighting their
struggles to make choices in the best interests of their children in the face
of seemingly overwhelming odds. These powerful accounts from the
mothers of removed children go to the very heart of key issues in the
contested history of the Stolen Generations.

NOTES

1. Ella Simon's autobiography identifies the stigma faced by some white Australians who worked with Aboriginal people; she comments "Even the white missionaries who came there to live used to be called 'black.' They were thought of as being
even worse [than Aboriginal people] precisely because they volunteered to live there."
Simon, *Through My Eyes*, 37.

2. Kidd, *The Way We Civilise*, 347.

3. Orford, "Commissioning the Truth," 854.

4. Barrie Dexter, in Barrie & Judith Dexter interviewed by Steven Guth, 24 March
1999, ORAL TRC 5000/21, National Library of Australia, 2–3.

5. A recent national study of the experiences of both Indigenous and non-Indigenous children who grew up in out-of-home care in Australia between 1930 and 1989
highlighted that almost every one of the 669 respondents had experienced some level

of abuse and maltreatment in care, so this was clearly endemic. Of these respondnts, 97 percent experienced "some type of maltreatment"; 87 percent experienced emotional abuse; 82 percent verbal abuse; 82 percent physical abuse by adults; 67 percent physical abuse by peers; over 60 percent experienced sexual abuse during their time in out-of-home care. Fernandez et al., *No Child Should Grow Up Like This*, 224.

6. Pattie Lees interviewed by Colleen Hattersley, 13 June 2001, ORAL TRC 5000/300, National Library of Australia, 22.

7. NSW Department of Communities and Justice, "The Adoption Process for Birth Parents."

8. NSW Department of Communities and Justice, "Written Information on Adoption. Additional Information for Parents of an Aboriginal Child," 4.

9. Lily Arthur interviewed by Anne Maree Payne, 30 October 2013, UTS Transcript RP4, 2.

10. Barbara Lange interviewed by David Woodgate, 30 March 2001, ORAL TRC 5000/250, National Library of Australia, 19.

11. Mervyn Pattemore interviewed by Glenys Dimond, 1 November 2000, ORAL TRC 5000/195, National Library of Australia, 2.

12. Alice Marbach interviewed by Deborah Somersall, 26 February 2000,ORAL TRC 5000/95, National Library of Australia, 14.

13. Les Penhall interviewed by Francis Good, 25 January & 1 February 2000, ORAL TRC 5000/105, National Library of Australia, 23.

14. Frank Gare, interviewed by W. J. E. Bannister, 11 March 1999, ORAL TRC 5000/14, National Library of Australia, Session 1, 00:42:52.

15. Alice Marbach interviewed by Deborah Somersall, 26 February 2000, ORAL TRC 5000/95, National Library of Australia, 25.

16. *Gladstone News Weekly*, "A Life Spent Serving Children and Others," 18–19.

17. *Gladstone News Weekly*, "A Life Spent Serving Children and Others," 19.

18. Les Penhall interviewed by Francis Good, 25 January & 1 February 2000, ORAL TRC 5000/105, National Library of Australia, 23.

19. Marjorie Harris interviewed by Glenys Dimond, 15 June 2001, ORAL TRC 5000/313, National Library of Australia, 101.

20. Keith McEwan interviewed by Gordon Dowell, 19 May 2000, ORAL TRC 5000/137, National Library of Australia, 16.

21. Keith McEwan interviewed by Gordon Dowell, 19 May 2000, ORAL TRC 5000/137, National Library of Australia, 27.

22. Frank Gare interviewed by W. J. E. Bannister, 11 March 1999, ORAL TRC 5000/14, National Library of Australia, Session 3, 00:43:03.

23. Dorothy Pyatt interviewed by Karen George, 6 December 2000, ORAL TRC 5000/222, National Library of Australia, 15.

24. *SA Aborigines Amendment Act* 1939, 40. (2).

25. Mervyn Pattemore interviewed by Glenys Dimond, 1 November 2000, ORAL TRC 5000/195, National Library of Australia, 14.

26. Mervyn Pattemore interviewed by Glenys Dimond, 1 November 2000, ORAL TRC 5000/195, National Library of Australia, 14–15.

27. Annie Ozies interviewed by Gary Lee, 15 August 2000, ORAL TRC 5000/158, National Library of Australia, 46.

28. Anne Ronberg interviewed by Eileen Moseley, 2 April 2001, ORAL TRC 5000/242, National Library of Australia, 22.

29. Sharon Kinchela, in Sharon Kinchela, Rosie Matthews & Debbie Kinchela interviewed by Colleen Hattersley, 28 March 2001, ORAL TRC 5000/248, National Library of Australia, 45.

30. Bolt, "High Price of Not Testing the Truth on 'Stolen Generations.'" My emphasis.

31. Windschuttle, *The Fabrication of Aboriginal History*, 17.

32. van Krieken, "Rethinking Cultural Genocide," 139.

33. Wolfe, "Settler Colonialism and the Elimination of the Native," 388. I would also note here Katherine Ellinghaus's insight that "assimilliation, which can be seen as a benign ideology compared with some of the more violent aspects of colonization, could also lead to unbelievably cruel and inhumane practices." Ellinghaus, *Taking Assimilation to Heart*, 218.

34. Quoted in Haebich, *Broken Circles*, 45.

35. Windschuttle, *The Fabrication of Aboriginal History*, 18.

36. Eileen Moseley interviewed by Anne Ronberg, 27 March 2001, ORAL TRC 5000/241, National Library of Australia, 15.

37. Trudy (Gertrude) McMahon interviewed by Ann-Mari Jordens, 19 May 2000, ORAL TRC 5000/116, National Library of Australia, 11.

38. Dorothy Pyatt interviewed by Karen George, 6 December 2000, ORAL TRC 5000/222, National Library of Australia, 45.

39. Macleod, *Patrol in the Dreamtime*, 165.

40. Colin Macleod interviewed by Gordon Dowell, 16 February 2000, ORAL TRC 5000/90, National Library of Australia, 14.

41. Les Penhall interviewed by Francis Good, 25 January & 1 Feb 2000, ORAL TRC 5000/105, National Library of Australia, 20.

42. Quoted in Shino Kinishi, "The Four Fathers of Australia," 36–37.

43. Frank Gare, interviewed by W. J. E. Bannister, 11 March 1999, ORAL TRC 5000/14, National Library of Australia, Session 1, 00:42:52.

44. Dorothy Pyatt interviewed by Karen George, 6 December 2000, ORAL TRC 5000/222, National Library of Australia, 44.

45. Keith McEwan interviewed by Gordon Dowell, 19 May 2000, ORAL TRC 5000/137, National Library of Australia, 14–15.

46. Annie Mullins interviewed by Lyn McLeavy, 30 September 2000, ORAL TRC 5000/280, National Library of Australia, 35. Ella Simons makes a similar comment in her autobiography published in 1978, commenting that she didn't really fit in to either the white or Aboriginal community. Simon, *Through My Eyes*, 33.

47. Marjorie Harris interviewed by Glenys Dimond, 15 June 2001, ORAL TRC 5000/313, National Library of Australia, 72.

48. For example, Cec Fisher believed his grandmother was sent away as her near-white children were an embarrassment to the white community—"So the easiest was to send her away, because Aboriginal people in them days had no rights, they were wards of the state, and they didn't know the law and couldn't fight back." Cec (Cecil) Fisher interviewed by Lyn McLeavy, 24 September 2000, ORAL TRC 5000/231, National Library of Australia, 14.

49. See, for example, Williams & Wingfield, *Down the Hole, Up the Tree, Across the Sandhills . . . Running from the State and Daisy Bates*.

50. See Goodall, "'Saving the Children'"; Manne, "Aboriginal Child Removal and the Question of Genocide, 1900–1940."

51. *Genocide Convention* 1948 Article II (d). Patrick Wolfe described the "abundant evidence of genocide being practised in post-war Australia on the basis of Article II (d) alone." Wolfe, "Settler Colonialism and the Elimination of the Native," 401.

52. Alice Marbach interviewed by Deborah Somersall, 26 February 2000, ORAL TRC 5000/95, National Library of Australia, 13.

53. Les Penhall interviewed by Francis Good, 25 January & 1 February 2000, ORAL TRC 5000/105, National Library of Australia, 20.

54. Macleod, *Patrol in the Dreamtime*, 165.

55. See, for example, John Leslie Wood interviewed by Barbara Erskine, 23 November 1999, ORAL TRC 5000/69, National Library of Australia; Judith Stubbs interviewed by Ann-Mari Jordens, 22 October 2000, ORAL TRC 5000/175, National Library of Australia; Doris Kartinyeri interviewed by Sue Anderson, 17 November 2000, ORAL TRC 5000/223, National Library of Australia; Rosemary Wanganeen interviewed by Sue Anderson, 9 May 2001, ORAL TRC 5000/261, National Library of Australia; Kathy Donovan interviewed by John Maynard, 3 April 2001, ORAL TRC 5000/264, National

Library of Australia; Trevor Deshong interviewed by Colleen Hattersley, 31 July 2001, ORAL TRC 5000/295, National Library of Australia; Sylvia Neary interviewed by Jane Watson, 16 March 2001, TRC 5000/251, National Library of Australia.

56. Barrie Dexter, in Barrie & Judith Dexter interviewed by Steven Guth, 24 March 1999, ORAL TRC 5000/21, National Library of Australia, 6.

57. George Tippett interviewed by Gordon Dowell, 18 May 2000, ORAL TRC 5000/170, National Library of Australia, 22.

58. Julie Wilson interviewed by Frank Heimans, 30 January 2001, ORAL TRC 5000/226, National Library of Australia, 57.

59. The provision of school education is largely a state responsibility in Australia. Austin discusses the poor quality of educational provision for Aboriginal children in the Northern Territory and the reluctance of some white authorities for Aboriginal people to receive any education—Austin, "Cecil Cook, Scientific Thought and 'Half-Castes' in the Northern Territory 1927–1939,'" 119. Burridge describes the "debased curriculum" offered to Aboriginal children in NSW ("Classroom Perspectives on Australia's Contact History," 287) while Goodall highlights that access to public schools was a battleground between white and Aboriginal parents in rural towns in NSW (*Invasion to Embassy*, 110). Ellinghaus describes Victoria's Aboriginal education provision as "rudimentary at best" (*Taking Assimilation to Heart*, 106); Kidd highlights the lack of trained teachers on some Aboriginal missions and reserves in Queensland as late as the 1960s (*The Way We Civilise*, 239).

60. Clara Coulthard interviewed by Sue Anderson, 12 December 2000, ORAL TRC 5000/210, National Library of Australia, 27.

61. Mervyn Pattemore interviewed by Glenys Dimond, 1 November 2000, ORAL TRC 5000/195, National Library of Australia, 15.

62. Mervyn Pattemore interviewed by Glenys Dimond, 1 November 2000, ORAL TRC 5000/195, National Library of Australia, 17.

63. Swain, "History of Child Protection Legislation," Appendix 2.

64. Mervyn Pattemore interviewed by Glenys Dimond, 1 November 2000, ORAL TRC 5000/195, National Library of Australia, 39.

65. Nannup, Marsh & Kinnane, *When the Pelican Laughed*, 45.

66. Nannup, Marsh & Kinnane, *When the Pelican Laughed*, 69.

67. Nannup, Marsh & Kinnane, *When the Pelican Laughed*, 120.

68. Simon, *Through My Eyes*, 162.

69. Frank Gare, interviewed by W. J. E. Bannister, 11 March 1999, ORAL TRC 5000/14, National Library of Australia, Session 2, 00:06:35.

70. Glynn Pritchard interviewed by Helen Belle Curzon-Siggers, 14 August 1999, ORAL TRC 5000/35, National Library of Australia, 66.

71. Mona Ngitji Ngitji Tur interviewed by Sue Anderson, 9 March 2001, ORAL TRC 5000/253, National Library of Australia, 40.

72. Christine Jacques interviewed by Karen George, 5 July 2000, ORAL TRC 5000/134, National Library of Australia, 35–36.

73. Read, "Clio or Janus?," 54–55.

NINE

Beyond Silence

Aboriginal Mothers' Experiences of Child Removal in the Stolen Generations Era

In the *Bringing Them Home* Report, Aboriginal mothers were chiefly defined by their absence and their silence. Behind this silence, the evidence that I have been able to gather suggests that Aboriginal mothers had diverse and complex stories to tell, stories which are not always easily categorized and may not fit our preconceived ideas about the mothers of the Stolen Generations.

What evidence is there about the experiences of Aboriginal mothers in the Stolen Generations era? For this chapter, I have focused on three main sources of information: interviews with Aboriginal mothers from the National Library of Australia's *Bringing Them Home* Oral History Project documenting mothers' experiences of child removal; the limited evidence available from within the *Bringing Them Home* Report; and the autobiographical writings of Aboriginal women living during the Stolen Generations era. While I would not argue that this sample of Aboriginal mothers' experiences is in any way comprehensive, even from this relatively small sample the range of factors contributing to child removal and the complexity of the situations Aboriginal mothers faced during this time is evident.

The stories mothers outlined in this chapter highlight that these mothers did exercise a degree of choice and agency, even within the severely constrained options that may have been available to them during the Stolen Generations era. Where they had some degree of choice, mothers often exercised it to achieve what they saw as the best possible outcome for their child or children.

My objective in this chapter is not to "fill" Aboriginal mothers' silence or provide a "voice to the voiceless." Rather, having identified the factors which may inhibit mothers from speaking about their experiences of human rights violations, I hope to consider here what enables them to speak—and to be heard.

It is important to note that I am defining "child removal" here very broadly, as any situation in which an Aboriginal mother was unable to care for her child or children due to circumstances beyond her control, and her children were subsequently raised by others. As I have outlined previously, I do not believe the categories that have most often been used to explore Aboriginal child removal in the Stolen Generations era, such as the concept of "forcible removal" or the idea of "consent," are actually helpful in understanding the experiences of many Aboriginal mothers or in exploring the difficult choices they were making. I have not excluded, as the *Bringing Them Home* Inquiry did, those circumstances where Aboriginal mothers made arrangements for extended family members to care for their children, as key to my focus on the Stolen Generations era as a violation of Aboriginal parental rights is capturing a broad range of experiences where Aboriginal mothers were unable to care for their children despite their wish to do so.

None of the accounts of child removal described by the Aboriginal mothers that I have been able to identify fit neatly within the classic Stolen Generations narrative of children being taken from their mother's arms by police or welfare officers. Indeed, Ruby commented that she had never seen the removal of two of her children as part of the Stolen Generations experience, because aspects of her experience differed from this dominant narrative of child removal:

> I still thought [the removal of my children] was something separate because I saw, I saw—like from that story, from those stories it was like, government officials, or police officers going out and grabbing those kids, and taking them away . . . there was a bit more subtlety about what happened to me, rather than blatant taken away, you know. So, I didn't equate it as the same thing . . . it didn't really dawn on me that that could be part of my experience as well . . . when we see the books and you think about Stolen Generations, it's about officers, government officials coming and taking them. . . . So I didn't equate my situation to that. But in retrospect when I think about it, even though it wasn't a government official that did it, it was still part of that code, that they could do better at raising our kids. [1]

"CHOICELESS CHOICES"? THE EXPERIENCES OF ABORIGINAL MOTHERS IN THE STOLEN GENERATIONS ERA

The idea of the "choiceless choice" is a concept applied by historian Lawrence Langer in the context of the Holocaust, where sometimes the only "choice" available to people was between abnormal and impossible options, as there were no "humanly significant alternatives . . . enabling an individual to make a decision, act on it, and accept the consequences, all within a framework that supports personal integrity and self-esteem."[2] Whilst not suggesting any simplistic equivalence between the situation of Aboriginal mothers in the Stolen Generations era and that of Holocaust victims, I would argue that Langer's notion of the "choiceless choice" has some resonance with the experiences of the mothers of the Stolen Generations, who faced situations in which they were not allowed to care for their children due to circumstances beyond their own control, and who then attempted to negotiate the best possible outcome for their child from the limited options available to them. Ruth Hegarty captures this concept in her second autobiographical book, *Bittersweet Journey*, when discussing her resignation to the situation she and her second daughter were in, trapped within the Cherbourg dormitory system:

> For us there was no way out. It was easy to fall into the pattern of rules and regulations. To avoid any trouble one obeyed rather than suffer the consequences.
> When you can't change anything, you live with what you've got and make the most of it.[3]

It is not surprising perhaps to learn that some Aboriginal mothers may not have identified with the idea of their children being part of the "Stolen Generations," as the factors which led to their experience of child removal were far more complicated—though no less tragic—than the experience of children being torn from their mothers' arms by government officials.

One of the challenges of human rights reporting is that the notion of being a "victim" is "grounded in passivity and denial of agency."[4] Feminist critiques of truth commissions have identified the need for such inquiries to recognize women's participation in a range of roles beyond that of passive victim, including as "fighters, survivors . . . household managers, and community leaders."[5]

Researchers have also noted the challenge of identifying Aboriginal women's agency; as Goodall comments, "most recent studies find it far easier to follow the overwhelming impacts of 'Protection' and 'Welfare' than to trace the way resistances have been negotiated, shaped or even cracked what often appears as the unchallengeable power of the state."[6] It is difficult to grasp any sense of the agency of Aboriginal parents in the face of government policies and practices of child removal, in part because the *Bringing Them Home* Report contained such limited evidence about their experiences; the focus in the Report is on parents' broken lives after the removal of their children,[7] undoubtedly a highly important issue but not necessarily capturing the whole story.

One mother's experience outlined in the *Bringing Them Home* Report is the case study of "Clare," who was interviewed by the Inquiry because she was herself removed as a child; the Report states:

> Clare was determined that her own two sons would not be taken from her and at one stage when they were quite young, she decided to board them with different relatives to ensure that her own status as a sole parent would not lead to their removal.[8]

A number of the mothers' interviews I have analyzed have clear parallels with Clare's experience; these mothers describe being in situations largely beyond their control and making the best choices available to them about the care of their children within severely constrained options. For example, Ruby "chose" to foster her son with family members rather than allow him to be institutionalized in the mission dormitory. Although desperately unhappy about being separated from her children, she "chose" to leave both her children with their foster families as she felt they were settled and happy and had integrated into these families (and in the case of her daughter she had no legal recourse to secure her return), and she "absconded" interstate to begin a new life and to break the pattern of mission control, forced employment, pregnancy and child removal that had dominated her adult life to this point.[9]

In terms of measuring the agency of Aboriginal mothers, I would argue that the *Bringing Them Home* Inquiry's dichotomous categories of "forcibly removed" or "not forcibly removed" failed to capture the complex reality of the choices and compromises being made by many Aboriginal mothers confronted with the removal of a child or children. One example is the case of Doris Pilkington, whose mother Molly's journey home when she was removed from her mother as a teenager became the basis for the acclaimed biography and film (*Follow the Rabbit Proof Fence* and *The Rabbit Proof Fence*). The sequel to the story is not as well-known but is related by Pilkington in *Under the Wintamarra Tree*, Pilkington's powerful autobiography detailing her own experiences as a removed child. Pilkington related how her mother Molly was sent to Moore River for a second time, this time with her two young daughters. Molly again absconded from the Moore River Settlement, once more following the rabbit-proof fence, this time carrying her eighteen-month-old daughter but leaving her other daughter (the author, Doris) behind:

> On 4 October 1941, ten years after her notorious first escape, Molly once again absconded from Moore River. Unable to carry both her children, Molly took her baby daughter Anna with her, knowing Doris would be cared for by her aunt, Gracie Fields.[10]

Pilkington poignantly described waiting by the boundary fence each day where mothers and children met at the Moore River Settlement, hoping to see her mother and sister, who never reappeared.[11] She related how, years later when she was finally reunited with her mother, she confronted her about why she had abandoned her:

> I didn't know that I'd been taken from my mother. I just thought she'd left me there at Moore River, that she took me there herself and then went back to Jigalong. I thought she'd just handed me over to the Government. Mum didn't. I asked her years later, why did she hand me over to the Native Affairs? She broke down, she told me that I'd been taken from her, that she had no rights as an Aboriginal mother, like so many others. If the Government wanted your children, you had no rights to prevent their removal. You just sat down to cry and mourn for your lost children. There was nothing else to do. [12]

Unlike *Follow the Rabbit Proof Fence,* which is a story emphasizing the triumph of a young girl over the systematic removal of Aboriginal children, *Under the Wintamarra Tree* emphasizes the powerlessness of Aboriginal mothers to prevent the removal of their children; although Molly makes a desperate "choice" in leaving Doris behind in the hope of saving her other child, her younger daughter was also eventually removed from her and was taken to Sister Kate's (a home in Perth) in 1944, and was never reunited with her mother. [13] Pilkington's autobiography contains moving personal accounts of the pain of separation from the perspective of both mother and child, their loneliness and despair, and the impact of child removal resonating throughout Indigenous families and communities. There is also a strong sense of the strength of Aboriginal communities, the bonds that developed between the removed children and the other carers who became mother figures to them, and the resilience of Aboriginal culture even under the impact of genocidal policies. The image of the Wintamarra tree is used by Pilkington to symbolize the enduring nature of Aboriginal culture, with deep roots sending up new shoots even when the tree appears on the surface to be dead. Pilkington also acknowledged that her own journey to reconnect with her family, her past and her culture at times led her to overlook the emotions her mother was experiencing, the trauma and pain of past events being revisited. [14]

In *Mum Shirl. An Autobiography,* one of the best-known Aboriginal mothers in Australia speaks of her life and work. Although not addressed in her autobiography, "Mum Shirl" is said to have earned her famous nickname when visiting prisoners; if a guard queried why she was visiting a particular prisoner, she would reply "'I'm his mum.'" [15] In her autobiography, Mum Shirl recounts her experience of relinquishing her three-year-old daughter Beatrice to be raised by her mother-in-law, as her own epilepsy made it too difficult for her to properly care for her child herself in an era before medication to treat the disease was available:

> I was able to take care of Beatrice until she was nearly three years old. But the epileptic fits, and the fear of the fits, kept me from letting her be and have the sort of normal life she should have.

So when she was almost three, I took her up to her father's people in Kempsey, although it almost broke my heart. She was an active little girl and she needed the sort of life I couldn't give her. My in-laws loved her, and took great care of her, and kept me informed about her all the time. I travelled up and down from Sydney to Kempsey to see her constantly.[16]

There seemed a particular poignancy in learning that the Aboriginal woman so widely renowned for her compassionate advocacy for prisoners and her work in caring for over sixty foster children was unable to care for her biological daughter.[17] Mum Shirl paid tribute to a number of "remarkable people," women in the Aboriginal community who have worked tirelessly and dedicated their lives to helping others, despite their own poverty and family worries. She commented, "All of these women, and more, were doing as much as I do and more. They never did get any medals, or recognition. They deserved all the rewards that could ever have been heaped upon them, but they didn't get any."[18] Mum Shirl described being seen as "an exception," a comment which implies that her dedicated care for others was seen by some as unusual for an Aboriginal mother; she emphasized that her role in caring for others was nothing exceptional but was in fact common in Aboriginal communities:

Many people have told me that they think I am an "exception," but I'm not . . . The difference now is they do think I am an exception, which has come to mean that many times I am allowed to do things that they would not let another Aboriginal person do. But there are many fine Aboriginal people who, with half a chance, would be doing what I am now doing, and many of them would be able to do it better because they have an educated mind. The difference seems to me to be that they are rarely given the chance.[19]

In another example of a "choiceless choice," Lesley McLennon described her difficult decision to relinquish her second son at birth in the hope that he could have an easier life; as a single mother she was struggling to provide for the one child she already had:

Interviewer: Why did you adopt him out?

Interviewee: Because I didn't want him to have a hard life like my son [Name].

Interviewer: It must have been a very hard decision.

Interviewee: It is. [My other son] used to say, "Mum, where's my brother?" You know. He used to ask me all the time, "where's my brother?"[20]

Ruby, who was being sent on a domestic service assignment where her baby could not accompany her, chose for her child to be placed with a close relative, rather than the only other alternative of the child being placed in institutional care on a mission. Ruby was at the time of the birth of her first child an unmarried teenager with no immediate family to support her. This case could not have been considered by the *Bringing Them Home* Inquiry, as children cared for by other Indigenous family or community members were not defined as "Stolen"; and indeed Ruby herself did not view the removal of this child as being part of the Stolen Generations:

> Interviewer: And what about you? So when, you know, back in 1997 when the Human Rights and Equal Opportunity Commission as it then was, you know, said "Oh we're going to have this big inquiry about the Stolen Generations." Were you aware of that when it was happening, or only after it was published? Did you know about the interviews they were doing, and the testimony?
>
> Interviewee: I didn't know about the interviews, but I knew that they were doing something like that. But then—I think for me that it was blocked off, that I didn't see my kids as being part of the Stolen Generation, you know?
>
> Interviewer: No, no, no.
>
> Interviewee: Although [my daughter] was, you know.
>
> Interviewer: Yes.
>
> Interviewee: But again, I didn't, I didn't see them like that because I thought they both went to very supportive families.
>
> Interviewer: Yes.
>
> Interviewee: And caring mothers . . .[21]

Ruby stated that she did not see her own experiences of child removal fitting within the framework of Stolen Generations cases. Ultimately, she "chose" to leave her first child with his Aboriginal foster family (as an alternative to being institutionalized due to her ongoing work assignments), as she believed he was settled and happy and that this was in his best interests:

> Interviewee: I didn't even know the word "Stolen" at that point.
>
> Interviewer: No, no.

Interviewee: I just knew that I couldn't disrupt the life that he's already had.

Interviewer: So, it sounds like you made a choice of what you thought was in his best interests?

Interviewee: I did.

Interviewer: Even though it was very hard and painful for you?

Interviewee: It was, you know. And because I knew who he was with . . . and they had a growing family, and he was really integrated into that.

Interviewer: And happy there?

Interviewee: He was happy there, like.[22]

She did not see the removal of two of her children as relating to the Stolen Generations, because the children were not removed by government officials, she knew where they were and maintained some level of contact with them, and they went to caring families and were well looked after. The definitional limits of the *Bringing Them Home* Inquiry, ruling out any investigation of intra-family and intra-community child separations, constructed "child removal" as only those removals of Aboriginal children to white institutions or families; this was overwhelmingly but not exclusively the case, as a situation quoted within the Report itself about the woman whose own mother had raised her children and refused to return them indicated.[23] The Report stated that the Inquiry did not investigate such intra-family and community cases as typically they did not involve "the application of laws, practices and policies of forcible removal." This is undoubtedly a complex issue given the important role of extended kin networks in Aboriginal families and child-rearing; however from the perspective of the mother, the impact of the removal is identical, in that she was denied the opportunity to raise her children. These cases would also not have fitted within the genocide argument made by the Inquiry—genocide, under the UN Convention, requires the forcible transfer of children from one group to another,[24] and transfers that took place *within* a "racial" group could not be deemed genocidal.

SEARCHING FOR "BLAMELESS VICTIMS"?

The emphasis placed by the *Bringing Them Home* Inquiry on the child victim, and the seemingly obvious oversight in not exploring whether those testifying had themselves also experienced the removal of their own children, suggests that an emphasis was being placed on construct-ing "innocent" and "blameless" children as the principal victims of child removal, those who could not be accused of having any culpability in their removal. Is it possible that because some mothers' stories did not neatly fit or somehow disrupted the overarching narrative that the *Bring-ing Them Home* Inquiry was attempting to create, these stories were not sought out during the Inquiry process, or were overlooked when the subsequent Report of the outcomes of the Inquiry was being compiled?

The narrative "role," in a sense, which is assigned to Aboriginal moth-ers in the dominant Stolen Generations narrative is typically to be pas-sive, helpless, grieving, and silent. Aboriginal mothers in Stolen Genera-tions stories are inevitably powerless to prevent their child's removal, grief-stricken after their removal, and then absent from their lives, to possibly reappear after many years at either a joyful or disappointing reunion.[25]

The reality, as we have seen from the experiences of interviewees and some autobiographical accounts, is that Aboriginal mothers' experiences of child removal were not always straightforward accounts of children being "snatched" from their arms but were sometimes more complex. These mothers' experiences are not always able to be understood in terms of simple dichotomies such as victim / oppressor, good mother / bad mother, victim / agent, present / absent. Rather than being passive vic-tims of government policy, Aboriginal mothers in the Stolen Generations era struggled to keep their families together and were often faced with agonizing choices such as surrendering one or more children in order to keep others, leaving a child behind (Doris Pilkington's mother) or surren-dering them to be raised by others (Mum Shirl's, Ruby's and Rita Hug-gins' experiences) because circumstances prevented them from caring for all of their children themselves.

Rather than being completely absent, a number of mothers managed to maintain some ongoing foothold in their children's lives after their removal—whether through letters, visits, phone calls, holiday visits, standing outside the fence of their children's school, or camping near the Homes their children had been relocated to—all actual examples of strat-egies used by Aboriginal mothers identified from the accounts of inter-viewees. In a powerful example of the lengths some parents went to, Eileen Moseley identified how her mother and father camped near the Home she was taken to so that they could maintain some contact with her:

> My mum and dad stayed down the creek to be closer to me. There was nothing illegal or wrong about it, and it wasn't stopped. But I was not allowed to sleep down there, down the creek with them any more . . . they just visited and they had to go back again. And I still remember that emptiness, you know, that went over me when I saw them walking away.[26]

Eunice Wright indicated how important these efforts to maintain contact made by parents and extended family were to the removed children:

> So I count meself lucky, not being taken away, but because I've been in contact with my family, you know, and I knew I had a family, and I knew I had people that cared for us, you know . . . Dad used to come up and see us . . . whenever he could afford it really, you know, two or three times I'd see him a year and then Mum, she used to come up when she got, after she got better and that. I remember she came up . . . she used to come up on the train, I remember, every Sunday, yeah, whenever she could afford the fare up. This is what I mean, this is where I'm saying I'm lucky because . . . That contact was kept up.[27]

Despite evidence about the efforts made by some Aboriginal mothers to maintain the integrity of their families, it is important nonetheless to acknowledge that there were at times situations in which they were powerless to act. Ruby described her traumatic experience of finding her one-week-old daughter gone when she returned from a medical appointment:

> I was just devastated that I didn't have, you know, came back to find my baby missing. But who could I go to, you know? . . . There was no one to go to about it . . . I went to my Aunt, but she said there's nothing we can do about it. So, you had that feeling of hopelessness, about how you can get things done, because we still weren't recognised . . . we had no redress. And so, there was no one I could turn to, to say that, you know, that's my child, she's taken, I don't know where—I didn't know, even know where she was at. I came home, and she was gone. Everything was packed up and gone. And I said, "Where's my baby, where's my baby." And they said, "Oh, she was sick, we needed to find her a good home." I said, "No," I said, "I can take care of her, I'll take her back home." And this—my Nan went off at me, she said, "Where's your baby, where's that baby? You don't give her to a Migaloo[28] woman. You bring her back." I said, "I didn't give her to anybody." So Nan was angry with me, because she thought I'd . . . Let her go, you know. And it took a long while before I could say no I didn't. I didn't, you know.[29]

This feeling of powerlessness reflects the reality of the constraints that existed on the rights of Aboriginal mothers, the lack of support available to them, and the lack of a legislative framework within to seek redress; after all, as numerous Stolen Generations legal cases have demonstrated, it has been extremely difficult to prove that removing Aboriginal children broke any Australian laws in existence at the time of their removal.[30]

SPEAKING OUT

Some Aboriginal mothers described making the difficult decision to speak out about their experiences, a decision made largely in the hope that doing so will promote awareness and understanding. Reflecting on compiling her life experiences into an autobiography, Alice Nannup commented, "I had to tell those things because they are the truth, and part of doing this is the hope that all people, young, old, black, white, will read this book and see how life was for people in my time." [31]

One mother who did choose to speak out and provide a highly detailed account of her experiences of child removal is Heather Vicenti, who experienced the temporary or permanent removal of five of her seven children at various stages, and wrote about her experiences in her autobiography, *Too Many Tears*. In stark contrast to Daisy Corunna's reticence to speak about her past, Vicenti's detailed description highlights a number of the factors that impacted upon Aboriginal mothers, including state and federal legislation, work requirements, unequal custody rights, differential access to social security benefits leading to charges of child neglect, and the tragic deaths of a number of her children, including a death in custody. Vicenti's personal account is accompanied by reproductions of a number of official documents and letters pertaining to her experiences which provide valuable insights into child removal policies and practices. I have discussed Vicenti's case in some detail below, as such an in-depth account of child removal in the Stolen Generations era told from the perspective of an Aboriginal mother is incredibly rare.

"TOO MANY TEARS": THE AUTOBIOGRAPHY OF HEATHER VICENTI

Vicenti was a twenty-year-old unmarried mother when her first child was born in January 1956. This child was initially adopted by his paternal grandmother as Vicenti's request to marry the baby's white father was rejected by the Protector of Aborigines. [32]

In another example of the "choiceless choice" exercised by Aboriginal mothers, Vicenti decided that she would prefer her son to be raised in a family environment rather than being institutionalized as she herself had been (Vicenti was raised at Moore River and Roelands). Despite intense pressure from authorities to relinquish him for adoption, including being informed that she had no authority to prevent his removal as he was a ward of the state, Vicenti "chose" instead for her son to be adopted by his father's family. [33] In her perception, this decision gave her a degree of control over her son's care arrangements.

Vicenti was sent out to work as a domestic servant in Albany soon after the birth of her son Kim. Vicenti wrote to the Native Welfare Department asking for her son's return, and was successful in securing his return when he was about six months old—with, as has been discussed previously in chapter 3, the assistance of the WA Commissioner of Native Welfare, who wrote a letter in his capacity as Vicenti's legal guardian objecting on her behalf to the adoption.[34] This letter is significant and highlights the need to avoid making broad generalizations about the roles played by various organizations and individuals in child removal processes. However, despite regaining custody of her son, within less than twelve months Vicenti had placed him in Sister Kate's Home as the arrangements she had put in place to care for her son while she was working had fallen through; the letter from a patrol officer on Vicenti's Native Welfare file dated 12 March 1957 states that this arrangement was "by mutual consent," and that Vicenti would pay maintenance of £2 per week for his care.[35]

In 1958 Vicenti married a German migrant and had another baby; the newly-married couple were able to again secure Kim's return.[36] Now living in Carnarvon, Vicenti was subjected to ongoing surveillance by Native Welfare, receiving regular visits from the local Native Welfare officer; a letter from this patrol officer is reproduced in her autobiography, outlining his request for information on Vicenti's "caste" as, ominously, this "could have some effect on the future of her child."[37] Vicenti had another baby, a daughter, in 1959; in 1962 the family relocated to Perth, and the marriage ended while Vicenti was expecting her fourth child. Despite being awarded maintenance payments from her ex-husband, these were never paid, and Vicenti and her children were left in dire financial circumstances.

I have referred in chapter 4 to the discrepancies in the welfare assistance given to Aboriginal and non-Aboriginal women experiencing financial difficulties, and as discussed earlier, Vicenti's autobiography contains reproductions of a series of letters she received from the Native Welfare Department outlining the differential status of herself as a "half-caste" and her children as "quarter-caste" in access to welfare payments that she sought after her marriage ended.[38] These letters highlight the ludicrousness of welfare payments being racially-based—a child in need is surely a child in need regardless of its "racial classification"; but also highlight how difficult such policies—based on supposed gradations of blood quantum—were to administer in practice.

At the height of Vicenti's financial struggles, her fourth child Ricci was born in January 1963; he was immediately placed by officers of the Native Welfare Department in a home for children awaiting adoption. Struggling to support herself and her other children, ineligible for benefits, sole parent to a young family of four children, Vicenti was advised by both the Department of Child Welfare and the Department of Native Welfare that she should seek work to maintain herself and her children; because of her desperate circumstances she made the difficult decision to surrender Ricci.[39] As Vicenti was herself removed as a child, she did not have a network of extended family to draw upon for support. She describes being constantly monitored by Native Welfare at this time and believes it was because she was seen as an easy target.

However, in another example of Aboriginal mothers' agency even in situations of extremely limited options, Vicenti again decided to exercise her own choices rather than those being forced upon her. She made an informal arrangement for a white female friend who was involved in advocating for Aboriginal rights to raise Ricci, rather than surrendering him formally for adoption. This led to what Vicenti herself describes as "a bizarre chain of events,"[40] with Ricci's foster mother taking Ricci and another Aboriginal boy to live in Russia in 1964. The mother of the other child had a change of heart and contacted the newspapers alleging the children had been kidnapped; the story created a media storm and it was insinuated that Vicenti had sold her child or had been duped by Communists. An article published in *The West Australian* about the removal of the boys on 24 February 1964 stated:

> Mrs Heather Vicenti . . . had readily agreed when Mrs Smith had suggested her son John[41] (15 months), should go to stay with her for an indefinite period. "I knew Mrs Smith could give John a better life and education than I could," said Mrs Vicenti.[42]

Vicenti's "ready agreement" to the fostering arrangement is similar to the "mutual consent" of her earlier arrangement to place her eldest child in Sister Kate's; what she saw as the best choice from a number of bad options available to her. Vicenti, however, maintained that it was the right decision and was made in Ricci's best interests.[43] She did not see Ricci again until he was ten years old. Vicenti also highlighted the irony of being criticized for allowing her son to be "kidnapped" at a time when white authorities were engaged in Aboriginal child removals on a widespread scale.

Vicenti's fifth child was born in April 1964, shortly after the media furor; Vicenti believes that her high profile due to the negative newspaper coverage of Ricci's foster arrangements had made her even more of a target for welfare authorities, and shortly afterwards all four of her remaining children were removed.[44]

Vicenti was summoned to appear in the Perth Children's Court in January 1965. The extract from the court transcript provided in Vicenti's autobiography indicated that the magistrate, after what appeared to be a very cursory consideration of the family's circumstances, was satisfied that the children were neglected on the basis that Vicenti had recently requested food from a night shelter for her children. This highlights the double-bind that other Aboriginal interviewees also related: when mothers asked authorities for assistance, this was then used against them to justify removal of their children. Vicenti's children were committed to the care of the Child Welfare Department until they reached the age of 18 years; the court transcript extract poignantly concluded "Mother weeps."[45] Vicenti was unable to regain custody of her children despite her ongoing efforts; she eventually decided to relinquish her baby son for adoption, believing that this would be in his best interests, but refused repeated requests by the foster parents to adopt her daughter, who was six at the time she was removed and who Vicenti knew would remember her. Vicenti clearly had her own sense of what was in the best interests of each of her children and made differing decisions for each of them regarding their placement to the best of her ability given the severe constraints she was operating under. However, Vicenti argued that the child welfare system was designed to remove children rather than to reunite families, and parents were inevitably worn down by its relentless internal logic. She commented, "The people who administered the Child Welfare Act gave little thought to the organisation of access to children and the ultimate reunification of families."[46]

Vicenti describes the devastating impact the loss of her children had on her:

> I can never forget the day when my world fell apart. My life is divided in time by that day—before my children were taken, and after my children were taken. The pain of it never leaves. . . . My life was destroyed that day, and the lives of my children. They cut the bonds that tied us all together.[47]

Vicenti had two other children with a new partner in 1969 and 1970, however she lived in constant dread that they too would be taken from her.[48]

All of Vicenti's children eventually returned to her as adults, another common theme in Stolen Generations narratives that speaks to the resilience of Aboriginal families; however, she ultimately lost four of her seven children in tragic circumstances. Vicenti also discovered that her daughter Marcia had had a child at sixteen and relinquished the child for adoption; Vicenti was never informed or offered the opportunity to care for her granddaughter.

Vicenti described her motivations for speaking out and sharing her story:

> Of those who did have their children taken, many do not wish to speak of an experience that was so terribly painful. Just writing my story has been a confrontation with the past, some of it my darkest nightmare. I tell my story in the hope that the lesson may be learned. . . . Although my story is sad, it is far from unique. The whole history of our people is sad. I do not look for sympathy, but our stories must be told. They must be told so that the themes are never repeated. We must all be vigilant.[49]

The experience of reading Vicenti's frank and powerful autobiography is harrowing. Understanding requires empathy, and many of the challenges some Aboriginal mothers face—dealing with extreme poverty, fighting to keep their children, caring for extended family and community members, dealing with courts and the juvenile and adult justice systems—have little in common with those facing middle class white mothers. As Vicenti's account highlights, one thing that happens when Aboriginal mothers speak out about their experiences of child removal and their struggles in raising their family is that people make judgments about their parenting and some may find it lacking, which is undoubtedly a factor which contributes to many mothers' ongoing silence. Vicenti's autobiography powerfully demonstrates that some lives are "too messy" to be neatly contained within humanitarian discourses.[50] While some of the decisions Vicenti made in relation to her children may seem to demonstrate questionable judgment, bearing in mind the immense financial and social difficulties she was facing as a single Aboriginal mother without family or effective welfare support, it is difficult not to have sympathy for her plight. Even the most bizarre aspect of her account, the surrendering of Ricci and his removal overseas, seems more explicable in the context of the imminent threat of the removal of all her children and the extreme poverty the family was then living in; at least through this decision she was able to exercise some element of control over his ongoing care arrangements.

BEING HEARD: THE IMPORTANCE OF PUBLIC RECOGNITION

Community recognition, awareness and acceptance of the Stolen Generations has undoubtedly been a factor in enabling some people to speak about their experiences of child removal. Despite my comments about the role of the dominant Stolen Generations narrative in silencing Aboriginal mothers, it is also important to acknowledge that for many Aboriginal people who were removed as children, it is a validating narrative and one which has enabled their stories to emerge.

A number of interviewees mentioned their pain and hurt when politicians or others questioned the legitimacy of their experiences or refused to apologize:

> This year has been a very hard year, the year 2000, because of the Howard government will not apologise for the atrocities put on the children that were removed. . . . I will still battle to get an apology from the government, which I would like in turn a sincere apology from the government and a set up of a reparations tribunal for all the hurt that's happened to everybody.[51]

Work undertaken with Holocaust survivors has found that denial of the truth of one's experiences can also silence; some stories require an empathetic listener to be told.[52] For some interviewees who were removed as children, the issue is not about being able to speak about their experiences, but knowing that their stories have been heard and appropriately responded to.[53] Others highlighted the need to move beyond symbolic gestures such as an apology to address the issue of compensation; they wanted real assistance to help them to deal with the ongoing impact of child removal on their lives. When asked about her views on compensation, Deirdre Heitmeyer commented:

> People that say, "Oh, but we didn't do it," well, they're living on the privileges of what really happened . . . you're where you are today because of the privileges that your ancestors stole . . . it is about recognition, you know, and it's about if we wipe it out of our mind it'll go away so let's not talk about it, don't talk about it, let's just forget it, you know. And they say forgive and forget, and yet that society that we live in is very big on remembering their great moments in history, but if it looks bad on them they just write it out of their history books.[54]

A range of opinions were expressed by Aboriginal interviewees in relation to the issue of compensation for members of the Stolen Generations, with strong views expressed both for and against it; whereas for white interviewees the issue of compensation is often inextricably linked to questioning the veracity of Stolen Generations stories and the motivations of those who tell them. Sue Gordon, who was herself removed as a child, believed compensation should have been given to the mothers whose children were removed:

> Anybody who should have got compensation, as far as I am concerned, was my mother. She was the person who suffered most, because I had no idea, I was four. There would have been an initial loss, but after that I just existed. But my mother had the knowledge for over thirty years of me, and trying to find me. So should she have been compensated for thirty years of suffering?[55]

In the case of Sue's mother however, it was too late for her to receive compensation, as she had already passed away.

"THE SYMPATHY OF BITTER EXPERIENCE": DOES "SPEAKING OUT" CONTRIBUTE TO HEALING?

Speaking out about human rights violations is seen as both a moral and legal imperative in Western culture.[56] Research has also been undertaken—including research by and with Indigenous peoples—which suggests that speaking about traumatic events, if undertaken in a sensitive and safe environment where the consequences of speaking are carefully managed, can actually contribute to the participants' sense of acknowledgment of the wrongs they have experienced, validate their pain and anger and can contribute to their healing.[57] However, even where speaking out has a therapeutic benefit, it can operate to keep the identification of the harms done and the focus for future healing on the individual, obscuring the wider systemic issues that might have caused the damage or harms in the first place, and the broader structural issues that might need to be addressed to prevent the violation happening again.[58] Reflecting on Stolen Generations testimonies in the context of narrative therapy, Kennedy and Wilson have emphasized the need to address the social, historical and power dimensions of Stolen Generations narratives, arguing that "what is healing in speaking about separation is not speaking *per se*, but rather challenging the particular historical relations of speaking and listening."[59] This takes us back to Miriam-Rose Ungunmerr-Baumann's concept of *dadirri* and her call for non-Indigenous Australians to take the time to listen to Aboriginal people.[60] Listening has been described as "a form of ethical responsiveness which recognises a duty to the story of the other";[61] and the corollary of the longstanding but recently-renewed Indigenous calls for "Voice" is the need for non-Indigenous Australians to hear.

What differentiates speech as therapy from speech as testimony is the expectation of the speaker that social change will result from their speech. A number of interviewees spoke about the importance to them of ensuring that the policies and practices of Aboriginal child removal never happened again; when asked about the issue of compensation one interviewee responded:

Interviewee: Well money can't bring back something that. . . . Money doesn't compensate you from being taken away from your mother, no money, no amount of money can give you back your parents.

Interviewer: What would you ask for?

Interviewee: That it never happens again. That it's something that'll never happen again in this country. And of course I don't think anybody, no matter who you are, has got the right to take children away because the colour of your skin is different from somebody else's.[62]

Sometimes speaking about experiences that have long been held close can be liberating for the speaker and can help them to mend other relationships in their lives. Reflecting on the process of telling her life story as part of an oral history project, Patsy Cohen commented to her research collaborator Margaret Somerville that "the telling had taken a load off her mind and how she had never spoken of many of these things before. She said how it had made a difference in her relationship to her now grown-up children."[63]

Based on their therapeutic work with Holocaust survivors, Felman and Laub argue that speaking about experiences of suffering is essential, as silence is oppressive and survivors whose stories remain untold begin to doubt their own reality:

Some have hardly spoken of it, but even those who have talked incessantly feel that they have managed to say very little that was heard.

> *None find peace in silence, even when it is their choice to remain silent. . . .*
> *The "not telling" of the story serves as a perpetuation of its tyranny. . . . The*
> *longer the story remains untold, the more distorted it becomes in the survi-*
> *vor's conception of it, so much so that the survivor doubts the reality of the*
> *actual events.* [64]

Kathy Donovan, who was removed as a child and who experienced the
removal of two of her own children in the post–Stolen Generations era,
was asked whether she saw speaking about her experiences as part of
healing, and responded:

> Yeah, but does anyone really listen? I mean, I think it's been beaten to
> death, you know, the Stolen Generation, the Stolen Generation. But it is
> out there, it is you know, and I'm only thirty-three and I've got three
> sisters and brothers. Three sisters that are younger than me, and it
> happened to my kids. So it's still happening. [65]

Sylvia Neary spoke about "coming out of silence" through her participation in recovery groups and meeting others who have had similar experiences. [66] In her autobiography Ella Simon made reference to "the sympathy of bitter experience," a term she used to describe the shared experience of Aboriginal and white women who found common ground in
their battle to improve local conditions and services. [67] Certainly many of
the interviewees who were removed as children spoke of receiving solace
and comfort from meeting others who had lived through the experience
of being removed and who could share with them intimate knowledge
and understanding of their pain. This is a solace that the mothers of the
Stolen Generations—who have primarily remained silent—cannot receive.

Learning more about Aboriginal mothers' experiences and perspectives on the removal of their children provides insights which are not
readily available from any other source. The stories of the mothers of the
Stolen Generations highlight the importance of thinking broadly about
the impact of human rights violations and ensuring that all parties who
are impacted by the violation are included in any subsequent investigation process.

While some argue that talking about past experiences is a key aspect
of healing, speaking out can be confronting, particularly for mothers of
removed children who have a lot at stake and very little of practical
benefit to gain. While theoretical debates abound about the therapeutic
benefits or harms of "speaking out" on an individual level, it is clear that
the context in which speech (or silence) occurs is vitally important, as is
the individual retaining some sense of control over their story and what
happens to it after it is told.

What enables some mothers to speak about their experiences of child
removal? The desire to raise awareness of their circumstances and to
prevent future repetition of similar violations are mentioned by a number

of people as important motivators. The importance of a receptive audience cannot be overstated; it is hard to speak into a vacuum, or if one believes the reception of one's story will be critical or hostile. For some, simply "being heard" is not sufficient; they want to move beyond symbolic gestures to practical measures that will address some of the real harms they have suffered and continue to suffer. We need to develop an "ethics of listening"[68] that will allow us to respond to these stories with compassion and justice.

The complex, sometimes messy stories of some Aboriginal mothers in the Stolen Generations era require knowledge of the structural disadvantages these mothers faced, an appreciation of the difficult choices they confronted, and a measure of empathy with their experiences to be properly heard and understood — and so they remain largely untold.

NOTES

1. "Ruby," interviewed by Anne Maree Payne, 13 September 2012, University of Technology Sydney, 49.

2. Langer, "The Dilemma of Choice in the Deathcamps," 225–226.

3. Hegarty, *Bittersweet Journey*, 6.

4. Nesiah, "Discussion Lines on Gender and Transitional Justice," 808.

5. Pankhurst, "Introduction," 12.

6. Goodall, "Assimilation Begins in the Home," 77.

7. See, for example, Human Rights and Equal Opportunity Commission, *Bringing Them Home*, 212.

8. Human Rights and Equal Opportunity Commission, *Bringing Them Home*, 224.

9. "Ruby," interviewed by Anne Maree Payne.

10. Pilkington, *Under the Wintamarra Tree*, 59.

11. Pilkington, *Under the Wintamarra Tree*, 79.

12. Pilkington, *Under the Wintamarra Tree*, 205.

13. *The Sydney Morning Herald*, "Daughter Dies with Her Story Still Incomplete."

14. Pilkington, *Under the Wintamarra Tree*, 203.

15. Aboriginal and Torres Strait Islander Commission News, "Mum Shirl."

16. Mum Shirl, *Mum Shirl. An Autobiography*, 24–25.

17. Although receiving no mention in her autobiography, a tribute to Mum Shirl published in *Aboriginal History* after her death indicates that "Shirley's own children were removed to AWB custody—the girls to Cootamundra; the boys to Kinchela. Through her own efforts she eventually regained custody of her children." Briscoe, "Colleen Shirley Smith, MBE, AM, 1928–98," xiv.

18. Mum Shirl, *Mum Shirl. An Autobiography*, 41.

19. Mum Shirl, *Mum Shirl. An Autobiography*, 38.

20. Lesley McLennon interviewed by Helen Belle Curzon-Siggers, 11 December 1999, ORAL TRC 5000/77, National Library of Australia, 30–31.

21. "Ruby," interviewed by Anne Maree Payne, 44.

22. "Ruby," interviewed by Anne Maree Payne, 24–25.

23. Human Rights and Equal Opportunity Commission, *Bringing Them Home*, 12.

24. *Genocide Convention* 1948 Article II(e).

25. It is interesting to note that a number of the autobiographical accounts of the reunions between mothers/extended family members and Stolen Generations children are anticlimactic, possibly reflecting the unrealizable expectations that have built up in the period leading up to the moment of reunion.

26. Eileen Moseley interviewed by Anne Ronberg, 27 March 2001, ORAL TRC 5000/241, National Library of Australia, 6.

27. Eunice Wright interviewed by Roderic Lacey, 26 July 2000, ORAL TRC 5000/152, National Library of Australia, 26–27.

28. White.

29. "Ruby," interviewed by Anne Maree Payne, 48.

30. Marchetti & Ransley, "Unconscious Racism," 538.

31. Nannup, Marsh, & Kinnane, *When the Pelican Laughed*, 217–218.

32. Vicenti and Dickman, "Too Many Tears," 73.

33. Vicenti and Dickman, "Too Many Tears," 77.

34. Vicenti and Dickman, "Too Many Tears," 80.

35. Vicenti and Dickman, "Too Many Tears," 81.

36. Vicenti and Dickman, "Too Many Tears," 86.

37. Vicenti and Dickman, "Too Many Tears," 85.

38. Vicenti and Dickman, "Too Many Tears," 96–97.

39. Vicenti and Dickman, "Too Many Tears," 98.

40. Vicenti and Dickman, "Too Many Tears," 106.

41. Ricci is renamed "John" by his adoptive mother.

42. Reproduced in Vicenti and Dickman, "Too Many Tears," 108.

43. Vicenti and Dickman, "Too Many Tears," 106.

44. Vicenti and Dickman, "Too Many Tears," 110.

45. Vicenti and Dickman, "Too Many Tears," 113.

46. Vicenti and Dickman, "Too Many Tears," 119.

47. Vicenti and Dickman, "Too Many Tears," 113.

48. Vicenti and Dickman, "Too Many Tears," 129.

49. Vicenti and Dickman, "Too Many Tears," 195.

50. Malkki, "Speechless Emissaries," 232.

51. Japarta Maurie Ryan, interviewed by Glenys Dimond, 29 December 2000, ORAL TRC 5000/233, National Library of Australia, 8–9.

52. Felman and Laub, *Testimony. Crises of Witnessing in Literature, Psychoanalysis, and History*, 68.

53. See, for example, Carol Kendall interviewed by John Maynard, 5 April 2001, ORAL TRC 5000/246, National Library of Australia, 44.

54. Deirdre Heitmeyer interviewed by John Maynard, 4 March 1999, ORAL TRC 5000/11, National Library of Australia, 6.

55. Sue Gordon interviewed by John Bannister, 12 October 1999, ORAL TRC 5000/52, National Library of Australia, 67.

56. See, for example Young, who identified in the context of Holocaust narratives the importance of the idea of "bearing witness" in the Judeo-Christian tradition, as well as the value placed upon the idea of being a witness in legal processes to investigate wrongdoing. Young, *Writing and Rewriting the Holocaust*, 18.

57. See, for example, Benabed, "An Indigenous Holistic Approach to Colonial Trauma and Its Healing"; Herman, *Trauma and Recovery*; Wesley-Esquimaux and Smolewski, "Historic Trauma and Aboriginal Healing."

58. Antze and Lambek argue that "there is nothing liberating in narrative per se. Merely to transfer the story from embodied symptoms to words is not necessarily either to integrate or to exorcise it" ("Introduction: Forecasting Memory," xix). They describe therapy as "a triumph over the political" (xxiv).

59. Kennedy and Wilson, "Constructing Shared Histories," 129.

60. Ungunmerr-Baumann, "Dadirri. Inner Deep Listening and Quiet Still Awareness."

61. Frow, "A Politics of Stolen Time," 364.

62. Edith Willoway interviewed by John Bannister, 13 December 2000, ORAL TRC 5000/265, National Library of Australia, 18.

63. Cohen and Somerville, *Ingelba and the Five Black Matriarchs*, xiii.

64. Felman and Laub, *Testimony. Crises of Witnessing in Literature, Psychoanalysis, and History*, 79. My emphasis.

65. Kathy Donovan interviewed by John Maynard, 3 April 2001, ORAL TRC 5000/264, National Library of Australia, 15.

66. Sylvia Neary interviewed by interviewed by Jane Watson, 16 March 2001, TRC 5000/251, National Library of Australia, 51.

67. Simon, *Through My Eyes*, 103.

68. Probyn, "The White Father: Denial, Paternalism and Community," 61.

Conclusion

Throughout this book I have explored issues around motherhood, silence and truth-telling, through in-depth analysis of the experiences of the mothers of the Stolen Generations. My research has focused on identifying Aboriginal mothers' experiences at the time of the removal of their children, but also on their subsequent experiences of engagement or disengagement with the *Bringing Them Home* Inquiry, which investigated whether the forcible removal of Indigenous children constituted a human rights violation. This book has identified structural barriers to mothering in the Stolen Generations era; the impact of negative perceptions of Aboriginal motherhood on child removal practices; and the factors impacting on Aboriginal mothers' decisions to speak or be silent about their experiences of child removal through the *Bringing Them Home* Inquiry and beyond.

MOTHERHOOD AND RACE

Intersectional analyses have emphasized that not all mothers are the same, and the relationship in Australia between the promotion of white motherhood and the denigration and active discouragement of Aboriginal motherhood during the Stolen Generations era has been acknowledged.[1] Motherhood is seen by some as having a special status and standing in black communities, operating as a site of resistance and liberation for black women, and this has provided an important counterpoint to white constructions of black motherhood as deviant and deficient.

This book has highlighted the very real impact of poverty, social disadvantage, racism and discrimination on Aboriginal motherhood in the Stolen Generations era, with the legacy of this history of disadvantage continuing to impact in manifest ways on Aboriginal families today. Welfare approaches tend to blame individual parents for their failings, and governments and welfare agencies remain unwilling or unable to identify and address structural and systemic disadvantages arising from issues such as poverty and the social impact of racial discrimination.[2] In the Stolen Generations era, systemic barriers to Aboriginal motherhood such as legal inequalities, discrimination in access to family-based social security payments, the impact of mission policies requiring mothers to work and removing children to mission dormitories and the heightened surveillance and supervision of Aboriginal families living on missions and reserves, all contributed significantly to Aboriginal child removal at this time. The deep impact of these structural issues on the ability of Aboriginal mothers to maintain the integrity of their families remains an under-acknowledged aspect of our understanding of the Stolen Generations era.

MOTHERHOOD AND HUMAN RIGHTS

When mothers become involved in human rights campaigns and truth-telling processes, it is often to protest against the violation of the rights of others rather than to defend their own rights; women testifiers have been described as "repositories of memory for the suffering of others."[3] This is a form of behavior that falls within what society defines as an appropriate role for mothers, who are expected to subsume their own needs and desires in those of people for whom they care, particularly their children.

Some inquiries investigating Indigenous child removal, such as the *Bringing Them Home* Inquiry in Australia and the Truth and Reconciliation Commission in Canada, have had a tendency to focus on the child victim rather than on other parties whose rights may have also been violated, such as parents, who were acknowledged in both of these processes as injured parties but who were not a major focus of investigation.[4] An interesting exception to the trend to view child removal as primarily a violation of the rights of the child has been the Australian inquiries into forced adoption, where a previously stigmatized group of mothers has actively campaigned for recognition of forced adoption practices as a violation of their rights, in an attempt to redefine society's perception of them as "bad" or uncaring mothers who abandoned their children.[5]

The limitations of human rights approaches, with their constrained definitions of who is a rights-holder and who has suffered a damage,[6] are highlighted by the case of the mothers of the Stolen Generations. The damage of the original violation has spread widely beyond the individuals removed and their parents to their extended families and wider communities, and indeed has impacted across generations. This is challenging for a human rights inquiry, grounded in notions of individual rights and freedoms, to encompass.

THE LEGACY OF THE STOLEN GENERATIONS ON ABORIGINAL MOTHERS

Bowlby defined one of the most important functions of the family as the passing on of parenting skills intergenerationally.[7] The impact of being raised in institutional care or in abusive or unloving foster care relationships on Aboriginal people's capacity to develop close relationships as adults and to function effectively in family life was addressed in the

Bringing Them Home Report, which described this impacting intergenerationally in cycles of child removal occurring within Aboriginal families.[8] Many comments were made by Aboriginal interviewees who were removed as children about the ways in which their removal impacted upon their own parenting and other adult relationships, exemplified in this comment by Deirdre Heitmeyer:

> As a mother too, I think we need help because what's our role-model? I don't have a role-model. But not only do I not have a role-model, my kids are the first kids in three generations to be with their natural mother. That's not right, and simply because of who our mothers were.[9]

The high level of intervention by various missionaries, reserve managers and welfare agencies in Aboriginal families over decades has also left a legacy, undermining parental authority and de-skilling Aboriginal parents. This book has highlighted the impact of generations of interventions by white authorities into Aboriginal families, to the detriment of these families. White interviewees who participated in various ways in the removal of Aboriginal children in the Stolen Generations era stated their belief that they were acting in the best interests of these children within the options available to them at the time; which leads me to reflect on what we are doing in this area today that future generations may look back on and condemn.

"SORRY MEANS YOU DON'T DO IT AGAIN": THE IMPACT ON CONTEMPORARY REMOVALS

Since the end of the Stolen Generations era, there has been a multiplication of bureaucracies concerned with intervening in the lives of Indigenous families.[10] There has been continuity in child removal practices despite attempted reforms such as the introduction of the Aboriginal Child Placement Principle, and state interventions in Indigenous families are justified as legitimate and benevolent because they are framed in terms of child welfare.[11]

The data in relation to the representation of Indigenous children in the child welfare system in Australia are stark. The situation continues to worsen, with a recent Productivity Commission *Closing the Gap* Annual Report indicating that rates of Indigenous children in out-of-home care have almost tripled in the past fifteen years.[12] An Independent Review into Aboriginal Out-Of-Home Care in NSW chaired by Professor Megan Davis highlighted the impact of intergenerational trauma on Aboriginal families, as well as finding a culture of noncompliance with the implementation of the Aboriginal Child Placement Principle and the failure to embed Aboriginal self-determination into the child protection system.[13]

This review also noted the important grassroots advocacy work being undertaken by community groups such as Grandmothers Against Removals.

Describing the idealized image of the "good mother" in Australia, Indigenous legal scholar Kylie Cripps has argued that "There is no room within this stereotype to accommodate experiences of racism, colonialism, classism, nor violence that may mediate individual actions and responsibilities of women as they navigate their 'motherhood.'"[14] Cripps highlights the correlation between domestic violence and the substantiation of child abuse allegations in Indigenous families; she also highlights the growing conceptualization of poverty and social isolation as "risk factors" for child protection agencies, rather than them being understood as systemic factors underpinning child neglect.[15] The history of the "child rescue" movement has left its legacy on contemporary child welfare; Swain and Hillel's study of the relationship between children, nation, race and empire argues that the image of the vulnerable child at risk "has been carefully constructed upon a denial or victimisation of the family and kin who, properly supported, are most likely to ensure its safety."[16]

In her exploration of state intervention into Indigenous families, Kylie Cripps reports the staggering rates of contemporary Indigenous child removal at ten times the rate of non-Indigenous children, and questions "whether, as a consequence of intention, poor policy or misguided practice, we are creating another stolen generation."[17]

Drawing parallels between historical Aboriginal child removal and contemporary removals due to juvenile justice mechanisms, Beresford and Omaji have also highlighted continuities between past and present child removal practices:

> Both systems undertook the removal of children while turning a blind eye to the underlying causes of Aboriginal social disadvantage, a disadvantage which has its historic roots in government policies towards Aboriginal people.[18]

Noting that Australian policy makers and child welfare practitioners have found it easier to remove Aboriginal children than to address the underlying social problems of Aboriginal communities, they argue that the removal of Aboriginal children "continues unabated" because "It is the convenient, politically acceptable way of dealing with the problems associated with extreme social disadvantage and racial marginalisation widely experienced by Aboriginal youth."[19] Cripps comments that "It is easy to blame the mother and/or the Indigenous community for the dysfunction that exists," while the role of the state in enabling the conditions of systemic poverty and neglect that many Aboriginal children live in is ignored.[20]

Today, community groups campaign to raise public awareness of the ongoing high levels of child removal that continue to impact on Aboriginal families. These campaigns call for child welfare agencies to take pro-active steps to ensure Aboriginal children remain with their families. Grandmothers Against Removals continues to campaign against Indigenous child removal and to ensure that welfare agencies comply with the Aboriginal Child Placement Principle, calling for the provision of re-sources to Indigenous families, "rather than the punishment and trauma of forced removal."[21]

Commenting on the complicity of the state in justifying the dispropor-tionate rates of removal of Indigenous children both in the past and to-day, Cripps highlights the need for welfare agencies to move away from pathologizing individual parents and provide real and meaningful sup-port for Indigenous families and communities, "with Indigenous partner-ship and collaboration at the core of all activities."[22] She emphasizes the importance of a rights-based approach to the issue of child removal, one in which the legacy of the past is acknowledged, to enable Aboriginal mothers "to utilise those rights to determine a safer future for themselves and for their children."[23]

UNTOLD SUFFERING: MOTHERHOOD, SILENCE AND TRUTH-TELLING

This book has focused on mothers' silence and speech in the wake of child removal, identifying the factors that inhibit mothers' speech as well as those that enable it. The silence of victims of human rights violations can be difficult to interpret, as it can be the result of their exclusion from investigative processes or a conscious choice being made by a victim or victims. Have the mothers of the Stolen Generations been silenced or have they chosen silence? The removal of Aboriginal children in Austra-lia has been conceptualized under the term "the Stolen Generations," and this construction of the violation has operated to silence some Aboriginal mothers, whose stories do not fit neatly within the dominant Stolen Gen-erations narrative. The complex "choiceless choices" that were made by Aboriginal mothers mean that they are not readily categorizable as "blameless victims," their stories are "messy" and challenging to analyze and require "deep listening" to hear. If their testimony is not actively sought in human rights processes, many mothers of removed children will remain silent, as they have much to lose but little of practical benefit to gain by speaking out.

While reasons for choosing silence can be complex, there are factors which inhibit mothers from speaking about their experiences of human rights violations in the particular context of child removal. These include fears of the consequences of speaking about issues such as rape, incest and sexual abuse (particularly the impact of this on the children who are born as a result of these violations); the impact of self-blame, the blame of family members and the blame of society; and the need to protect fragile family relationships that are in the process of being rebuilt. Silence may also be the result of cultural observations, victims' rejection of human rights mechanisms, or their sense of hopelessness and despair, their sense that speech is pointless and will only lead to further hurt. Speaking out, often unproblematically associated with healing in human rights processes, may be more difficult for some victims than others. If speech is indeed intrinsic to healing, how do we find a way to support mothers' speech, to provide a safe place where they can speak of their losses without the fear of judgment, and begin the process of rebuilding their lives?

WHAT ARE THE CIRCUMSTANCES THAT ENABLE MOTHERS TO SPEAK?

Can we identify the factors which enable mothers' speech? Some mothers who have spoken out in the aftermath of great tragedy, such as the Madres de la Plaza de Mayo, or other women who have spoken of their experiences of human rights violation after long maintaining silence, such as the Korean "comfort women," have found a way to turn their individual experiences of immense loss and suffering into positive campaigns for human rights. These examples highlight that the context within which speech about violations occurs is vital. In the case of the Madres, the revered status of mothers in Argentine culture provided a platform from which the Madres could speak and be heard.[24] Korean women subjected to sexual slavery in World War II chose to finally speak about their experiences due to a mix of personal motivations and the desire for apology;[25] but perhaps the time had also arrived when the Korean community and the international community were ready to hear and acknowledge their stories, and finally understood where the responsibility for what they had experienced should lie.[26]

It is not surprising that Aboriginal mothers, who rights in the Stolen Generations era were severely constrained by the impact of Aboriginal "protection" legislation, and whose capacity to love and care for their children was widely denigrated, responded to the removal of their children with grief and silence. However, is the Australian community, who responded with an outpouring of sympathy to the plight of removed Aboriginal children after the publication of the *Bringing Them Home* Report, truly ready even today to hear the stories of their mothers' experiences? As this book has demonstrated, perceptions about neglectful Aboriginal mothers were essential to the practice of child removal in the Stolen Generations era, they were its rationale and justification. Once you begin to question these perceptions, the whole edifice of Aboriginal child removal is revealed as racially discriminatory, undifferentiating in its impact and inhumane. Fundamentally, this is why some white people involved in child removals cannot let go of their negative perception of Aboriginal mothers and continue to insist that Aboriginal children were only ever removed for justifiable reasons, that all Aboriginal children benefited from their removal, and that their mothers were in any case neglectful, indifferent and "consented" to their removal.

American philosopher Richard Rorty argued that we need to view racially intolerant people as "deprived," lacking in both security and sympathy,[27] and called for a "sentimental education" that would enable us to recognize the humanity of people different from ourselves, to recognize that we share "similarities such as cherishing our parents and our children."[28] There is a need for "long, sad, sentimental stories" that build empathy between people, Rorty argued, as we can be "moved to action by sad and sentimental stories";[29] this shared empathy for human suffering rather than rational arguments about equality was what he believed would ultimately build support for human rights. While Aboriginal mothers have been unwilling or unable to speak about their experiences of child removal for a range of reasons, if Rorty's analysis is correct these untold stories may in fact be essential for the wider community's recognition and understanding of the pain and loss experienced by Aboriginal mothers. This raises important ethical issues about whether those who have suffered pain and injustice must also bear the responsibility for educating others about their experiences. However, there is a need to listen, to acknowledge the pain that has been inflicted on Aboriginal families, and to respond to their tales of loss and suffering with empathy and understanding, rather than judgment and criticism, if we truly wish to "hear" mothers' experiences of human rights violations.

HEALING THE PAST

Is it possible to find a way to heal the wounds of the past for Aboriginal women whose motherhood has been stolen from them?

Yvonne Mills discussed her ongoing sorrow at the damage that had been done to her relationship with her mother, and her regret at not being able to ask her mother about her experiences:

> All of it will never go away, it will never go away. Because you can never replace it, you can never go back over time and have like, your time again. You can never have that closeness that you should've had. And I guess the saddest part of it all is that when our mother was here, that we never talked more about it. And we would've learnt more about her and about how she felt and about what had happened.[30]

Alice Nannup's autobiography, *When the Pelican Laughed,* captures her bittersweet experience of returning home after an absence of forty-two years:

> It was hard to cope with the way I was feeling. I felt cheated, like deprived of so much, but there was nothing I could do about it now. It had all been out of my control, and there's no turning back the clock, it had all gone, and I was too late. . . . Uncle Paddy had this big long stick, and he was hitting it on the ground and crying as he spoke to me. He said, "This is the only one girl that went away and come back. Mobs of girls been away from here, and they never come back yet. We are proud of you, proud you've come back."[31]

Nannup's words capture the bitterness of coming home to losses that cannot be repaired; but also the resilience of family and community, who rejoice in the return of their stolen children. Words cannot repair the harm that has been suffered; and sometimes words are not necessary anyway: "I never spoke much about what had happened to me after I left with the Campbells. It was enough for me, and for them, that I'd finally been able to come back."[32]

Doris Pilkington spoke of the journey of healing, likening it to the wintamarra tree at her birthplace; and I would like to end with her message of hope and resilience:

> The wintamarra tree of my birthplace is a permanent reminder of the beginning of my life, and of the wonderful lady who gave birth to me here. . . . Although the tree at my birthplace is dead, the original tree, its roots are still there down in the earth, and four new trees have grown up. It's always been there, waiting for me to come and connect to my birthplace.[33]

NOTES

1. Fiona Paisley, for example, discusses the difference between being considered "race mothers" and "mothers of the race." See Paisley, "Feminist Challenges to White Australia," 269.

2. Dorothy Roberts mounts a scathing attack on racial bias in both the historical and contemporary child welfare system in America. See Roberts, *Shattered Bonds. The Color of Child Welfare.*

3. Franke, "Gendered Subjects of Transitional Justice," 822.

4. Like the *Bringing Them Home* Report, *They Came for the Children* (Truth and Reconciliation Commission of Canada 2012) is focused primarily on the impact of child removals on the child victims, and while it does address some aspects of removals in relation to parents, it makes no reference to specific issues for Indigenous mothers.

5. In contrast to the mothers of the Stolen Generations, Australian mothers who experienced forced adoption have in the past few decades broken the "social silence" about their experiences and have actively campaigned for acknowledgment that the removal of their babies was a violation of their parental rights, resulting in a number of state and federal level inquiries into past adoption practices. See, for example, Cole, *Releasing the Past: Mothers' Stories of Their Stolen Babies;* the Senate Community Affairs References Committee, "Commonwealth Contribution to Former Forced Adoption Policies and Practices"; as well as the formal apology from the Prime Minister, Julia Gillard, "National Apology for Forced Adoptions."

6. Rubio-Marín, "What Happened to the Women?," 31.

7. Bowlby, *Maternal Care and Mental Health*, 69.

8. Human Rights and Equal Opportunity Commission, *Bringing Them Home*, 222.

9. Deirdre Heitmeyer interviewed by John Maynard, 4 March 1999, ORAL TRC 5000/11, National Library of Australia, 12.

10. Carrington, "Aboriginal Girls and Juvenile Justice," 12.

11. Carrington, "Aboriginal Girls and Juvenile Justice," 14.

12. Steering Committee for the Review of Government Service Provision, *Overcoming Indigenous Disadvantage*, xxiii.

13. Independent Review of Aboriginal Children and Young People in OOHC, *Family is Culture Report 2019*.

14. Cripps, "Indigenous Children's 'Best Interests' at the Crossroads," 27.

15. Cripps, "Indigenous Children's 'Best Interests' at the Crossroads," 30.

16. Swain and Hillel, *Child, Nation, Race and Empire*, 175.

17. Cripps, "Indigenous Children's 'Best Interests' at the Crossroads," 25.

18. Beresford and Omaji, *Our State of Mind*, 223.

19. Beresford and Omaji, *Our State of Mind*, 229.

20. Cripps, "Indigenous Children's 'Best Interests' at the Crossroads," 31.

21. Grandmothers Against Removal, "A Fundraiser for Grandmothers Against Removals."

22. Cripps, "Indigenous Children's 'Best Interests' at the Crossroads," 31.

23. Cripps, "Indigenous Children's 'Best Interests' at the Crossroads," 32.

24. Pieper Mooney, *The Politics of Motherhood*, 2.

25. Chinkin speculates that the decision by these women to finally speak more than forty years after the violations they had experienced was based both on their desire for formal acknowledgment and a "meaningful apology," plus their practical need for "physical, personal and economic security for the last years of their lives" (Chinkin, "Peoples Tribunals: Legitimate or Rough Justice," 206).

26. Chinkin, "Women's International Tribunal on Japanese Military Sexual Slavery," 341.

27. Rorty, "Human Rights, Rationality, and Sentimentality," 124.

28. Rorty, "Human Rights, Rationality, and Sentimentality," 125.

29. Rorty, "Human Rights, Rationality, and Sentimentality," 126.

30. Yvonne Mills interviewed by Colleen Hattersley, 15 August 1999, ORAL TRC 5000/37, National Library of Australia, 28.

31. Nannup, Marsh & Kinnane, *When the Pelican Laughed*, 209.

32. Nannup, Marsh & Kinnane, *When the Pelican Laughed*, 211.

33. Pilkington, *Under the Wintamarra Tree*, 208.

Appendix I

Legislation Consulted

COMMONWEALTH OF AUSTRALIA

Invalid and Old-Age Pensions Act 1908 (Cth)
War Pensions Act 1914 (Cth)
Widows Pension Act 1942 (Cth)
Social Services Act 1959 (Cth)
Genocide Convention Act 1949 (Cth)

STATE AND TERRITORY

Australian Capital Territory

Aborigines Welfare Ordinance 1954 (ACT)

New South Wales

Aborigines Protection Act 1909 (NSW)
Aborigines Protection Amending Act 1915 (NSW)
Aborigines Protection (Amendment) Act 1936 (NSW)
Aborigines Protection (Amendment) Act 1940 (NSW)
Aborigines Protection (Amendment) Act 1943 (NSW)
Aborigines Act 1969 (NSW)

Northern Territory

Northern Territory Aboriginals Act 1910 (NT)
Aboriginals Ordinance 1911 (NT)
Aboriginals Ordinance 1918 (NT)
Aboriginals Ordinance 1953 (NT)
Welfare Ordinance 1953 (NT)

Queensland

Aboriginal Protection and Restriction of the Sale of Opium Act 1897 (Qld)

Aboriginal Protection and Restriction of the Sale of Opium Amendment Act 1934 (Qld)
The Adoption of Children Act 1935 (Qld)
Aboriginals Preservation and Protection Act 1939 (Qld)
Torres Strait Islanders Act 1939 (Qld)
Aboriginal and Torres Strait Islanders Act 1965 (Qld)

South Australia

An Ordinance for the Protection, Maintenance and Upbringing of Orphans and other Destitute Children and Aborigines Act 1844 (SA)
Aborigines Act 1911 (SA)
Aborigines (Training of Children) Act 1923 (SA)
Aborigines Act 1934 (SA)
Aborigines Act Amending Act 1939 (SA)
Aboriginal Affairs Act 1962 (SA)

Victoria

Aboriginal Protection Act 1869 (Vic)
Aboriginal Protection Act 1886 (Vic)
Aborigines Act 1890 (Vic)
Aborigines Act 1910 (Vic)
Aborigines Act 1915 (Vic)
Aborigines Act 1928 (Vic)
Aborigines Act 1957 (Vic)

Western Australia

An Act to prevent the enticing away the girls of the Aboriginal race from school or from any service in which they are employed 1844 (WA)
Aborigines Protection Act 1886 (WA)
Aborigines Act 1889 (WA)
Aborigines Act 1897 (WA)
Aborigines Act 1905 (WA)
Aborigines Act Amendment Act 1911 (WA)
Native Administration Act 1936 (WA)
Native Administration Amendment Act 1941 (WA)
Native (Citizenship Rights) Act 1944 (WA)
Native Welfare Act 1954 (WA)
Native Welfare Act Amendment Act 1960 (WA)
Native Welfare Act 1963 (WA)

Appendix II

List of Interviews Quoted

Interviewees, National Library of Australia Bringing Them Home *Oral History Project*

John Alexander interviewed by John Bannister, 8 & 15 June 1999, ORAL TRC 5000/30, National Library of Australia.

Clair Andersen & Jaye Clair interviewed by Lyn McLeavy, 20 July, 24 August & 15 September 2000 and 25 May 2001, ORAL TRC 5000/287, National Library of Australia.

George Bloomfield interviewed by John Maynard, 7 April 2001, ORAL TRC 5000/247, National Library of Australia.

Dawn Brown interviewed by Peter Bertani, 29 July 2000, ORAL TRC 5000/157, National Library of Australia.

Clara Coulthard interviewed by Sue Anderson, 12 December 2000, ORAL TRC 5000/210, National Library of Australia.

Trevor Deshong interviewed by Colleen Hattersley, 31 July 2001, ORAL TRC 5000/295, National Library of Australia.

Barrie & Judith Dexter interviewed by Steven Guth, 24 March 1999, ORAL TRC 5000/21, National Library of Australia.

Daphne Doney interviewed by Marnie Richardson, 2 September 2000, ORAL TRC 5000/177, National Library of Australia.

Kathy Donovan interviewed by John Maynard, 3 April 2001, ORAL TRC 5000/264, National Library of Australia.

Oomera (Coral) Edwards interviewed by Ann-Mari Jordens, 5 March 2000, ORAL TRC 5000/94, National Library of Australia.

Cec (Cecil) Fisher interviewed by Lyn McLeavy, 24 September 2000, ORAL TRC 5000/231, National Library of Australia.

Jackie Frail interviewed by Rob Willis, 6 July 2000, ORAL TRC 5000/162, National Library of Australia.

Frank Gare interviewed by W.J.E. Bannister, 11 March 1999, ORAL TRC 5000/14, National Library of Australia.

Sue Gordon interviewed by John Bannister, 12 October 1999, ORAL TRC 5000/52, National Library of Australia.

Marjorie Harris interviewed by Glenys Dimond, 15 June 2001, ORAL TRC 5000/313, National Library of Australia.

Ruth Hegarty interviewed by Helen Belle Curzon Siggers, 14 December 1999, ORAL TRC 5000/79, National Library of Australia.

Deirdre Heitmeyer interviewed by John Maynard, 4 March 1999, ORAL TRC 5000/11, National Library of Australia.

Debra (Chandler) Hocking interviewed by Lyn McCleavy, 16 May 2000 and 22 & 29 May 2001, ORAL TRC 5000/279, National Library of Australia.

Syd (Sydney James) Jackson interviewed by Helen Belle Curzon-Siggers, 26 July–7 September 2000, ORAL TRC 5000/184, National Library of Australia.

Christine Jacques interviewed by Karen George, 5 July 2000, ORAL TRC 5000/134, National Library of Australia.

Doris Kartinyeri interviewed by Sue Anderson, 17 November 2000, ORAL TRC 5000/223, National Library of Australia.

Ryan Kelly interviewed by John Maynard, 1 April 2001, ORAL TRC 5000/240, National Library of Australia.

Carol Kendall interviewed by John Maynard, 5 April 2001, ORAL TRC 5000/246, National Library of Australia.

Sharon Kinchela, Rosie Matthews & Debbie Kinchela interviewed by Colleen Hattersley, 28 March 2001, ORAL TRC 5000/248, National Library of Australia.

Audrey Ngingali Kinnear interviewed by Francine George, 25 February 1999, ORAL TRC 5000/7, National Library of Australia.

Barbara Lange interviewed by David Woodgate, 30 March 2001, ORAL TRC 5000/250, National Library of Australia.

Pattie Lees interviewed by Colleen Hattersley, 13 June 2001, ORAL TRC 5000/300, National Library of Australia.

Colin Macleod interviewed by Gordon Dowell, 16 February 2000, ORAL TRC 5000/90, National Library of Australia.

Alice Marbach interviewed by Deborah Somersall, 26 February 2000, ORAL TRC 5000/95, National Library of Australia.

Keith McEwan interviewed by Gordon Dowell, 19 May 2000, ORAL TRC 5000/137, National Library of Australia.

Lesley McLennon interviewed by Helen Belle Curzon-Siggers, 11 December 1999, ORAL TRC 5000/77, National Library of Australia.

Trudy (Gertrude) McMahon interviewed by Ann-Mari Jordens, 19 May 2000, ORAL TRC 5000/116, National Library of Australia.

Margaret Helen Meyer interviewed by Gordon Dowell, 19 April 2000, ORAL TRC 5000/110, National Library of Australia.

Keiran Michael interviewed by Phillip Connors, 17 September 1999, ORAL TRC 5000/41, National Library of Australia.

David Mills interviewed by Karen George, 26 July 2000, ORAL TRC 5000/151, National Library of Australia.

Yvonne Mills interviewed by Colleen Hattersley, 15 August 1999, ORAL TRC 5000/37, National Library of Australia.

Eileen Moseley interviewed by Anne Ronberg, 27 March 2001, ORAL TRC 5000/241, National Library of Australia.

Annie Mullins interviewed by Lyn McLeavy, 30 September 2000, ORAL TRC 5000/280, National Library of Australia.

Sylvia Neary interviewed by Jane Watson, 16 March 2001, ORAL TRC 5000/251, National Library of Australia.

Annie Ozies interviewed by Gary Lee, 15 August 2000, ORAL TRC 5000/158, National Library of Australia.

Mervyn Pattemore interviewed by Glenys Dimond, 1 November 2000, ORAL TRC 5000/195, National Library of Australia.

Les (Leslie Newton) Penhall interviewed by Francis Good, 25 January & 1 February 2000, ORAL TRC 5000/105, National Library of Australia.

Darren Perry interviewed by Karen George, 12 May 2000, ORAL TRC 5000/115, National Library of Australia.

Glynn Pritchard interviewed by Helen Belle Curzon-Siggers, 14 August 1999, ORAL TRC 5000/35, National Library of Australia.

Dorothy Pyatt interviewed by Karen George, 6 December 2000, ORAL TRC 5000/222, National Library of Australia.

Anne Ronberg interviewed by Eileen Moseley, 2 April 2001, ORAL TRC 5000/242, National Library of Australia.

Bill Rutter interviewed by Rob Willis, 12 April 1999, ORAL TRC 5000/18, National Library of Australia.

Japarta Maurie Ryan interviewed by Glenys Dimond, 29 December 2000, ORAL TRC 5000/233, National Library of Australia.

Jean Sibley interviewed by Phillip Connors, 16 November 1999, ORAL TRC 5000/148, National Library of Australia.

Judith Stubbs interviewed by Ann-Mari Jordens, 22 October 2000, ORAL TRC 5000/175, National Library of Australia.

Mary Terszak interviewed by John Bannister, 4 November 1999, ORAL TRC 5000/61, National Library of Australia.

George Tippett interviewed by Gordon Dowell, 18 May 2000, ORAL TRC 5000/170, National Library of Australia.

Mona Ngitji Ngitji Tur interviewed by Sue Anderson, 9 March 2001, ORAL TRC 5000/253, National Library of Australia.

Wilma Walker interviewed by Deborah Somersall, 14 August 1999, ORAL TRC 5000/36, National Library of Australia.

Rosemary Wanganeen interviewed by Sue Anderson, 9 May 2001, ORAL TRC 5000/261, National Library of Australia.

Vince Wenberg interviewed by Frank Heimans, 6 September 2001, ORAL TRC 5000/319, National Library of Australia.

Edith Willoway interviewed by John Bannister, 13 December 2000, ORAL TRC 5000/265, National Library of Australia.

Julie Wilson interviewed by Frank Heimans, 30 January 2001, ORAL TRC 5000/226, National Library of Australia.

John Leslie Wood interviewed by Barbara Erskine, 23 November 1999, ORAL TRC 5000/69, National Library of Australia.

Eunice Wright interviewed by Roderic Lacey, 26 July 2000, ORAL TRC 5000/152, National Library of Australia.

*Interviews Conducted by Anne Maree Payne**

Lily Arthur interviewed by Anne Maree Payne, 30 October 2013, UTS Transcript RP4.

Peter Read interviewed by Anne Maree Payne, 24 October 2013, UTS Transcript RP3.

"Ruby" interviewed by Anne Maree Payne, 13 September 2012, UTS Transcript RP1.

NOTE

Pseudonyms have been used for interviewees who wished to remain anonymous.

Bibliography

Aboriginal and Torres Strait Islander Commission News. "Mum Shirl." Accessed 4 November 2015. http://www.gooriweb.org/heroes/biogs/mum_shirl.html.

Allen, Judith A. *Sex & Secrets. Crimes Involving Australian Women since 1880*. Melbourne: Oxford University Press, 1990.

Antze, Paul and Michael Lambek. "Introduction: Forecasting Memory." In *Tense Past. Cultural Essays in Trauma and Memory*, edited by Paul Antze & Michael Lambek, xi–xxxviii. New York: Routledge, 1996.

Aolain, Finnuala Ni and Catherine Turner. "Gender, Truth & Transition." *UCLA Women's Law Journal*, vol. 16, no. 2 (Winter/Spring 2007): 229–279.

Appleby, Gabrielle, and Meghan Davis. "The Uluru Statement and the Promises of Truth." *Australian Historical Studies*, vol. 49, no. 4 (2018): 501–509.

Atkinson, Judy. *Trauma Trails, Recreating Song Lines: The Transgenerational Effects of Trauma in Indigenous Australia*. North Melbourne: Spinifex, 2002.

Atkinson, Sue and Shurlee Swain. "A Network of Support: Mothering across the Koorie Community in Victoria, Australia." *Women's History Review,* vol. 8, no. 2 (1999): 219–230.

Austin, Tony. "Cecil Cook, Scientific Thought and 'Half-Castes' in the Northern Territory 1927–1939.'" *Aboriginal History*, vol. 14, no. 1–2 (1990): 104–122.

Australian Human Rights Commission. "Submission to the United Nations Human Rights Committee." Accessed 4 May 2021. https://humanrights.gov.au/our-work/legal/submission-united-nations-human-rights-committee.

———. "Voices of Australia—Resource Sheet 5. Protection of Human Rights in Australia." Accessed 14 February 2013. http://humanrights.gov.au/education/voices_of_australia/5_2resource.html.

Australian Institute of Aboriginal and Torres Strait Islander Studies. "Explore the Sorry Books." Accessed 31 January 2020. https://aiatsis.gov.au/explore/articles/explore-sorry-books.

———. "Indigenous Australians: Aboriginal and Torres Strait Islander Peoples." Accessed 6 June 2016. http://aiatsis.gov.au/explore/articles/indigenous-australians-aboriginal-and-torres-strait-islander-people.

———. "Guidelines for Ethical Research in Australian Indigenous Studies." Accessed 27 February 2015. http://www.aiatsis.gov.au/_files/research/ethics.pdf.

———. "To Remove and Protect: Laws that Changed Aboriginal Lives." Accessed 23 November 2015. http://aiatsis.gov.au/archive_digitised_collections/remove/index.html.

Australian Law Reform Commission. "Essentially Yours: The Protection of Human Genetic Information in Australia." ALRC Report 96. Accessed 29 August 2015. www.alrc.gov.au/publications/report-96.

Back, Les. *The Art of Listening*. Oxford: Berg, 2007.

Barkan, Elazar. *The Guilt of Nations. Restitution and Negotiating Historical Injustices*. Baltimore, MD: The Johns Hopkins University Press, 2000.

Barnes, Nancy. *Munyi's Daughter. A Spirited Brumby*. Henley Beach, SA: Seaview Press, 2000.

Benabed, Fella. 2009, "An Indigenous Holistic Approach to Colonial Trauma and Its Healing." *Literary Paritantra (Systems)*, vol. 1, no. 1 & 2, *Basant* (Spring 2009): 83–91.

Beresford, Quentin and Paul Omaji. *Our State of Mind: Racial Planning and the Stolen Generations*. South Fremantle: Fremantle Arts Centre Press, 1998.

Bird, Carmel, ed. *The Stolen Children. Their Stories*. Milsons Point: Random House, 1998.

Bird Rose, Deborah. "The Silence and Power of Women." In *Words and Silences. Aboriginal Women, Politics and Land*, edited by Peggy Brock, 92–116. Crows Nest: Allen & Unwin, 2001.

Blunt, Alison and Gillian Rose. "Introduction: Women's Colonial and Postcolonial Geographies." In *Writing Women and Space. Colonial and Postcolonial Geographies*, edited by Alison Blunt and Gillian Rose, 1–28. London: The Guilford Press, 1994.

Bock, Gisela. "Antinatalism, Maternity and Paternity in National Socialist Racism." In *Maternity and Gender Politics. Women and the Rise of the European Welfare States, 1880s–1950s*, edited by Gisela Bock & Pat Thane, 213–234. London: Routledge, 1991.

Bolt, Andrew. "High Price of Not Testing the Truth on 'Stolen Generations.'" *Herald Sun* (Melbourne Australia), October 8, 2014. https://www.heraldsun.com.au/news/opinion/andrew-bolt/high-price-of-not-testing-the-truth-on-stolen-generations/news-story/4de6b2144951acd810807e5ebc5267a5.

———. "I Wasn't Stolen—Aboriginal Leader's Shock Admission." *Herald Sun* (Melbourne, Australia), 23 February 2001. https://infoweb-newsbank-com.ezproxy.lib.uts.edu.au/apps/news/document-view?p=AUNB&docref=news/0FCE911AEE5349FC.

Bowlby, John. *Maternal Care and Mental Health. A Report Prepared on Behalf of the World Health Organization as a Contribution to the United Nations Programme for the Welfare of Homeless Children*, 2nd ed. Geneva: World Health Organization, 1952.

Brewster, Anne. *Reading Aboriginal Women's Autobiography*. South Melbourne: Sydney University Press, 1996.

Briscoe, Gordon. "Colleen Shirley Smith, MBE, AM, 1928–98." *Aboriginal History*, vol. 21 (1997): xii–xv.

Brock, Peggy. "Aboriginal Families and the Law in the Era of Segregation and Assimilation, 1890s–1950s." In *Sex, Power and Justice. Historical Perspectives of Law in Australia*, edited by Diane Kirkby, 133–149. Melbourne: Oxford University Press, 1995.

Brounéus, Karen. "Truth-Telling as Talking Cure? Insecurity and Retraumatization in the Rwandan Gacaca Courts." *Security Dialogue*, vol. 39, no. 1 (2008): 55–76.

Brown, Wendy. *States of Injury. Power and Freedom in Late Modernity*. Princeton: Princeton University Press, 1995.

Burridge, Nina. "Classroom Perspectives on Australia's Contact History." In *Historical Thinking for History Teachers: A New Approach to Engaging Students and Developing Historical Consciousness*, edited by Tim Allender, Anna Clark and Robert Parkes, 279–298. Crows Nest: Allen & Unwin, 2019.

Butalia, Urvashi. *The Other Side of Silence. Voices from the Partition of India*. London: Hurst & Company, 2000.

Carmody, Broede. "'So Many Mistruths': Sunrise Cops Heat Over Aboriginal Adoption Segment." *The Sydney Morning Herald*, March 13, 2018. https://www.smh.com.au/entertainment/tv-and-radio/so-many-mistruths-sunrise-cops-heat-over-aboriginal-adoption-segment-20180313-p4z46h.html.

Carrington, Kerry. "Aboriginal Girls and Juvenile Justice: What Justice? White Justice." *Journal for Social Justice Studies*, Special Edition Series, Contemporary Race Relations, vol. 3 (1990): 1–18.

Charbonneau, Sinéad, Robina Thomas, Caitlin Janzen, Jeannine Carrière, Susan Strega and Leslie Brown. "Storying the Untold. Indigenous Motherhood and Street Sex Work." In *Mothers of the Nation. Indigenous Mothering as Global Resistance, Reclaiming and Recovery*, edited by D. Memee Lavell-Harvard & Kim Anderson, 163–178. Bradford: Demeter Press, 2014.

Chinkin, Christine. "Peoples' Tribunals: Legitimate or Rough Justice." *Windsor Yearbook of Access to Justice*, vol. 24, no. 2 (2006): 201–220.

———. "Women's International Tribunal on Japanese Military Sexual Slavery." *The American Journal of International Law*, vol. 95, no. 2 (April 2001): 335–341.

Choo, Christine. *Mission Girls. Aboriginal Women on Catholic Missions in the Kimberley, Western Australia, 1900–1950*. Crawley: University of Western Australia Press, 2001.

Clare, M. *Karobran. The Story of an Aboriginal Girl.* Chippendale: Alternative Publishing Cooperative Limited, 1978.

Clark, Anna. *History's Children: History Wars in the Classroom.* Sydney: UNSW Press, 2008.

Clarke, Una. *Things Are So Much Better than They Used to Be. My Memoirs.* Australia: Self-published, 1992.

Clements, Theresa. *From Old Maloga (The Memoirs of an Aboriginal Woman).* Prahran: Fraser & Morphet, 1930.

Cohen, Patsy and Margaret Somerville. *Ingelba and the Five Black Matriarchs.* North Sydney: Allen & Unwin, 1990.

Cohen, Stanley. *States of Denial. Knowing about Atrocities and Suffering.* Cambridge: Polity, 2001.

Cole, Christine A. ed. *Releasing the Past: Mothers' Stories of Their Stolen Babies.* Bondi: NSW Committee on Adoption and Permanent Care, 2008.

Commonwealth of Australia. "Aboriginal Welfare." Initial Conference of Commonwealth and State Aboriginal Authorities, held at Canberra, 21st to 23rd April 1937. Accessed 16 December 2019. https://aiatsis.gov.au/sites/default/files/catalogue_resources/20663.pdf.

———. "Final Report of the Referendum Council." Accessed 23 September 2019. https://www.referendumcouncil.org.au/sites/default/files/report_attachments/Referendum_Council_Final_Report.pdf.

———. "Find & Connect. History & Information about Australian Orphanages, Children's Homes & Other Institutions." Find & Connect Web Resource Project. Accessed 5 November 2015. http://www.findandconnect.gov.au.

Conor, Liz. "'Black Velvet' and 'Purple Indignation': Print Responses to Japanese 'Poaching' of Aboriginal Women." *Aboriginal History*, vol. 37 (2013): 51–76. http://doi.org/10.22459/AH.37.2013.

Cowlishaw, Gillian. "Infanticide in Aboriginal Australia." *Oceania*, vol. 48, no. 4 (June 1978): 262–283.

Crawford, Evelyn, as told to Chris Walsh. *Over My Tracks.* Ringwood: Penguin, 1993.

Cripps, Kylie. "Indigenous Children's 'Best Interests' at the Crossroads: Citizenship Rights, Indigenous Mothers and Child Protection Authorities." *International Journal of Critical Indigenous Studies*, vol. 5, no. 2 (2012): 25–35.

Cummings, Barbara. *Take This Child . . . From Kahlin Compound to the Retta Dixon Children's Home.* Canberra: Aboriginal Studies Press, 1990.

Cuthbert, Denise. "Stolen Children, Invisible Mothers and Unspeakable Stories: The Experiences of Non-Aboriginal Adoptive and Foster Mothers of Aboriginal Children." *Social Semiotics*, vol. 11, no. 2 (2001): 139–154.

Cuthbert, Denise and Marian Quartly. "'Forced Adoption' in the Australian Story of National Regret and Apology." *Australian Journal of Politics and History*, no. 1 (2012): 82–96.

Davis, Megan. "Moment of Truth: Correspondence." *Quarterly Essay*, no. 70 (2018): 81–91.

Dewar, Mickey. "The Literary Construction of 'Half-Caste' in the 1930s: Gender, Sexuality and Race in the Northern Territory." In *Connection and Disconnection: encounters between settlers and Indigenous people in the Northern Territory*, edited by Tony Austin and Suzanne Parry, 177–204. Darwin: NTU Press, 1998.

Docker, John. "Recasting Sally Morgan's *My Place*: The Fictionality of Identity and the Phenomenology of the Converso." *Humanities Research*, vol. 1 (1998): 3–22. http://doi.org/10.22459/HR.01.1998.

Dodson, Mick. "National Inquiry into the Separation of Aboriginal and Torres Strait Islander Children from Their Families." Accessed 17 August 2017. https://www.humanrights.gov.au/news/speeches/site-navigation-56.

Dow Coral. "Sorry: The Unfinished Business of the Bringing Them Home Report." *Parliament of Australia*. Accessed 19 May 2019. https://www.aph.gov.au/About_

Parliament/Parliamentary_Departments/Parliamentary_Library/pubs/BN/0708/
BringingThemHomeReport#_ftn27.

Drake-Brockman, Judith. *Wongi Wongi: To Speak*. Carlisle, WA: Hesperian Press, 2001.

Eades, Diane. *Courtroom Talk and Neocolonial Control*. Berlin: Mouton de Gruyter, 2008.

Edmund, Mabel. *No Regrets*. St Lucia: University of Queensland Press, 1992.

Ellinghaus, Katherine. *Taking Assimilation to Heart. Marriages of White Women and Indigenous Men in the United States and Australia, 1887–1937*. Lincoln: University of Nebraska Press, 2006.

Fannin, Maria. "Labour Pain, 'Natal Politics' and Reproductive Justice for Black Birth Givers." *Body & Society*, vol. 25, no. 3 (2019): 22–48.

Feldman, Martha S., Kaj Skoldberg, Ruth Nicole Brown and Debra Horner. "Making Sense of Stories: A Rhetorical Approach to Narrative Analysis." *Journal of Public Administration Research and Theory*, vol. 14, no. 2 (2004): 147–170.

Felman, Shoshana and Dori Laub. *Testimony. Crises of Witnessing in Literature, Psychoanalysis, and History*. London: Routledge, 1992.

Fernandez, Elizabeth, Jung-Sook Lee, Hazel Blunden, Patricia McNamara, Szilvia Kovacs and Paul-Auguste Cornefert. *No Child Should Grow Up Like This: Identifying Long Term Outcomes of Forgotten Australians, Child Migrants and the Stolen Generations*. Kensington: University of New South Wales, 2016.

Foucault, Michel. "Method." In *The History of Sexuality. An Introduction*, vol. 1, 92–102. New York: Pantheon Books, 1978.

Franke, Katherine M. "Gendered Subjects of Transitional Justice." *Columbia Journal of Gender and Law*, vol. 15, no. 3 (2006): 813–828.

Frow, John. "A Politics of Stolen Time." *Meanjin*, vol. 57, no. 2 (1998): 351–367.

Gelder, Ken. "Aboriginal Narrative and Property." *Meanjin*, vol. 50, no. 2/3 (Winter-Spring 1991): 353–365.

Georges, Nick, Steven L. Guthridge, Shu Quin Li, John R. Condon, Tony Barnes, and Yuejen Zhao, "Progress in Closing the Gap in Life Expectancy at Birth for Aboriginal People in the Northern Territory, 1967–2012." *The Medical Journal of Australia*, vol. 207, no. 1 (2017): 25–30. doi: 10.5694/mja16.01138.

Gigliotti, Simone. "Unspeakable Pasts as Limit Events: The Holocaust, Genocide, and the Stolen Generations." *Australian Journal of Politics and History*, vol. 49, no. 2 (2003): 164–181.

Gillard, Julia. "National Apology for Forced Adoptions." *Commonwealth of Australia*. Accessed 15 January 2015. https://www.ag.gov.au/About/ForcedAdoptionsApology/Documents/Nationalapologyforforcedadoptions.PDF.

Gilligan, Carol. *In a Different Voice. Psychological Theory and Women's Development*. Cambridge, MA: Harvard University Press, 1982.

Gladstone News Weekly. "A Life Spent Serving Children and Others." *Gladstone News Weekly (Our Community)*, August 27, 2011. http://www.gladstonenews.com.au/pastissues/Issue252.pdf.

Goodall, Heather. "Assimilation Begins in the Home: The State and Aboriginal Women's Work as Mothers in New South Wales, 1900s to 1960s." In *Aboriginal Workers. Special Issues of Labour History*, edited by Ann McGrath and Kay Saunders, no. 69 (November 1995): 75–101.

———. "Challenging Voices: Tracing the Problematic Role of Testimony in Political Change." *Australian Literary Studies*, vol. 22, no. 4 (Oct 2006): 513–518.

———. *Invasion to Embassy. Land in Aboriginal Politics in New South Wales, 1770–1972*. St Leonards: Allen & Unwin, 1996.

———. "Too Early Yet or Not Soon Enough? Reflections on 'Sharing' Histories as Process." *Australian Historical Studies*, vol. 33, no. 118 (2002): 7–24.

———. "'Saving the Children.' Gender and the Colonisation of Aboriginal Children in NSW, 1788 to 1990." *Aboriginal Law Bulletin*, no. 20 (1990). http://www.austlii.edu.au/au/journals/AboriginalLB/1990/20.html.

Grandmothers Against Removals. "A Fundraiser for Grandmothers Against Removals." Accessed 20 May 2016. https://www.facebook.com/events/986438714773927/.

Greenfield, Susan C. "Introduction." In *Inventing Maternity. Politics, Science and Literature, 1650–1865*, edited by Susan C. Greenfield & Carol Barash, 1–33. Lexington: The University Press of Kentucky, 1999.

Grimshaw, Patricia, Marilyn Lake, Ann McGrath, and Marian Quartly. *Creating a Nation*. Ringwood: McPhee Gribble, 1994.

Guilliatt, Richard. "Their Day in Court." *The Sydney Morning Herald*, 20 November 1999. http://www.smh.com.au/national/their-day-in-court-20130526-2n51u.html.

Haebich, Anna. *Broken Circles. Fragmenting Indigenous Families 1800–2000*. Fremantle: Fremantle Arts Centre Press, 2000.

Haskins, Victoria. "'Could You See to the Return of My Daughter': Fathers and Daughters under the New South Wales Aborigines Protection Board Child Removal Policy." *Australian Historical Studies*, vol. 34, no. 121 (2008): 106–121.

Hegarty, Ruth. *Bittersweet Journey*. St Lucia: University of Queensland Press, 2003.

———. *Is That You, Ruthie?* St Lucia: University of Queensland Press, 1999.

Herman, Judith. *Trauma and Recovery. The Aftermath of Violence—From Domestic Abuse to Political Terror*. New York: Basic Books, 1992.

hooks, b. *Yearning: Race, Gender, and Cultural Politics*. Boston: South End Press, 1990.

Huggins, Rita and Jackie Huggins. *Auntie Rita*. Canberra: Aboriginal Studies Press, 1996.

Human Rights and Equal Opportunity Commission. *Bringing Them Home. Report of the National Inquiry into the Separation of Aboriginal and Torres Strait Islander Children from Their Families*. Sydney: Commonwealth of Australia, 1997.

———. "The National Inquiry into the Separation of Aboriginal and Torres Strait Islander Children from Their Families, Bringing Them Home." Accessed 18 April 2016. http://humanrights.gov.au/sites/default/files/content/pdf/social_justice/submissions_un_hr_committee/6_stolen_generations.pdf.

———. "Submission to the Senate Legal and Constitutional References Committee's Inquiry into the Stolen Generation." Accessed 10 May 2016. https://www.humanrights.gov.au/sites/default/files/content/pdf/social_justice/stolen_senate_submission.pdf.

Independent Review of Aboriginal Children and Young People in OOHC. *Family Is Culture Report 2019*. https://www.familyisculture.nsw.gov.au/__data/assets/pdf_file/0011/726329/Family-Is-Culture-Review-Report.pdf.

Janeway, Elizabeth. *Powers of the Weak*. New York: Alfred A. Knopf, 1980.

Joint Select Committee on Constitutional Recognition Relating to Aboriginal and Torres Strait Islander Peoples. *Final Report*, Commonwealth of Australia, 2018. Viewed 7 April 2020. https://www.aph.gov.au/Parliamentary_Business/Committees/Joint/Former_Committees/Constitutional_Recognition_2018/ConstRecognition/Final_Report.

Jopson, Debra. "A Real Nowhere Man." *The Sydney Morning Herald*, August 26, 2005. http://www.smh.com.au/news/national/a-real-nowhere-man/2005/08/25/1124562981265.html.

Kartinyeri, Doris E. *Kick the Tin*. North Melbourne: Spinifex Press, 2000.

Kennedy, Marnie. *Born a Half-Caste*. Canberra: Australian Institute of Aboriginal Studies, 1985.

Kennedy, Roseanne and Tikka Jan Wilson. "Constructing Shared Histories: Stolen Generations Testimony, Narrative Therapy and Address." In *World Memory. Personal Trajectories in Global Time*, edited by Jill Bennett and Roseanne Kennedy, 119–139. New York: Palgrave MacMillan, 2003.

Kidd, Rosalind. *The Way We Civilise. Aboriginal Affairs—The Untold Story*. St Lucia: University of Queensland Press, 1997.

Konishi, Shino. "The Four Fathers of Australia: Baz Luhrmann's Depiction of Aboriginal History and Paternity in the Northern Territory." *History Australia*, vol. 8, no. 1 (2011): 23–41.

Krog, Antjie. *Country of My Skull. Guilt, Sorrow, and the Limits of Forgiveness in the New South Africa*. New York: Three Rivers Press, 2000.

Krog, Antjie, Nosisi Mpolweni-Zantsi and Kopano Ratele. "The South African Truth and Reconciliation Commission (TRC): Ways of Knowing Mrs Konile." In *Handbook of Critical and Indigenous Methodologies*, edited by Norman K. Denzin, Yvonna S. Lincoln, and Linda Tuhiwai Smith, 531–545. Thousand Oaks, CA: Sage, 2008.

Ladner, Joyce A. "Introduction to Tomorrow's Tomorrow. The Black Woman." In *Feminism and Methodology*, edited by Sandra Harding, 74–83. Bloomington: Indiana University Press, 1987.

Lake, Marilyn. *Getting Equal. The History of Australian Feminism*. Sydney: Allen & Unwin, 1999.

———. "A Revolution in the Family: The Challenge and Contradictions of Maternal Citizenship in Australia." In *Mothers of a New World. Maternalist Politics and the Origins of Welfare States*, edited by Seth Koven & Sonya Michel, 378–395. New York: Routledge, 1993.

Langer, Lawrence L. "The Dilemma of Choice in the Deathcamps." *Centrepoint: A Journal of Interdisciplinary Studies*, vol. 4, no. 1 (Fall 1980): 222–231.

Langford, Ruby. *Don't Take Your Love to Town*. Ringwood: Penguin Books, 1988.

Lugosi, Nicole V. T. "'Truth-Telling' and Legal Discourse: A Critical Analysis of the Neil Stonechild Inquiry." *Canadian Journal of Political Science*, vol. 44, no. 2 (2011): 299–315.

Macleod, Colin. *Patrol in the Dreamtime*. Rockhampton: Central Queensland University Press, 2003.

Malinowski, Bronislaw. *The Family Among the Australian Aborigines. A Sociological Study*. London: University of London Press, 1913.

Malkki, Liisa H. "Speechless Emissaries. Refugees, Humanitarianism, and Dehistoricization." In *Siting Culture. The Shifting Anthropological Object*, edited by Karen Fog Olwig and Kirsten Hastrup, 223–254. London: Routledge, 1997.

Manjoo, Rashida. "Gender Injustice and the South African Truth and Reconciliation Commission." In *Gendered Peace. Women's Struggles for Post-War Justice and Reconciliation*, edited by Donna Pankhurst, 137–154. London: Routledge, 2008.

Manne, Robert. "Aboriginal Child Removal and the Question of Genocide, 1900–1940." In *Genocide and Settler Society. Frontier Violence and Stolen Indigenous Children in Australian History*, edited by Dirk A. Moses, 217–243. New York: Berghahn Books, 2004.

———. *In Denial. The Stolen Generations and the Right*. Melbourne: Black Inc., 2001.

Marchetti, Elena and Janet Ransley. "Unconscious Racism: Scrutinizing Judicial Reasoning in 'Stolen Generation' Cases." *Social & Legal Studies*, vol. 14, no. 4 (2005): 533–552.

Markus, Andrew. "Legislating White Australia, 1900–1970." In *Sex, Power and Justice. Historical Perspectives of Law in Australia*, edited by Diane Kirkby, 237–251. Melbourne: Oxford University Press, 1995.

McCaslin, Wanda D. and Denise C. Breton. "Justice as Healing. Going Outside the Colonizers' Cage." In *Handbook of Critical and Indigenous Methodologies*, edited by Norman K. Denzin, Yvonna S. Lincoln & Linda Tuhiwai Smith, 511–529. Thousand Oaks, CA: Sage, 2008.

McConnochie, Keith, David Hollinsworth and Jan Pettman. *Race and Racism in Australia*. Wentworth Falls: Social Science Press, 1988.

McCorquodale, John. "The Legal Classification of Race in Australia." *Aboriginal History*, vol. 10, no. 1 (1986): 7–24.

McDonald, Connie Nungulla with Beryl Stirling. *Finding Myself*. Ourimbah: Bookbound Publishing, 2007.

McDonald, Connie Nungulla with Jill Finnane. *When You Grow Up*. Broome: Magabala Books, 1996.

McGee-Sippel, Lorraine. *Hey Mum, What's a Half-Caste?* Broome: Magabala Books, 2009.

McGregor, Russell. "Governance, not Genocide. Aboriginal Assimilation in the Postwar Era." In *Genocide and Settler Society. Frontier Violence and Stolen Indigenous Chil-*

dren in Australian History, edited by Dirk A. Moses, 290–306. New York: Berghahn Books, 2004.

McKenna, Mark. "Moment of Truth: History and Australia's Future." *Quarterly Essay,* no. 69 (2008).

Mellor, Doreen and Anna Haebich, eds. *Many Voices. Reflections on Experiences of Indigenous Child Separation.* Canberra: National Library of Australia, 2002.

Mertus, Julie. "Truth in a Box: The Limits of Justice through Judicial Mechanisms." In *The Politics of Memory: Truth, Healing and Social Justice,* edited by Ifi Amadiume and Abdullahi An-Na'im, 142–161. London: Zed Books, 2000.

Mok, Jeannie. *Cherbourg Dorm Girls.* Fortitude Valley: Multicultural Community Centre, 2005.

Moreton-Robinson, Aileen. "When the Object Speaks, A Postcolonial Encounter: Anthropological Representations and Aboriginal Women's Self-Presentations." *Discourse: Studies in the Cultural Politics of Education,* vol. 19, no. 3 (July 2007): 275–289.

Morgan, Sally. *My Place,* Fremantle: Fremantle Arts Centre Press, 1987.

Mum Shirl with the assistance of Bobbi Sykes. *Mum Shirl. An Autobiography.* Richmond, VA: Heinemann, 1981.

Nakata, Martin. *Disciplining the Savages: Savaging the Disciplines.* Canberra: Aboriginal Studies Press, 2007.

Nannup, Alice, Lauren Marsh, and Stephen Kinnane. *When the Pelican Laughed.* South Fremantle: Fremantle Arts Centre Press, 1992.

National Library of Australia. "Bringing Them Home Oral History Project." Accessed 21 August, 2015. http://nla.gov.au/nla.cat-vn833081.

National Museum of Australia. "1908: Legislation Introduction National Age and Invalid Pensions." Accessed 18 December 2015. http://www.nma.gov.au/online_features/defining_moments/featured/age_and_invalid_pensions.

Nesiah, Vasuki. "Discussion Lines on Gender and Transitional Justice: An Introductory Essay Reflecting on the ICTJ Bellagio Workshop on Gender and Transitional Justice." *Columbia Journal of Gender and Law,* vol. 15, no. 3 (2006): 799–812.

———. "Gender and Truth Commission Mandates." International Centre for Transitional Justice. Accessed 14 June 2010. http://www.ictj.org/static/Gender/0602.GenderTRC.eng.pdf.

New South Wales Department of Communities and Justice. "The Adoption Process for Birth Parents." Accessed 3 February 2020. https://www.facs.nsw.gov.au/families/adoption/birth-parents/the-process/chapters/before-consent.

———. "Written Information on Adoption. Additional Information for Parents of an Aboriginal Child." Accessed 3 February 2020. https://www.facs.nsw.gov.au/download?file=349075.

Oguro, Susan, Anne Maree Payne and Sally Varnham. "Integrating Human Rights Education into Schools: Legislation, Curriculum and Practice." *International Journal of Law & Education,* vol. 20, no. 1 (2015): 5–19.

O'Neill, Cate. "Child Endowment Act 1941." Find & Connect. History & information about Australian orphanages, children's homes & other institutions. Accessed 17 December 2015. http://www.findandconnect.gov.au/ref/australia/biogs/FE00090b.htm.

O'Reilly, Andrea. *Toni Morrison and Motherhood: A Politics of the Heart.* Albany: State University of New York Press, 2004.

Orford, Anne. "Commissioning the Truth." *Columbia Journal of Gender and Law,* vol. 15, no. 3 (2006): 851–882.

Oscar, June. "June Oscar's 2020 Vision: Reaching Our Potential as a Nation Begins with Truth-Telling." *The Guardian.* January 31, 2020. https://www.theguardian.com/australia-news/2020/jan/31/june-oscars-2020s-vision-reaching-our-potential-as-a-nation-begins-with-truth-telling.

Paisley, Fiona. "Feminist Challenges to White Australia, 1900–1930s." In *Sex, Power and Justice. Historical Perspectives of Law in Australia,* edited by Diane Kirkby, 252–269. Melbourne: Oxford University Press, 1995.

Pankhurst, Donna. "Introduction." In *Gendered Peace. Women's Struggles for Post-War Justice and Reconciliation,* edited by Donna Pankhurst, 1–30. London: Routledge 2008.

Parry, Naomi. "'Such a Longing': Black and White Children in Welfare in New South Wales and Tasmania, 1880–1940." PhD diss., University of New South Wales, 2007.

Payne, Anne Maree. "'For All of Us, For None of You': Practical Reconciliation." In *Does the Media Fail Aboriginal Political Aspirations? 45 Years of Media Reporting of Key Political Moments,* edited by Amy Thomas, Andrew Jakubowicz, and Heidi Norman, 138–155. Canberra: Department of Aboriginal Affairs and Aboriginal Studies Press, 2019.

———. "'To the Exclusion of the Rights of the Mother': Legal Barriers to Aboriginal Mothering in the Stolen Generations Era." *Law & History,* vol. 7, no. 1 (2020): 123–165.

———. "Untold Suffering? Motherhood and the Stolen Generations." PhD Thesis, University of Technology Sydney, 2016. https://opus.lib.uts.edu.au/bitstream/10453/90276/6/01front.pdf.

Pettman, Jan. *Living in the Margins. Racism, Sexism and Feminism in Australia.* North Sydney: Allen & Unwin, 1992.

———. "Racism, Sexism and Sociology." In *Intersexions. Gender/Class/Culture/Ethnicity,* edited by Gill Bottomley, Marie de Lepervanche and Jeannie Martin, 187–202. North Sydney: Allen & Unwin, 1991.

Pettman, Jan Jindy. "Race, Ethnicity and Gender in Australia." In *Unsettling Settler Societies. Articulations of Gender, Race, Ethnicity and Class,* edited by Daiva Stasiulis and Nira Yuval-Davis, 65–93. London: Sage, 1995.

Pieper Mooney, Jadwiga E. *The Politics of Motherhood. Maternity and Women's Rights in Twentieth-Century Chile.* Pittsburgh: University of Pittsburgh Press, 2009.

Pilkington, Doris. *Follow the Rabbit-Proof Fence.* St Lucia: University of Queensland Press, 1996.

———. *Under the Wintamarra Tree.* St Lucia: University of Queensland Press, 2002.

Pilkington, Doris, interviewed by Anne Brewster. "The Stolen Generations: Rites of Passage: Doris Pilkington Interviewed by Anne Brewster." *Journal of Commonwealth Literature,* vol. 42, no. 1 (2007): 143–159.

Poff, Deborah C. "The Importance of Story-Telling: Research Protocols in Aboriginal Communities." *Journal of Empirical Research on Human Research Ethics,* vol. 1, no. 3 (2006): 27–28.

Probyn, Fiona. "The White Father: Denial, Paternalism and Community." *Cultural Studies Review,* vol. 9, no. 1 (2003): 60–76.

Read, Peter. "Clio or Janus? Historians and the Stolen Generations." *Australian Historical Studies,* vol. 33, no. 118 (2002): 54–60.

———, ed. *Down There with Me on the Cowra Mission. An Oral History of Erambie Aboriginal Reserve, Cowra, New South Wales.* Sydney: Pergamon Press, 1984.

———. "How Many Separated Children?" *Australian Journal of Politics and History,* vol. 49, no. 2 (2003): 155–163.

———. *A Rape of the Soul So Profound. The Return of the Stolen Generations.* St. Leonards: Allen & Unwin, 1999.

———. *The Stolen Generations: The Removal of Aboriginal Children in New South Wales 1883 to 1969.* Occasional Paper (no. 1). Sydney: New South Wales Ministry of Aboriginal Affairs, 1981.

———. *Tripping Over Feathers. Scenes in the Life of Joy Janaka Wiradjuri Williams. A Narrative of the Stolen Generations.* Crawley, Western Australia: UWA Publishing, 2009.

Reconciliation Australia. "Truth-Telling about the Past, the Present and the Future." Accessed 10 October 2018. https://www.reconciliation.org.au/truth-telling-about-the-past-the-present-and-the-future/.

Reys, Shelley. "Unfinished Business—Reparations and Reconciliation." Australian Human Rights Commission. 14 December 2012. https://humanrights.gov.au/our-work/aboriginal-and-torres-strait-islander-social-justice/unfinished-business-reparations-and.

Rich, Adrienne. *Of Woman Born. Motherhood as Experience and Institution*. London: Virago, 1977.

Rintoul, Stuart. "The Dispossession of Lowitja O'Donoghue." In *The Best Australian Essays 2001*, edited by Peter Craven, 106–116. Melbourne: Black Inc., 2001.

———. *The Wailing. A National Black Oral History*. Melbourne: William Heineman, 1993.

Roberts, Dorothy E. "Racism and Patriarchy in the Meaning of Motherhood." In *Mothers in Law. Feminist Theory and the Legal Regulation of Motherhood*, edited by Martha Albertson Fineman and Isabel Karpin, 224–249. New York: Columbia University Press, 1995.

———. *Shattered Bonds. The Color of Child Welfare*. New York: Basic Civitas Books, 2002.

Rolls, Mitchell. "The Changing Politics of Miscegenation." *Aboriginal History*, vol. 29 (2005): 64–76. http://doi.org/10.22459/AH.29.2011.

Rorty, Richard. "Human Rights, Rationality, and Sentimentality." *Headline Series*, no. 318 (Winter 1998): 116–126.

Ross, Fiona C. *Bearing Witness. Women and the Truth and Reconciliation Commission in South Africa*. London: Pluto Press, 2003.

Roughsey, Elsie (Labumore). *An Aboriginal Mother Tells of the Old and the New*. Fitzroy: McPhee Gribble, 1984.

Rowley, Charles D. *Outcasts in White Australia. Aboriginal Policy and Practice—Volume II*. Canberra: Australian National University Press, 1971.

Rubio-Marín, Ruth. "What Happened to the Women? Gender and Reparations for Human Rights Violations." *Advancing Transitional Justice Series*, no. 1. New York: International Center for Transitional Justice, Social Science Research Council, 2006.

Rudd, Kevin. "Apology to Australia's Indigenous Peoples." Australian Government. Accessed 15 January 2016. http://www.australia.gov.au/about-australia/our-country/our-people/apology-to-australias-indigenous-peoples.

Ruddick, Sara. *Maternal Thinking. Towards a Politics of Peace*. London: The Women's Press, 1989.

Russell, Lynette. "'Dirty Domestics and Worse Cooks': Aboriginal Women's Agency and Domestic Frontiers, Southern Australia, 1800–1850." *Frontiers: A Journal of Women Studies*, vol. 28, no. 1 and 2 (2007): 18–46.

Sanger, Carol. "Mother from Child: Perspectives on Separation and Abandonment." In *Mothers in Law. Feminist Theory and the Legal Regulation of Motherhood*, edited by Martha Albertson Fineman and Isabel Karpin, 27–42. New York: Columbia University Press, 1995.

Scarry, Elaine. *The Body in Pain. The Making and Unmaking of the World*. Oxford: Oxford University Press, 1985.

Scott, Joan W. "The Evidence of Experience." *Critical Inquiry*, vol. 17, no. 4 (Summer 1991): 773–797.

Scott, Shirley. "Why Wasn't Genocide a Crime in Australia? Accounting for the Half-Century Delay in Australia Implementing the Genocide Convention." *Australian Journal of Human Rights*, vol. 10, no. 1 (June 2004): 159–178.

Secretariat of National Aboriginal and Islander Child Care. "Sorry Business." Accessed 9 December 2015. http://www.supportingcarers.snaicc.org.au/connecting-to-culture/sorry-business/.

Senate Community Affairs References Committee. "Commonwealth Contribution to Former Forced Adoption Policies and Practices." Commonwealth of Australia. Accessed 1 June 2016. http://www.aph.gov.au/Parliamentary_Business/Committees/Senate/Community_Affairs/Completed_inquiries/2010-13/commcontribformerforcedadoption/report/index

Shaw, Danny. "Myths and Facts about Aborigines and Social Security." *Indigenous Law Bulletin*, vol. 4, no. 19 (March 1999): 20–21.

Simkin, Emma. "Debate Rages Over Stolen Generations Phrase." In *PM*, edited by Mark Colvin, *Australian Broadcasting Corporation*, 2001. https://www.abc.net.au/pm/stories/s251005.htm.

Simon, Ella. *Through My Eyes*. Melbourne: Rigby Ltd, 1978.

Stack, Carol B. *All Our Kin. Strategies for Survival in a Black Community*. New York: Harper & Row, 1974.

Stasiulis, Davia and Nira Yuval-Davis. "Introduction: Beyond Dichotomies—Gender, Race, Ethnicity and Class in Settler Societies." In *Unsettling Settler Societies. Articulations of Gender, Race, Ethnicity and Class*, edited by Davia Stasiulis and Nira Yuval-Davis, 1–38. London: Sage, 1995.

Steering Committee for the Review of Government Service Provision. *Overcoming Indigenous Disadvantage. Key Indicators 2020 Report*. Productivity Commission, Canberra. https://www.pc.gov.au/research/ongoing/overcoming-indigenous-disadvantage/2020/report-documents/oid-2020-overcoming-indigenous-disadvantage-key-indicators-2020-report.pdf.

Stephens, Tony. "Mother's Regret Carried to Grave." *The Sydney Morning Herald*, February 13, 2008. https://www.smh.com.au/news/national/mothers-regret-carried-to-grave/2008/02/12/1202760301397.html.

Swain, Shurlee. "History of Child Protection Legislation." Royal Commission into Institutional Responses to Child Sexual Abuse. Accessed 9 September 2015. http://www.childabuseroyalcommission.gov.au/documents/published-research/historical-perspectives-report-1-history-of-instit.pdf.

Swain, Shurlee and Margot Hillel. *Child, Nation, Race and Empire. Child Rescue Discourse, England, Canada and Australia, 1850–1915*. Manchester: Manchester University Press, 2010.

The Sydney Morning Herald. "Daughter Dies with Her Story Still Incomplete." *The Sydney Morning Herald*, January 15, 2004. https://www.smh.com.au/national/daughter-dies-with-her-story-still-incomplete-20040115-gdi5s5.html.

Terszak, Mary. *Orphaned by the Colour of My Skin. A Stolen Generation Story*. Maleny Qld: Verdant House, 2008.

Truth and Reconciliation Commission of Canada. *They Came for the Children. Canada, Aboriginal Peoples, and Residential Schools*. Winnipeg: Truth and Reconciliation Commission of Canada, 2012.

Tucker, Margaret. *If Everyone Cared. Autobiography of Margaret Tucker, M.B.E.* South Melbourne: Grosvenor, 1977.

Tuhiwai Smith, Linda. *Decolonizing Methodologies. Research and Indigenous Peoples*. 2nd ed. London: Zed Books, 2012.

Ungunmerr-Baumann, Miriam-Rose. "Dadirri. Inner Deep Listening and Quiet Still Awareness." Emmaus Productions. Accessed 11 May 2016. http://www.dadirri.org.au/wp-content/uploads/2015/03/Dadirri-Inner-Deep-Listening-M-R-Ungunmerr-Bauman-Refl1.pdf.

van Krieken, Robert. "Rethinking Cultural Genocide: Aboriginal Child Removal and Settler-Colonial State Formation." *Oceania*, vol. 75, no. 2 (December 2004): 125–151.

Vatan, Florence, and Marc Silberman. "After the Violence: Memory." In *Memory and Postwar Memorials: Confronting the Violence of the Past*, edited by Marc Silberman and Florence Vatan, 1–14. Basingstoke: Palgrave Macmillan, 2013.

Vicenti, Heather and Deborah Dickman. *Too Many Tears. An Autobiographical Account of Stolen Generations*. St Albans, Aus.: Meme Media, 2008.

Walker, Della. *Me and You. The Life Story of Della Walker as Told to Tina Coutts*. Canberra: Aboriginal Studies Press, 1989.

Ward, Glenyse. *Unna You Fullas*. Broome: Magabala Books, 1991.

———. *Wandering Girl*. Broome: Magabala Books, 1987.

Wesley-Esquimaux, Cynthia C. and Magdalena Smolewski. "Historic Trauma and Aboriginal Healing." Aboriginal Healing Foundation. Accessed 9 May 2012. http://www.ahf.ca/downloads/historic-trauma.pdf.

West, Ida. *Pride Against Prejudice. Reminiscences of a Tasmanian Aborigine.* Canberra: Australian Institute of Aboriginal Studies, 1987.

Williams, Edna Tantjingu and Eileen Wani Wingfield. *Down the Hole, Up the Tree, across the Sandhills . . . Running from the State and Daisy Bates.* Alice Springs: Jukurrpa Books, 2000.

Wilson, Richard. *The Politics of Truth and Reconciliation in South Africa: Legitimizing the Post-Apartheid State.* Cambridge: Cambridge University Press, 2001.

Windschuttle, Keith. *The Fabrication of Aboriginal History.* Sydney: Macleay Press, 2009.

Wolfe, Patrick. "Settler Colonialism and the Elimination of the Native." *Journal of Genocide Research*, vol. 8, no. 4 (2006): 387–409.

Woodrow, Marjorie. *One of the Lost Generation.* Narromine NSW: Self-published, 1990.

Woollacott, Angela. *Gender and Empire.* London: Palgrave, 2006.

Young, James E. *Writing and Rewriting the Holocaust. Narrative and the Consequences of Interpretation.* Bloomington: Indiana University Press, 1988.

Index

Aboriginal Child Placement Principle, 99, 163, 164

Aboriginal child removal: contemporary removals, 163–165, 168n2; difference between Aboriginal and non-Aboriginal child removals, 5, 58, 59, 67, 71, 96, 125; due to death or illness of parent, 95, 108; due to education, 36, 63, 90, 102, 123, 124, 130–133; due to "half-caste" status, 5, 58, 63, 64, 124–128, 136n48; due to mission policy, 85, 86–88; due to perceptions of neglect, 5, 11–12, 58, 68, 75, 85–86, 90, 91, 93, 99–104, 111, 117, 124, 125, 126, 127, 131, 134, 151, 164, 166; due to the requirement for mothers to work, 3, 11, 75, 77–81, 82, 149; fear of, 11, 82, 85, 88–90; gendered removal of Aboriginal girls, 13, 57, 63, 107, 129, 172; intergenerational impacts of, 19, 45, 162, 163; interstate, 63, 132–133; intra-family removal, 145–146; powerlessness of Aboriginal parents to prevent, 37, 57, 60, 80, 81, 85, 88, 110–111, 117, 143, 147–148; racial discrimination in, 125–126

Aboriginal children's homes, 44, 58, 62, 105, 130, 147; The Bungalow, 122; Colebrook Home, 53; Cootamundra Girls' Home, 157n17; Kinchela Boys' Home, 157n17; Oodnadatta Children's Home, 133; Retta Dixon Home, 78, 105, 131; St Mary's Hostel, 131–132; Sister Kate's Children's Cottage Home, 23, 96, 143, 149, 151

Aboriginal families, state intervention in, 3, 36, 63, 81, 82, 90, 108, 163, 164

Aboriginal missions and reserves, 4, 11, 68, 69, 71, 74, 77, 78, 79, 85, 86, 88, 94, 97, 103, 109, 110, 121, 128, 129, 130, 132, 133, 137n59, 142, 145, 161, 163; Brewarrina Mission, 88; Cherbourg Mission, 79–80, 101, 140–141; Cowra Mission, 85–86; Croker Island, 94, 101; Daintree Mission, 87, 101, 120, 121, 129; Doomadgee Mission, 87; Erambie Reserve, 85–86; Moore River Settlement, 88, 96, 132, 142–143, 149; Palm Island, 43, 86; Phillip Creek Mission, 107, 120, 123–124; Purfleet Mission, 66n51; Roelands Mission, 69, 96, 149; Umeewarra Mission, 101, 123; Yarrabah Mission, 87

Aboriginal parental rights, constraints on, 56–57; lack of judicial review, 60–61; legal guardianship status of, 3, 57, 58–60, 121

Aboriginal Protection Board, NSW, 56, 59, 60, 61, 62, 63, 66n51, 70–71, 86

Aboriginal protection legislation, impact of: Australian Capital Territory, 56, 61–62, 171; New South Wales, 56, 57, 58, 59, 60, 61–62, 63, 64, 65n31, 65n37, 65n42, 66n52, 171; Northern Territory, 4, 56, 58, 60, 61, 63, 64, 77, 171; Queensland, 4, 56, 58, 60, 61, 64, 171–172; South Australia, 4, 53, 56, 58, 61, 63, 64, 172; Tasmania, 4, 56, 60, 64; Victoria, 4, 56, 60, 61, 64, 172; Western Australia, 4, 56, 57, 58, 61, 63, 102, 172

Aboriginals Ordinance 1918 (NT), 63, 65n34

Aboriginals Ordinance 1953 (NT), 65n35

Aboriginals Preservation and Protection Act 1939 (Qld), 60

Aboriginal women's autobiographical narratives, 8, 15n39, 20, 34, 41, 42, 57, 60, 62, 66n51, 67, 69, 71, 72, 73–74, 79, 81, 88, 94, 96, 98, 104, 105, 108, 132, 134n1, 136n46, 139, 140, 142–144, 147, 148, 150, 151–152, 156, 167–168

Aborigines Act 1915 (Vic), 65n43

Aborigines Act Amendment Act 1911 (WA), 65n33

Aborigines Amendment Act 1939 (SA), 123

Aborigines Protection (Amendment) Act 1940 (NSW), 65n31, 66n52

Aborigines Protection (Amendment) Act 1943 (NSW), 63

Aborigines Protection Amending Act 1915 (NSW), 60, 65n37

Aboriginal Protection and Restriction of the Sale of Opium Act 1987 (Qld), 65n29

Aborigines Welfare Ordinance Act 1954 (ACT), 56, 66n52

adoption, 1, 5, 6, 14n25, 41, 42, 54, 60, 106, 110, 111, 119–120, 122, 123, 149, 150, 151, 162, 168n5; cross-cultural issues in, 98–99, 127

The Adoption of Children Act 1935 (Qld), 60

Agency of Aboriginal mothers, 48, 139, 141–142, 151

alcoholism as a factor in child removal, 44, 85–86, 104, 117

Alexander, John, 40, 50n44, 51n55, 173

anti-miscegenation, 10, 57

anti-natalism, 70

APB. *See* Aboriginal Protection Board, NSW

apologies, role of in transitional justice, 166, 168n5, 169n25

Apology to Australia's Indigenous Peoples, 13; impact of Howard government's refusal to apologise, 22, 153

apprenticeships, 58, 77

Arthur, Lily, viii, 119

assimilation, 4, 34, 63, 86, 96, 124, 136n33

"benefits" of removal to Aboriginal children, beliefs about, 12, 37, 109, 110, 118, 123, 130, 166

best interests of the child, perceptions of, 2, 12–13, 56, 99, 111, 118, 134, 145–146, 151, 163, 164

birth rate, decline in white, 57, 68

"blameless victims," the search for, 146, 165

Bloomfield, George, 104, 113n63, 114n64, 173

Bolt, Andrew, 14n27, 53, 125

Bowlby, John, 111, 162

Bringing Them Home Inquiry, vii, 1, 3, 5, 6, 11, 13n2, 13n4, 17–28, 36, 38, 43, 45, 99, 119, 124, 129, 140, 142, 145, 146, 161, 162; attacks on credibility of, 13n4, 25, 103

Bringing Them Home Report, vii, 1, 7, 13, 17, 18–19, 20, 22, 24, 25, 45, 54, 55, 56, 57, 77, 86, 103, 139, 141–142, 146, 162

Brown, Dawn, 47–48, 51n78, 173

certificate of exemption from Aboriginal Protection legislation, 68, 69

child abandonment, 41–42, 105–106

child abuse, 5, 12, 41, 45, 103, 107, 118, 134n5, 164

child maintenance payments, 61, 64, 149–150

child removal policies and practices, 2, 3, 4, 6, 8, 11, 13n2, 20, 21, 45, 81, 91, 141, 146, 149, 155, 168n5; Australian Capital Territory, 56, 61–62; New South Wales, 4, 56, 57, 58, 59, 61, 62, 63, 70, 85, 86, 88, 137n59; Northern Territory, 4, 56, 58, 60, 61, 62, 63, 71, 77, 78, 110, 114n98, 120, 132, 137n59; Queensland, 4, 56, 58, 60, 61, 64, 69, 70, 71, 86, 137n59; South Australia, 4, 53, 56, 58, 61, 63, 106, 119–120, 132; Tasmania, 4, 56, 60, 63, 64, 132; Victoria, 4, 56, 60, 61, 63, 98, 132, 137n59; Western Australia, 4, 56, 57,

58, 60–61, 63, 88, 102–103, 111, 132
"choiceless choices," 131, 140, 144, 149, 165
Clarke, Una, 58, 94, 101
Clements, Theresa, 15n39, 108
compensation for child removal, 24, 46, 55, 153, 154, 155
Conference of Commonwealth and State Aboriginal Authorities 1937, 72, 107
consent, 3, 11–12, 53–54, 56, 58, 64n1, 87, 91, 99, 117, 119–123, 131, 140, 149, 151, 166
Corunna, Daisy, 34–37, 149
Corunna, Gladys, 36–37, 73
cottage mothers, 94, 98, 101, 126
Cubillo and Gunner v. Commonwealth, 107
custody rights, 56, 58–60, 63, 117, 149, 151, 157n17

dadirri, 9, 154
Dexter, Barrie, 118, 130
Dodson, Mick (Michael), vii, 1, 18
domestic service, 35, 77, 132; impact on child removal, 36, 41, 77, 78, 79, 80, 145, 149
domestic violence and child removal, relationship between, 100, 117, 122, 125, 164
Doney, Daphne, 88, 91n21, 173
Donovan, Kathy, 51n57, 136n55, 156, 159n65, 173
Drake-Brockman, Alice, 36–37
Drake-Brockman, Judith, 50n35

Edmund, Mabel, 96
education: as a factor in child removal, 63, 80, 90, 102, 123, 124, 130–133, 151; standard provided to Aboriginal children in the Stolen Generations era, 12, 117, 130, 137n59
Edwards, Oomera (Coral), 104
eugenics, 10, 57
extended family, importance of in Aboriginal communities, 47, 68, 79, 94, 95, 97–98, 99, 100, 104, 146, 148, 152, 162

fatherhood, 3, 14n11
fathers, 3–4, 35, 37, 48, 62, 106, 119; Aboriginal fathers, 3–4, 14n11, 14n13, 109, 120, 122, 144, 147; adoptive and Foster fathers, 111, 127; white fathers of Aboriginal children, 3, 14n14, 53, 64, 73, 122, 149
Follow the Rabbit Proof Fence, 94, 142, 143
forced adoption, 5, 14n25, 14n26, 119, 162, 168n5
forcible removal, 3, 12, 13n2, 19, 20–21, 26, 37, 77, 86, 91, 99, 117, 123–124, 129, 140, 146, 161
foster-care arrangements, 19, 20, 58, 99, 142, 145, 151, 162
foster mothers, 44, 47, 101, 110, 132, 144, 151
foster parents, 43, 49, 63, 98, 101–102, 117, 151
Frail, Jackie, 50n41, 65n50, 99, 113n32, 173

Gare, Frank, 55, 61, 102, 103, 110, 111, 121, 123, 132
genocide, 13n2, 31, 118, 125; finding of the *Bringing Them Home* Inquiry, 5, 18, 19, 55, 99, 124, 129, 146; forcible transfer of children, 129, 146; Holocaust, 70, 140, 153, 155, 158n56; imposing measures to prevent live births, 129; Rwandan, 31; UN Convention on the Prevention and Punishment of the Crime of Genocide, 55, 124, 129
Goodall, Heather, 32, 53, 70–71, 86, 90, 137n59, 141
Gordon, Sue, 50n39, 154, 158n55, 173
Grandmothers Against Removals, 113n33, 163, 164

Haebich, Anna, 61, 68, 70, 71, 86, 88, 103, 108, 109
"half-caste," Aboriginal people classified as, 5, 10, 58, 63, 64, 69, 74–75, 96, 122; beliefs about acceptance of within Aboriginal communities, 107–109, 126–128;

white concerns about population growth of, 57, 68, 70, 129

Harris, Marjorie, 46, 51n71, 107, 114n82, 122, 135n19, 136n47, 173

healing the wounds of the past, 41, 83n22, 158n57, 167–168; role of speech in, 22, 25, 27, 31, 154–157, 165

Hegarty, Ruth, 15n39, 50n40, 74, 79–80, 140–141, 174

Heitmeyer, Deirdre, 29n40, 51n58, 90, 92n29, 99, 113n37, 153–154, 158n54, 162–163, 169n9, 174

Howard, John, 13n4, 22, 53, 64n3, 153

Huggins, Jackie, viii, 41

Huggins, Rita, 73, 79

human rights, 17, 18, 31, 32, 37, 54, 55, 141, 154, 161, 165, 166, 167; limitations of human rights inquiry processes, 1, 21, 21–28, 46, 48–49, 156, 162; parental rights, 21; rights of mothers, 162, 166, 167

Human Rights and Equal Opportunity Commission, 13n2, 18, 145

infant mortality, 70, 75n17, 109, 114n98

infanticide, beliefs about, 107–109. *See also* Aboriginal child removal

institutionalisation of Aboriginal children, 4, 71, 79–80, 88, 94–95, 96, 100, 133, 142, 145, 149

intergenerational trauma arising from child removal, 27, 90, 104, 163

Invalid and Old Age Pensions Act 1908 (Cth), 72

Kartinyeri, Doris, 15n39, 136n55, 174

Kelly, Molly, 82, 88, 142–143, 147

Kelly, Ryan, 15n29, 65n50, 174

Kendall, Carol, 22, 29n31, 50n21, 158n53, 174

Kidd, Rosalind, 69, 70, 71, 86, 101, 117, 137n59

Kinchela, Sharon, 44, 51n60, 100, 113n39, 125, 135n29, 174

Kinnear, Audrey Ngingali, 89, 91n22, 174

kinship networks, importance of, 35, 94, 95, 98

Lange, Barbara, 106, 114n74, 119–120, 135n10, 174

Langer, Lawrence, 140

Langford, Ruby, 15n39, 62, 105

Lees, Pattie, 43, 51n56, 65n50, 118–119, 135n6, 174

Link-Up NSW, 1, 9, 18, 39, 44

Macleod, Colin, 107, 110, 113n59, 114n79, 115n103, 126, 136n39, 136n40, 174

Madres de la Plaza de Mayo, 166

Manne, Robert, 13n4, 64n1

Marbach, Alice, 101–102, 110, 113n48, 115n102, 120, 121, 135n12, 135n15, 136n52, 174

maternal health, Aboriginal women's, 70, 114n98

maternity wards, discrimination in, 96–97

McEwan, Keith, 98, 111, 112n30, 115n105, 122, 127, 135n20, 135n21, 136n45, 174

McLennon, Lesley, 38, 42, 50n37, 51n52, 144, 157n20, 174

McMahon, Trudy (Gertrude), 46, 51n74, 95, 96, 105–106, 112n9, 114n72, 126, 136n37, 174

Meyer, Margaret Helen, 98, 112n31, 174

Mills, Yvonne, 23, 29n35, 50n38, 65n50, 167, 169n30, 174

miscegenation, concerns about, 10, 13, 57, 63

mission dormitories, 77, 79, 86, 97, 124, 161

Morgan, Sally, 15n39, 34, 35, 36–37, 41, 73

Moseley, Eileen, 125, 136n36, 147, 158n26, 175

motherhood, 1–2, 8, 10, 11, 13, 17, 67, 70, 81, 82, 97, 107, 109, 161, 164, 167; social construction of, 2

mothering, 1, 10, 47, 49, 64, 80–81, 88, 90–91, 111, 161; cultural differences in approaches to, 93–95, 105–106

Mullins, Annie, 78, 82n3, 82n4, 82n5, 82n6, 82n7, 87, 91n14, 136n46, 175

Mum Shirl, 15n39, 62, 81, 104, 105, 106, 143–144, 147, 157n17

My Place , 15n39, 34, 35, 36

Nannup, Alice, 15n39, 72, 73, 96–97, 132, 148, 167–168

"National Apology for Forced Adoptions," 168n5

National Library of Australia's *Bringing Them Home* Oral History project, viii, 6, 14n10, 16n59, 21, 22, 26, 40, 61, 95, 98, 105, 119, 139, 173–176

Native Administration Act 1936 (WA), 63

Native Welfare Act 1963 (WA), 102

Neary, Sylvia, 6, 15n30, 136n55, 156, 159n66, 175

neglect, perceptions of, 5, 11–12, 21, 58, 68, 75, 85–86, 90, 91, 93, 99–104, 107, 111, 117, 124, 125, 126, 127, 131, 134, 151, 164, 166

Neville, A. O., 107, 110, 121, 127

nomadic lifestyle, impact on child removal, 68, 69, 71, 72, 96, 102

nuclear family structure, attempts to impose on Aboriginal families, 86, 100

O'Donoghue, Lowitja (Lois), 53, 64n1

oral history, 6–7, 10, 17, 67, 85, 87, 155

An Ordinance for the Protection, Maintenance and Upbringing of Orphans and Other Destitute Children and Aborigines Act 1844 (SA), 65n28

Origins Forced Adoptions Support Network, viii, 119

Out of Home Care, 104, 134n5, 163

Ozies, Annie, 124, 135n27, 175

Parkerville Children's Home, 36, 37

patrol officers, accounts of role in Aboriginal child removal, 6, 61, 102, 107, 110, 117, 120–121, 126, 149–150

Pattemore, Mervyn, 78, 82n2, 107, 114n68, 114n80, 115n104, 120, 123–124, 131, 135n11, 135n25, 135n26, 137n61, 175

Penhall, Les (Leslie Newton), 29n42, 29n43, 51n72, 120, 121–122, 135n13, 136n41, 175

Perry, Darren, 41–42, 50n50, 175

Pilkington Garimari, Doris, 15n39, 82, 88, 94–95, 142–143, 168

police, accounts of role of in Aboriginal child removal, 6, 87, 89, 100, 101, 102, 121, 123, 126, 128, 140

Pritchard, Glynn, 132, 137n70, 175

Pyatt, Dorothy, 101, 104, 113n42, 114n69, 123, 135n23, 136n38, 175

rape/sexual assault, 32–34, 35, 49, 165. *See also* sexual abuse

Rabbit Proof Fence , 142

Read, Peter, 11, 35, 45, 50n22, 85, 134, 176

records: Aboriginal parents' access to, 106; concerns about accuracy of, 6, 7, 15n29, 38, 133; discovery of information held on, 43, 61

To Remove and Protect, 54

reproductive rights, attempts to restrict Aboriginal women's, 107, 129

restorative justice, 25, 27

retributive justice, 25, 26

Ronberg, Anne, 124, 135n28

Royal Commission into Aboriginal Deaths in Custody, 18

"Ruby," 33–34, 47, 48, 50n16, 50n17, 51n77, 57, 65n21, 65n22, 79, 80, 82n8, 82n9, 83n12, 89, 91n23, 140, 142, 145–146, 147, 148, 157n1, 157n9, 157n21, 157n22, 158n29, 176

Rudd, Kevin, 13

Ruddick, Sarah, 3, 117

Russell, Lynette, 109

Rutter, Bill, 88, 91n20, 175

Ryan, Japarta Maurie, 95, 112n11, 158n51, 175

segregation on the basis of race, 4, 18, 63, 90, 96–97

self-determination, 163

Senate Inquiry into the Stolen Generations, 13n3

sexual abuse, 12, 33, 45, 125, 129, 134n5, 165. *See also* rape/sexual assault

Sibley, Jean, 87, 91n15, 175

silence, 8, 27, 31; in Aboriginal English, 32, 46; cultural differences in use of, 32; due to denial, 153–154; due to sorry business and cultural obligations, 46; in human rights inquiry processes, 1, 32, 46; as an Indigenous knowledge-management strategy, 32; outlier accounts and, 23–24; use of as a coping mechanism within families, 37–38, 42

silence of Aboriginal mothers about their experiences of child removal, 11, 17, 40, 49, 139, 140, 147, 165, 166; due to blame, 11, 41–44, 49, 152, 165; due to guilt, shame and self-blame, 45, 49, 165; due to sexual assault, 32–34, 165; due to trauma, 23, 38–39, 41; to preserve family relationships, 37–38, 47–48, 165; as resistance, 36, 48–49

Simon, Ella, 15n39, 66n51, 71, 104, 108, 132, 134n1, 136n46, 156

single mothers, 44, 73, 106, 114n73, 152

single parents, 12, 73, 78, 95

social security, 3, 57; Baby Bonus, 69, 74; Child Endowment, 62, 67, 70–72, 73, 74, 102; maternity allowance, 67, 68–69, 71, 72, 73, 74; paid in rations instead of cash, 11, 73–74; racial discrimination in access to, 3, 8, 11, 12, 21, 64, 67–75, 100, 102, 149; Single Mothers' pension, 73, 114n73; War Widows' pension, 73; Widows' pension, 73

Social Services Act 1959 (Cth), 72

sorry business in relation to child removal, 46, 51n69

South Australian Children's Welfare and Public Relief Board, 119–120

speaking out, 148–149, 152, 156, 165, 166; risks of, 31, 32, 48, 156, 165; benefits attributed to, 22, 41, 154–156

state surveillance of Aboriginal mothers, 3, 11, 82, 85–86, 150

state wards, 54, 58, 61, 136n48, 149

Stolen Generations, definitional debates about the, 1, 3, 9, 11, 21, 53, 54, 119, 125

Stolen Generations Alliance, viii, 9

Stolen Generations era, 55, 59, 61, 95, 103, 109, 117, 119, 140; contested history of, 1, 12, 99, 118, 134; historical sources about, 6–8; number of children removed during, 6; overview of, 4–5; racial discrimination not unlawful during, 55, 148

Stolen Generations narratives, 140, 147, 152, 153, 154

stolen wages, 78

Stubbs, Judith, 24, 29n39, 50n46, 136n55, 175

Terszak, Mary, 15n39, 23, 29n36, 175

testimony, 11, 17, 18, 19, 23, 24, 25, 31, 45, 64, 109, 155, 165

training institutions, 4, 63, 130

transitional justice, 19, 25, 26

truancy, impact on child removal, 90, 102, 123, 131

Truth, UN Resolution on the Right to, 25

Truth Commissions, 141; Canadian Truth and Reconciliation Commission, 162, 168n4; South African Truth and Reconciliation Commission (SATRC), 21, 23, 25, 36, 45

truth-telling, 1, 17, 18, 25, 26, 28, 31, 36, 48, 134, 161, 162

Tuhiwai Smith, Linda, 9, 27

Tur, Mona Ngitji Ngitji, 133, 137n71, 175

Under the Wintamarra Tree , 88, 94, 142, 143

Uluru Statement from the Heart, 17, 26

United Aboriginal Mission, 53, 63, 133

Vicenti, Heather, 15n39, 57, 60–61, 69, 74, 89, 149–152

voluntary relinquishment of children, 105–106

Walker, Wilma, 87, 91n12, 91n13, 175

War Pensions Act 1914 (Cth), 73

Welfare Ordinance 1953 (NT), 58, 65n32
white people: attitudes towards child
    removal, 8, 12, 93, 100, 103, 105, 109,
    110–111, 117–118, 120, 123, 126–127,
    129, 130, 134; beliefs about
    Aboriginal mothers' capacity to
    love and care for their children, 22,
    82, 93, 109–110, 115n100, 166;

    criticisms of the *Bringing Them Home*
    Inquiry, 25, 103
Wilson, Julie, 39, 42, 44, 50n42, 50n43,
    51n53, 51n59, 130, 137n58, 175
Wilson, Sir Ronald, vii, 18, 103
Windschuttle, Keith, 99, 125
Wright, Eunice, 112n12, 148, 158n27,
    176

About the Author

Anne Maree Payne works in the School of Communication at the University of Technology Sydney (UTS), where she teaches a range of subjects relating to Aboriginal history, gender, diversity, citizenship, and sociology. After nearly two decades working in equity and diversity, she completed a master's in human rights at the London School of Economics and her PhD at UTS in 2016. Her current research interests include human rights (particularly of mothers), truth-telling, and white Australian attitudes towards Aboriginal people. Most recently she has written an entry in the *Elgar Encyclopaedia of Human Rights* on "Mothers, rights of," and coauthored a report for the Australian Institute of Aboriginal and Torres Strait Islander Studies (AIATSIS) on the need for a National Resting Place for the care of Indigenous Ancestral Remains.